OCEAN STEAMERS

A History of Ocean-going Passenger Steamships
1820–1970

THE FIRST STEAM BOAT, THE COMET, BUILT BY
HENRY BELL, 1811
WHO BROUGHT STEAM NAVIGATION INTO PRACTICE IN EUROPE.

OCEAN STEAMERS

A History of Ocean-going Passenger Steamships
1820–1970

JOHN ADAMS FRSA

New Cavendish Books

London

A White Mouse publication, an imprint of
New Cavendish Books Ltd

First edition published in Great Britain by
White Mouse Editions, 1993
Copyright © New Cavendish Books, 1993

Designer: Jacky Wedgwood
Editor: Narisa Chakra
Production: Allen Levy

Typeset by Wyvern Typesetting Ltd, Bristol.

Printed and bound in Hong Kong under the supervision of Mandarin
Offset, London

New Cavendish Books Ltd
3 Denbigh Road, London W11 2SJ

ISBN 0 904568 89 X

Acknowledgements

I should like to thank the following for their help with my
researches into the histories of the ocean steamers described in
this book:

Birmingham City Library
Birmingham University Library
Keith Byass
The Cunard Line
The late John H Isherwood
The Keeper of Maritime History, Southampton
Alan B Mallett
The National Maritime Museum, Greenwich
P & O Line
The Science Museum, South Kensington
University of Liverpool Archives
The World Ship Society

My thanks are also due to Narisa Chakra for her editorial
prowess in correcting my original typescript and to Jacky
Wedgwood for so expertly dealing with innumerable layout
problems.

Publishers Note

*Much of the illustrative material, particularly in the middle section of
this book is drawn from a wide range of contemporary sources and in
some instances the colour reproduction reflects the unusual tints and
screening employed at that time. Likewise professional colour
transparencies of liners particularly the less well known ships of the fifties
and sixties are surprisingly rare. Once again the reproductions of some
illustrations must be viewed in the light of the standards of that time.*

Cover illustration showing the MAURETANIA funnels by kind
permission of the Cunard Line Limited

Picture credits

New Cavendish Books would like to thank the following for their help
with this publication and for permission to reproduce copyright
material. They would also like to thank Henry Maxwell for advice on
the text.

John Adams Collection pages 6, 16, 17, 22, 23, 25 (*above*), 55
(*below*), 62 (*left*), 88, 89, 90 (*above*), 92 (*below*), 94 (*above*), 96, 97 (*left*),
99 (*above left*), 101, 102 (*below left*), 103, 104 (*above/below right, below
left*), 105 (*above/below right, inset*), 107 (*above right, below left*), 108, 110,
112, 114 (*above*), 115 (*above*), 116 (*left*), 117 (*left, right*), 118, 119 (*left,
right, below*), 120, 121 (*below left*), 122, 123, 125, 126, 127, 128 (*above*),
129 (*left, below right*), 130, 131, 132, 133, 134 (*below centre*), 135, 136,
137, 138, 140, 141 (*above, below*), 142 (*below*), 143, 144 (*below, inset*),
146 (*below*), 147 (*above, inset*), 148, 149, 150 (*below right/left*), 153, 158,
161 (*below*), 162 (*above left*), 163 (*left*), 167 (*above left*), 168 (*above
left/right*), 172 (*above right, below*), 173 (*above right*), 176 (*below*), 178
(*above right, below*), 179 (*below right*), 180, 184 (*below right*), 185 (*above
right*), 196 (*below left*), 197 (*above left, below left/right*), 198 (*below*), 199,
200 (*above right*)

John Adams Collection/Illustrated London News pages 13, 29,
30, 33, 34, 35, 36, 37, 39, 40 (*right*), 41, 42, 43, 44, 45, 46, 47, 48, 49
(*below*), 50, 51, 52, 53, 54, 55 (*above*), 56, 58, 59, 60, 61, 64, 65, 66–67
(*centre, right*), 68, 69, 70, 71, 73, 74, 75, 76, 77, 78, 79, 80, 81 (*below*),
82 (*below*), 83, 84, 85, 86, 87, 90 (*below*), 93 (*below*)

P M Alexander/Millbrook House pages 139, 142 (*above left/right*),
145 (*above*), 146 (*above left/right*), 150 (*above*), 152, 156, 158 (*below right*),
160, 161 (*above left/right*), 166 (*above left/right*), 168 (*below right*), 169,
170, 171, 172 (*above left*), 173 (*above left*) 177, 178 (*inset*), 179 (*above
left/right*), 181, 184 (*below left*), 185 (*below right*), 186 (*below*), 187 (*below
left*), 188 (*above right*), 189, 190, 191, 193 (*above left*), 194 (*below*)

Cunard Line Ltd pages 118 (*above right*), 200 (*above left*), 201

J Arthur Dixon page 197 (*above right*)

Documentation pages 40 (*left*), 57, 62 (*right*), 63, 66 (*above right*),
66–67 (*below*), 72, 81 (*above*), 82 (*above*), 98, 109, 111, 119 (*centre right*),
128 (*below left/right*), 129 (*inset*), 133 (*right*), 134 (*above, below, left/right*),
141 (*above left*), 144 (*right*), 145 (*right*), 147 (*inset*), 151, 154, 157, 159,
162 (*right*), 163 (*right, above/below*), 164, 165, 166 (*left*), 167 (*below
left/right, above right*), 168 (*left*), 174, 175, 176, 179 (*left*), 183, 194 (*left*),

Elizabeth Kirby Collection pages 91, 92 (*above*) 95, 97 (*right*), 99
(*below left/right*), 100, 102 (*above left*), 104 (*above left*), 105 (*below left*),
106, 107 (*above left*), 114 (*below*)

National Maritime Museum pages 14, 15, 21, 24, 27, 28

P & O Group Library pages 18, 49 (*above*), 94 (*below*), 147 (*below
right*), 154 (*below centre*), 194 (*above right*), 195

Science Museum pages 12, 25 (*below*), 26, 30, 32, 162 (*below*)

World Ship Society pages 196 (*below right*), 198 (*above left*)

Every effort has been made to trace and acknowledge all copyright
holders. The publisher apologises for any omissions.

Contents

Big Steamers
1914–1918

'OH, WHERE are you going to, all you Big Steamers,
    With England's own coal, up and down the salt seas?'
'We are going to fetch you your bread and your butter,
    Your beef, pork, and mutton, eggs, apples, and cheese.'

'And where will you fetch it from, all you Big Steamers,
    And where shall I write you when you are away?'
'We fetch it from Melbourne, Quebec, and Vancouver –
    Address us at Hobart, Hong-Kong, and Bombay.'

'But if anything happened to all you Big Steamers,
    And suppose you were wrecked up and down the salt sea?'
'Then you'd have no coffee or bacon for breakfast,
    And you'd have no muffins or toast for your tea.'

'Then I'll pray for fine weather for all you Big Steamers,
    For little blue billows and breezes so soft.'
'Oh, billows and breezes don't bother Big Steamers,
    For we're iron below and steel-rigging aloft.'

'Then I'll build a new lighthouse for all you Big Steamers,
    With plenty wise pilots to pilot you through.'
'Oh, the Channel's as bright as a ball-room already,
    And pilots are thicker than pilchards at Looe.'

'Then what can I do for you, all you Big Steamers,
    Oh, what can I do for your comfort and good?'
'Send out your big warships to watch your big waters,
    That no one may stop us from bringing you food.

'For the bread that you eat and the biscuits you nibble,
    The sweets that you suck and the joints that you carve,
They are brought to you daily by all us Big Steamers –
    And if any one hinders our coming you'll starve!'

Rudyard Kipling

Preface

My lifelong interest in ocean steamers began in the great days of steam when magnificent liners plied the oceans of the world. I well remember that during the First World War, when I was five or six, I would often read Rudyard Kipling's poem 'Big Steamers' before going to bed and would fall asleep dreaming of travel and adventure on the high seas.

Living well away from the sea probably made it all the more exciting as I had no real idea of what an ocean steamer was like. The seeds of my fascination had nevertheless been sown.

Later when I went away to boarding school in the early 1920s, my friends and I would write away to the big shipping companies, who were mostly situated around Cockspur Street in London, if I remember correctly. We would then eagerly await the arrival of fat envelopes, or bundles, of beautiful, coloured postcards. These were carefully collected and hoarded, and have survived to illustrate many of the ships mentioned in this book.

The majority of my career was spent in writing about and presenting programmes on my other great love – steam railways. But the 'Big Steamers' were not forgotten and when I retired and had time to browse in bookshops I realised that, while there were hundreds of books on railways and tens of books on warships, ocean-going passenger steamers were relatively neglected. Accordingly, ten years ago I dug out my old post-cards and began to research the subject in depth, collecting many other fascinating illustrations along the way. The work was certainly interesting to me and I hope that this book will enable the reader to share my love of ocean steamers which was kindled all those years ago.

JOHN ADAMS
September 1992

Introduction

In that extraordinary period, known to history as the Industrial Revolution, nothing was more remarkable than the application of steam power to the subjugation of the oceans.

The development of steam power at sea, from the first tentative attempts, taken with the diminutive SAVANNAH of 1819, wherein the engine was used merely as an auxiliary to sail, but which managed to reach Liverpool from Georgia, USA, in 28 days, was at first hesitant. It required a further nineteen years before the first Atlantic crossing under continuous steam power was made. This was by the paddle steamer SIRIUS in 1838.

Water and coal were the early bugbears. The earliest steamships had no condensers. The only water available for their boilers was sea water. Every two days or so the steam engines had to be stopped and the boilers scaled to remove the clogging deposits of salt. Necessity, as always, being the mother of invention, it was not too long before condensers were available, allowing the fresh water to be recycled, as we would now say, and this difficulty was largely overcome. Coal, however, was another matter. Coal required extensive bunkers, drawing on the space available for cargo and passengers, and necessitating the costly transportation of huge tonnages to remote strategic points along the way, aptly termed coaling stations. And it was the absence of such strategic stations across the vast distances of the Pacific which so greatly delayed the coming of the steamship to the Southern Hemisphere.

Coal, too, had other inconveniences. Coaling at these points was, to the very end, a dreadful business, with clouds of coal dust penetrating to every corner of a vessel and making even the open decks like places in the Black Country. Worse still was the toll it took of stokers and firemen whose lives were spent in appalling conditions, for ever shovelling and straining in the intense heat and dust of the stokeholds.

But gradually, and against all the formidable obstacles, the steamship opened up the oceans as the steam locomotive was opening up the continents, and constant technical improvements, and ever larger and faster vessels made ocean travel for the multitude a commonplace.

Here, in this entralling 'Valhalla' of past steamships, the great evolution is unfolded. Thanks to the author's acute eye for the significant detail and the important development, we can see the wood as well as the trees. Nothing significant escapes his attention, and the book is not only an invaluable reference work but, thanks to its discriminating division into periods, the thread of the story is never lost. There it all lies for our inspection – from wood to iron, from iron to steel, from paddle to screw, from reciprocating engine to turbine. The first real transatlantic regular service owed its inauguration to the foresight and determination of Samuel Cunard, who, in 1840, ordered from the builders four small and identical paddlers, and inaugurated a twice-monthly service from Liverpool to Boston. The first of these was, of course, the BRITANNIA, immortalised by Charles Dickens, and hers was the honour of being the first steamship to be entrusted with the Mails. The first screw steamer, and the first to be built of iron, to cross the Atlantic was Brunel's famous GREAT BRITAIN, of 1848, which crossed from Liverpool to New York in 15 days, carrying 1,100 tons of coal in her bunkers.

The last Cunard paddle-steamer was the SCOTIA, which was built of iron and burned 140 tons of coal a day in her furnaces. The last wooden transatlantic to be built was the ARABIA, of 1853, just one year after the first artificial refrigerator had been installed in a ship, the CLEOPATRA, heralding an enormous advance in ships' catering. Steerage, in the 1850s, were expected to bring their own beds and bedding with them. In 1862 the PS SCOTIA crossed from New York to Queenstown in 8 days 3 hours. The era of the 'Atlantic Greyhound' and the 'Blue Riband' was in sight.

And, of course, towering in stature over all this decade was Brunel's mighty GREAT EASTERN, the indubitable progenitor of all the super-liners of the 20th century. The author rightly devotes a separate chapter to this unique vessel.

What day-to-day life at sea was like in those adolescent days of the steamship can be savoured in an early chapter, where Dickens' deathless account of his crossing in the BRITANNIA is extensively quoted from. But it would be wrong to imagine that, apart from the horrors of sea-sickness, and the ever-present risk of bodily injury from the ship's often violent motion, the actual appointments were primitive. Saloons were richly decorated in silks and velvets, with costly panellings, fine carpets and were furnished with opulent settees and chairs. But it was not until 1871 that the first vessel to have steam heating pipes in the public rooms instead of stoves appeared, and 1878 before a liner, the White Star Line's ADRIATIC, was lit by gaslight.

Thereafter progress in all aspects was both rapid and sustained. The OCEANIC of 1899, of 17,040 gross tonnage and nearly 700 feet in length, was the last liner of the 19th century to be built and the first to exceed the dimensions of Brunel's GREAT EASTERN.

And then, early in the 20th century, exploded the revolutionary steam turbine, which paved the way for all the great express liners of our day, whose names were household words, and whose proportions rivalled those of the great cathedrals, and, some might think, their majesty was well.

Liners became ever larger, ever faster, ever more luxurious and spacious. Dickens' BRITANNIA, if stripped of masts and funnel, could have nestled comfortably within the main dining saloon of the QUEEN MARY. Four propellors replaced two on the faster liners, passengers could telephone from ship to shore;

swimming pools, often of Pompeian splendour, were almost *a sine qua non*, and meals on board were Lucullan banquets. But perhaps of all these advances, the most welcome and the most beneficial was the substitution of oil for coal as fuel. This took place on a large scale in the years immediately following the First World War. Gone now were those struggling gangs of men – rightly called 'the Black Squad' – sweating their hearts out and choking their lungs out below the water-line. Gone were the horrors of coaling days. In their place a handful of immaculate engineers controlled a few nozzles and boiler rooms were as salubrious as sun-decks.

And so it continued, and seemed set to continue, until, almost literally, from the skies, there dropped a predator, in the guise of the jumbo jet aircraft, which in a few short years consigned the whole race of these bejewelled leviathans to extinction.

The 'express liner' is no more. Those few which survive have been reconstructed as cruising yachts, and mooch along at half their previous speeds. Even the once ubiquitous mail ship is a thing of the past. The leisure industry has taken over, and virtually all new passenger tonnage is for cruising or car-ferrying. It was in truth a 'belle epoque', and this splendid volume is a reminder of it. Unconventional – some might say outlandish – are some of today's cruising liners; and as each new and extra-vagant *fille de joie* follows another down the slipways, luxuriance no doubt advances while leisure, maybe, recedes.

CAPTAIN GORDON WALKER, DSC

CHAPTER 1

Life on Board

Many of us imagine a sea voyage as a holiday in which we are pampered with the utmost luxury in a ship with stabilisers and all modern aids to make our vessel ride any rough weather without our suffering 'mal du mare', but it was not like this in the early days, and those who made long voyages across the oceans had to endure spartan conditions. It would be hard to imagine just what it was like, if some of the early travellers had not left us diaries of their journeys.

In 1841 Charles Dickens travelled to America in Cunard's first paddle-steamer the BRITANNIA, sailing from Liverpool on New Year's Day and arriving in Boston 21 days later. He gave an account of the voyage in his book *America*, from which a short extract gives a flavour of the trip:

'It is the third morning. I am awakened out of my sleep by a dismal shriek from my wife, who demands to know whether there's any danger. I rouse myself, and look out of the bed. The water-jug is plunging and leaping like a lively dolphin; all the smaller articles are afloat, except my shoes, which are stranded on a carpet-bag, high and dry, like a couple of coal barges. Suddenly I see them spring in the air, and behold the looking-glass, which is nailed to the wall, is sticking fast upon the ceiling. At the same time the door entirely disappears, and a new one is open in the floor. Then I begin to comprehend that the state-room is standing on its head.

'Before it is possible to make any arrangement at all compatable with this novel state of things the ship rights. Before one can say "Thank Heaven!", she is wrong again. Before one can say she is wrong, she seems to have started foreward, and to be a creature actually running of its own accord, with broken knees and failing legs, through every variety of hole and pitfall and stumbling constantly. Before one can so much as wonder, she takes a high leap into the air. Before she has well done that, she takes a deep dive into the water. Before she has gained the surface, she throws a summerset. The instant she is on her legs, she rushes backwards. And so she goes on staggering, heaving, wrestling, leaping, diving, jumping, pitching, throbbing, rolling, and rocking, and going through all these movements, sometimes by turns and sometimes altogether: until one feels disposed to roar for mercy. A Steward passes. "Steward!". "Sir?"

"What is the matter? What do you call this?"
"Rather a heavy sea on, Sir, and a head-wind."

* * *

'I say nothing of what may be called the domestic noises of the ship: such as the breaking of glass and crockery, the tumbling down of stewards, the gambols overhead of loose casks and truant dozens of bottled porter, and the very remarkable and far from exhilarating sounds raised in their various state-rooms by the seventy passengers who were too ill to get up to breakfast. I say nothing of them: for although I lay listening to this concert for three or four days, I don't think I heard it for more than a quarter of a minute, at the expiration of which time, I lay down again, excessively sea-sick.
A description of one day will serve for all the rest.

'The weather continued obstinately and almost unprecedentedly bad, we usually straggled into this cabin, more or less faint and miserable, about an hour before noon, and lay down on the sofas to recover; during which interval, the Captain would look in to communicate the state of the wind, the moral certainty of its changing to-morrow (the weather is always going to improve to-morrow at sea), the vessel's rate of sailing, and so forth. Observations there were none to tell us of, for there was no sun to take them by.

'The Captain being gone, we compose ourselves to read, if the place be light enough; and if not, we doze and talk alternately. At one, a bell rings, and the stewardess comes down with a steaming dish of baked potatoes, and another of roasted apples; and a plate of pig's face, cold ham, salt beef; or perhaps a smoking mass of rare hot collops. We fell upon these dainties; eat as much as we can (we have great appetites now); and as long as possible about it. If the fire will burn (it will sometimes) we are pretty cheerful. If it won't, we all remark to each other that it's very cold, rub our hands, cover ourselves with coats and cloaks and lie down again to doze, talk, and read (provided as aforesaid) until dinner-time. At five, another bell rings, and the stewardess reappears with another dish of potatoes – boiled this time – and store of hot meat of various kinds: not forgetting the roast pig, to be taken medicinally. We sit down at table again (rather more cheerfully than before); prolonging the meal with a rather mouldy dessert of apples, grapes, and oranges; and drink our wine and brandy-and-

Charles Dickens' cabin
aboard the BRITANNIA

On 21 September 1874, Joseph Sams, who was an emigrant to Australia, sailed from Gravesend in the steamer NORTHUMBERLAND, calling at Plymouth on 23 September and leaving again at 7.30pm the same day. Fortunately he kept a diary of his voyage. How the diary survived and found its way back to England is a mystery – however, it did, and has been published in book form by the National Maritime Museum. A short extract follows:

Sept 24th Thursday. As I feel first rate today will give a slight description of the ship. Her name is the NORTHUMBER-LAND and she is owned by Money, Wigram & Sons of Blackwall, London. Her tonnage is 2,178 tons register, 500 horse power, she is painted black and white and looks very graceful in the water which she rides very well. She has an auxiliary screw that will propel her at a speed of $10\frac{1}{2}$ knots an hour at highest. Her sailing speed will at times reach 16 knots an hour, not having experienced of her sailing I can say nothing at present about her on that point. When under steam she rides very nice but has a slight drawback this journey owing to being heavily laden in the bow which causes her to pitch more than usual, thereby shipping many seas, but I find that her cargo in the bow is coal, therefore by degrees she will get lighter. She has three masts but of her sailing qualities more anon. The forepart of the vessel is inhabited by 3rd class passengers of whom there are between 1 & 2 hundred people. Midship is appropriated to the 2nd Class there being 77 including my humble self. The after part is solely at the use of the 1st Class passengers who number about 85. The 3rd class have their rations given to them and have to make up their own food, take it to the cookhouse and afterwards fetch it and take it to their mess room. In the 2nd they have nothing to do with the cooking etc., a bell rings for breakfast at 8, dinner at 1 & tea at 5, and we assemble in the 2nd Class Saloon where we are provided with food, etc. the style of which I will more fully detail at a later period. The first class live like fighting cocks and it is rather galling to see all the pastry etc. and good things taken under your very nose from the galley to the Chief Saloon.

'The Captain, Mr Shinner, is according to account a very homely man & looks so. The First Mate Mr Tyces is also a pleasant looking fellow with a propensity for scratching his head, and he is not lazy, for he does it with both hands. Our Steward is named Pat Brodie a very decent fellow and will do anything for us. I mean to enjoy myself.

'The ship is what they call a wet decked one, so bought a pair of top boots at Plymouth. We have two cows on board, several pigs, ducks, geese, poultry, sheep in abundance. Several pigs and parrots and the forecastle is like a young farm yard. The ship's company contains 38 seamen, baker, carpenter, butcher, poultryman and officers, with several middies. Most of the cabins are swarmed with bugs and some

water. The bottles and glasses are still on the table, and the oranges and so forth are rolling about according to their fancy and the ship's way, when the doctor comes down, by special nightly invitation, to join our evening rubber: immediately on whose arrival we make a party at whist, and as it is a rough night and the cards will not lie on the cloth, we put the tricks in our pockets as we take them. At whist we remain with exemplary gravity (deducting a short time for tea and toast) until eleven o'clock or thereabouts; when the Captain comes down again, in a sou'wester hat tied under his chin and a pilot coat: making the ground wet where he stands. By this time the card-playing is over, and the bottles and glasses are again upon the table; after an hour's pleasant conversation about the ship, the passengers, and things in general, the Captain (who never goes to bed, and is never out of humour), turns up his coat collar for the deck again; shakes hands all round; and goes laughing out into the weather as merrily as to a birthday party.'

Poor Dickens!

of the fellows are afraid to undress. Our cabin being next to the doctor's shop we are freed from such marauders.

September 26th Saturday. Up at 7. A most beautiful morning and very hot, the sun streaming down so that it was difficult to find any shade. Began the regulation dinners today. Soup or bouille and preserved meat, made into pies, & rice. The soup was the best thing I have yet tasted on board. Last night there was a good deal of romance about, or rather just starting, the fellows having got about as far as the waists. I rather expect we shall soon see more in this line, as we near the line.

21st October, Wednesday. Up at 7.30. Screw up during night. Fair wind on the quarter, very cold, ship laying over very much. It is quite winter weather & we expect snow. During the afternoon the wind freshened & at 5 p.m. is blowing half a gale, sea about 20 feet high & ship every now & then laying over to the water's edge, very few of us on deck & everyone hanging on by the skin of their teeth, going about 14 knots an hour, this is the first day we have had of sea weather & and I enjoyed it wonderfully, imagine me with top boots on, muffler, reefer & seal cap on, hanging on anywhere, helping the sailors & altogether having a rare time of it, the luck is when a fellow goes over, as when he is falling he's sure to catch hold of the nearest person to him & therefore there is

generally 2 or 3 down at once in the water etc. I have not had a spill yet but several near squeaks. Having now had experience of the sailing quality of the ship I have pleasure in saying it is much better than steam as she will go faster by 4 or 5 knots an hour, but is a very wet ship, the water comes over her in rare form and she dives a good deal; however with all this she is not so dusty. I am sorry to say we have a rather mediocre lot of seamen and I would rather not be in a heavy gale with them, but to make up for it we have a most superior class of officers & the Captain is very careful & could not be bettered. One grand point with him is he 'NEVER DRINKS' more than a little beer with his dinner. The officers led the way up the rigging today when the wind got too high and they had to reef the mainsail. It was a pretty sight, the first time we have seen all hands on board, there were 27 men on the main yard reefing like so many bees.

29th October, Thursday. Up at 7.30. Dead calm, wind got up about 8 but as it happened against us, steam up at 8 & screw going again, after breakfast came on to snow & has been doing so all day, very cold on deck & very miserable. Much warmer in cabins owing to the engines. Last night the storekeeepr got drunk again & after several tricks had been played him was put in irons & had to walk the poop for an hour or two all in the cold.'

NORTHUMBERLAND
1,898 tons
270 x 38 feet
1871

Cuzco
Orient Line
1871

In 1885 Andrew Crawford and his wife Jessie travelled to Australia and back. Their outward journey was made in the sailing ship PATRIACH and their return voyage was in the Orient Line's CUZCO and it is part of this voyage that is recorded below, again from a National Maritime Museum publication.

The Crawfords boarded the CUZCO on Friday 26 June 1885 at Williamstown, which is a suburb of Melbourne, and sailed at 4.00 pm that day. There were a large number of steerage passengers, about 37 in the second class, but very few first class. A Mr Anderson – a partner in the Orient Line was on board with the Australian manager of the company. On Wednesday 1 July, the CUZCO put in at Albany in King George's Sound, Western Australia to allow Mr Anderson and his escort to disembark.

'On Monday 6th July the ship rolled about severely and sitting at meals was no easy task. Heavy seas were frequently shipped and many on deck got drenched, including our two selves. Played whist in the evening, and at supper a tremendous sea came over the bows and somehow got through the sky-light to the astonishment of those sitting underneath. We were fortunately out of it by this time, but those who found their stout had been mixed with salt water looked as if they didn't like it. The wind continued right against us and we are now a day behind our time already, the record in speed for the last few days being very low.

'Tuesday (the next day) showed signs of improvement, the wind having changed a little more aft and enabling the ship to get up and sail, the sea, however, is still high and several tumbles and slight accidents occurred on deck; one young lady getting her foot sprained, another lady tumbled or rather rolled out of bed during the night, and as her bunk was the top one the sensation must have been unpleasant and peculiar, though no bones were broken. As a parting kick in the storm CUZCO treated us to one of her best rolls just before tea. Happening to be on deck at the time I can vouch for it being a good one. As she heeled over to something like an angle of 45° and her rails got under water, I began to think of home and wondered whether she meant to come back again or would turn round and come up on the other side. She seemed to quiver and shake for a minute then pulled herself together and wriggled back and we breathed again, but it spoiled my tea remembering as I did that a sister-ship the AUSTRAL turned completely over in Sydney Harbour a year or two ago and gave nobody a chance of getting out. Most of the sick have now appeared on deck and everybody is beginning to know everybody else and everybody's history. We have ladies on board who wear marriage rings and pass themselves off as widows, and are neither one thing nor the other, and so we get to hear all sorts of nice little titbits of scandal. In the evening our steamer has all sails set and is going along at a great rate and we hope to make up some of our lost time.

'To-day (Wednesday) has been the best, we have had full speed since dawn and it has been a pleasure to be on deck, the wind is favourable and the record for the last 24 hours is nearly 300 miles. The piano keeps going at a great rate and it comes to be a question with some, whether it will be thrown overboard or shut up and someone bribed to lock it and loose the key. (excessive use of the piano was due to rehersals for the ship's concert at the end of the week). A sensation has been caused by the discovery of a stowaway secreted 'down among the coals'. How he has lived all this time is a mystery, but it is generally supposed he must have been fed by some of the crew. He is quite a young man and will be put to the roughest kind of work – probably as a stoker.'

Andrew Crawford finished his account of his voyage with the following comment:

'Although a sea voyage is beneficial from a health point of view, the mode of transit is slow and somewhat monotonous. A good sailing ship with good weather and a short voyage, say six weeks, is certainly preferable to a steamer, but after that time the journey gets tiresome, especially when no land is seen or places touched at and nothing to vary the same routine every day. The steamer has advantages of better feeding arrangements, carrying as most steamers do, a refrigerator from which is sent to the table all sorts of delicacies from milk, fresh as from the cow, to oysters as good as from Billingsgate or vegetables from Covent Garden. A steamer, however, has other drawbacks, a continual throbbing or vibrating motion caused by the engines and propeller, a disagreeable odour sent forth from the cook's galley, the heat from the engines and boilers and a feeling of soot and dustiness on every thing you touch on deck. Cleanliness and quietness commend the sailing vessel.'

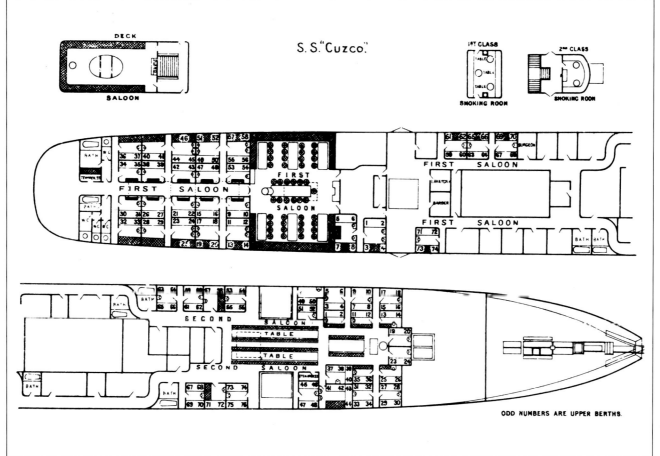

The interior layout of the CUZCO

In October 1910 a young English lady sailed from Southampton on the North German Lloyd steamer PRINZ LUDWIG bound for the Far East. Born of an American mother, the English 'School for Young Ladies' had turned Alice into an elegant eighteen year-old, a slender young woman with Titian hair and a rosy complexion. She spoke German and French fluently, and had a natural ease of manner that charmed young and old alike. Moreover, she had a beautiful singing voice, and in two years time would be returning to Paris for further training.

She did not know when she boarded the PRINZ LUDWIG that she was embarking on a momentous journey. Her chaperone was a lady, who, with her little daughter, was going out to Shanghai to join her husband. With them at the Surgeon-Commander's table, were two German Naval Lieutenants, going to join their ships in Chinese waters, and a British Royal Naval Captain.

The ship was run with strict Germanic discipline and a great deal of saluting went on. The British officer was in mufti, but apparently German officers wore uniform all the time. This meant that, whenever the ship's Captain appeared the German officers sprang to their feet.

Parties went ashore at Gibraltar and at Algiers,

where the ship was 'coaled' and became filthy dirty, having previously been scrubbed from top to bottom. Underneath the routine life, lay the barely suppressed excitement of the passengers and crew, for the identity of a certain Count and Countess on the passenger list due to embark at Genoa on 3rd November.

On the morning of the day of departure from Genoa the PRINZ LUDWIG was delayed some hours when an enourmous amount of luggage (30 trunks) was brought aboard for these two special passengers. The secret was revealed to Alice, crowding the decks with the rest, when Crown Prince William and Crown Princess Cecilie of Germany were piped aboard at noon. With ceremonial pomp the band played and the Royal Hohenzollern standard with the motto 'God with Us' was broken at the mast-head – so much for travelling incognito!

An entourage of twenty haughty personages followed. The grandes dames held themselves upright, the men were formidable with horizontally striped ties and cliff colours. Most were military friends of the Prince, from the upper nobility, sporting vainglorious 'Kaiser Bill' moustaches, while others wore goatee beards.

After a rough passage through the Bay of Naples, the Crown Prince and Princess came down to dine in the First-class saloon. The Crown Prince heard Alice rehearsing in the Music Room for a concert that night and stayed to listen. Afterwards he complimented her

Four illustrations from *Life on Board* by Harry Furniss P & O East of Suez

on her singing, she giving him a deep curtsey and thanking him.

When they were sailing in the Eastern Mediterranean with the sun blazing down, the ship's officers and naval 'naughty boys' (as Alice called her shadows) changed into tropical kit of spotless white. The men of the royal party relaxed in deck trousers held up by leather belts and open necked shirts with sleeves rolled up. The women appearing hatless in their tucked and appliquéd dresses. The Prince invited Alice to play a game of shuffleboard.

At the Grand Ball the Crown Prince, in full dress, with orders and medals clanking, danced with Alice not one but several times, the German Fraus watching none too pleased at the 'Englanderin' stealing the show. It

was well known that their musical Prince had a penchant for attractive Anglo-American girls with beautiful voices. After he left, she danced non-stop with her 'naughty boys', and the handsome von Arnould from the entourage who 'danced beautifully'. He promptly fell in love with her and she with him, and in her diary that night she wrote 'It was the loveliest evening of my life!'

On the final night, Alice was invited to the Captain's champagne dinner for his royal guests. Afterwards Alice danced again with the Crown Prince, and the next day 20 November, she witnessed the landing in Colombo to a 21-gun salute.

A fairy-tale voyage in contrast to the journeys made by Charles Dickens, Joseph Sams and the Crawfords.

Port Said

Above and right:
P & O Pencillings

Warm Weather

In the Bay

Life on a troop-ship in World War II

It was at RAF West Kirby in May 1941 that '60 Draft' were awaiting their boat overseas, the only clue to our destination the tropical kit with which we had been issued, and such was security that our only other clue was that the equipment for recreational facilities which we were taking with us, were all consigned by the manufacturers to '23 SFTS, RAF Heany, Bulawayo, Southern Rhodesia'! On the morning of Whit-Sunday we had to be on parade by 4.30am with all our kit, and after breakfast we collected rations for 24 hours, as we were told we should be embarking at Greenock. By 8.00am all 2,000 of us had been transported to West Kirby station on the Wirral electric line to take us to Lime Street Station, Liverpool. At James Street our train stopped for about 15 minutes when the doors opened and the order 'Everybody Out' was given. We formed up in column of threes, marched out of the station, round the corner and onto the HIGHLAND BRIGADE which was lying at the quay usually occupied by the Isle of Man steamers.

The HIGHLAND BRIGADE should not really come into this book as she was a motor-vessel, but I trust the reader will forgive a little author's license as, apart from the diesel fumes, life was very similar to that on steam troop-ships. A vessel of 14,131 tons, she was 544 × 69 feet and her twin screws were driven by Burmeister and Wain diesels to give a service speed of 15 knots. Built by Harland & Wolff she was completed in 1929 for the Nelson Line and transferred to Royal Mail Lines in 1932. In her normal life, she was a frozen meat ship which plied between Buenos Aires and London and in addition to her cargo had accommodation for about 600 passengers.

Being a member of the 'other ranks', we were accommodated in what were normally refrigeration holds with hammocks slung at night to the refrigeration pipes in the roof above the daytime benches and tables. There being no daylight in our quarters we spent most of our life on deck. We had to collect our food at meal times from the ship's galley, which was at the other end of the ship, our quarters being at what was known to us as the 'sharp end'. We sailed from Liverpool at dusk on Whit-Monday and next morning met up with the remainder of our convoy off the Western Isles. We now had about 40 ships with an escort of the cruiser CITY OF BIRMINGHAM and six lease-lend ex-American destroyers. Life on board was pretty monotonous and a great part of our days was spent sitting on our life-jackets and reading. Breakfast was at 8.00am, and most days for the first week we had boat-drill at 10.00am. We had our main meal of the day at 1.00pm and high-tea at 5.30pm. At 9.00pm those who wanted to could go to the crew's galley with their tin mug and have it filled with hot cocoa and have a 'thick captain' biscuit to dunk in it. Whatever has happened to 'thick captains'? Life was interspersed with various ships duties such as 'anti-submarine' watch in 24 hour shifts with two watches of four hours on and then eight hours off. This duty came round about every ten days, better than cleaning lavatories!

The only way we could tell which way we were going was by the daily correction for our watches, which was given out, the length of day and how cold it got. We must have headed north-west from Scotland to somewhere near Greenland, and then gone down the East coast of America as far as about Florida, before cutting across the Atlantic to Freetown. At Freetown the whole convoy was serviced with fresh water and fuel, which took a week. The only fresh water on board was for drinking and cooking. All washing facilities used salt water, and even with special sea-water soap a lather was most difficult to obtain, and after rinsing left you feeling sticky. Having been in tropical temperatures for about two weeks, we were all decidedly smelly. However, nature has its way, about our third day in Freetown we had a real tropical rain-storm and within minutes we had 2,000 airmen on deck all quite naked having a good wash with real soap! It was rumoured that the FRANCONIA also in the convoy had nurses on board and that they were doing the same as us! Our Captain was not very good at keeping his position in the convoy and on two occasions we were treated to one of the destroyers coming along-side at full speed and using their loud-hailer to say 'Captain of the HIGHLAND BRIGADE, with the Commodore's compliments, will you please keep your station'.

It was after we left Freetown and were running down the West coast of Africa that we discovered some loose boards in the floor of our hold and extracted a case of tinned salmon and one of tinned apricots, which were a great delicacy and supplemented our ships rations. However it must be said that when one considers that the ship's facilities were having to cater for 2,000 men, they worked wonders. Eventually we reached Durban, some of the convoy having gone into Cape Town. We had taken six weeks for the voyage and most of the time had sailed at 11–12 knots, the speed of the slowest ship.

CHAPTER 2

Early Days, Wooden Ships
1819–1858

In its time the steamship was as great an advance over the sailing vessel, in the mode of travel, as the change over from piston-engined aircraft to the jet and later the supersonic Concorde. Before the advent of steam, a crossing from Bristol to New York could take anything up to five or six weeks according to weather and wind. Such trips were often hazardous and several ships sank on their maiden voyages with serious loss of lives.

It is generally thought that the first major application of steam as a means of propulsion, albeit auxiliary, was in 1819 with the wooden ship SAVANNAH which was built in New York and had a single cylinder auxiliary engine of 90 horsepower fitted to drive two collapsible paddle-wheels. According to contemporary records this little ship of 320 tons crossed the Atlantic from Savannah in Georgia, USA to Liverpool in $27\frac{3}{4}$ days and apparently the engines were used for approximately 80 hours out of a total 663 hours at sea. Shortly after this trip attempts were made to sell her to various Scandinavian countries without success and she returned to her home port in America under sail without the use of steam. Her engines were removed and she spent the rest of her life as a sailing vessel. However the seed had been sown.

SAVANNAH
320 tons
1819

ROYAL WILLIAM
364 tons
160 x 28 feet
Quebec & Halifax
Steam Navigation Co.
1831

1825–1830

In 1825 a company called The American & Colonial Steam Navigation Company was registered in London, with a nominal share capital of £600,000, the objects of the company being to operate a line of steamships between Valentia Harbour in County Kerry on the south west coast of Ireland and America. Public enthusiasm was not very great and only £30,000 of the £600,000 was raised and the company, having to 'cut its coat according to the cloth', placed an order for one wooden paddle steamship of 436 tons with J. H. Duke of Dover to be named CALPE. Some time before she was completed it was realised that the whole venture was not economically viable and the vessel was sold in a partly completed state to the Netherlands Navy who had her completed and named CURACAO. In the years 1827, 1828 and 1829 she made round trips from Amsterdam to Paramaribo in Dutch Guiana (now Surinam), remaining in the Netherlands Navy until she was broken up in 1850. Although she spent her whole active life as a naval vessel, she was designed as a passenger carrying ship to ply the North Atlantic.

1830–1839

Another early attempt to carry passengers across an ocean with a steamship was made in 1831 by the ROYAL WILLIAM which had been built for the Quebec & Halifax Steam Navigation Company by Campbell and Black of Quebec. She was of wooden construction of 364 tons, 160 feet long and 28 feet beam. The paddles were driven by two-cylinder side-lever engines which would give an estimated speed of 6 knots. She started life operating between Quebec and Halifax (Nova Scotia) in her first year but in 1832 was employed between Quebec and Picton (Nova Scotia). However she was not a money-maker and eventually her owners decided to try and sell her in England. To this end the ROYAL WILLIAM, after leaving Quebec, sailed from Picton on 18 August 1833 with seven passengers, a full bunker of coal (a little over 300 tons) and a small quantity of cargo. Cowes (Isle of Wight) was reached on 8 September, a voyage of only 22 days. The engines had been used for 75% of the time, although every fourth day a boiler wash-out was required to remove salt. The ROYAL WILLIAM proceeded to Gravesend

(London) arriving on 12 September. No sale was effected and she was chartered to the Portuguese Government who, after using her for coastal services for a year, eventually bought her and renamed her ISABEL SECUNDE and transferred her to their navy. In 1836 while on naval patrol she became the first steamship to fire a gun in anger. She remained with the navy until 1840.

The SOPHIA JANE, a small vessel of only 256 tons, had a wooden hull and had been built in 1826 by Barnes & Miller who were said to be pupils of James Watt. Miller certainly had connections with Watt in the late 1780s in methods of applying steam power to boats and produced his first experimental steamboat in 1788. This was a small paddle-boat that had been built at Dalswinton near Glasgow for which Boulton & Watt of the Soho Foundry in Birmingham had built an engine. It seems probable that the Miller who was a pioneer in experimenting with steam propulsion for ships was connected with the Miller who, with Barnes, built the SOPHIA JANE which also had an engine built by Boulton & Watt. (James Watt had died in 1819). The

SOPHIA JANE was 126 feet long by 20 feet beam and the 50 horse power engines drove the side paddle-wheels. She was originally constructed to carry passengers to and from various Channel ports in England and France. It would appear that her voyage to Australia was speculative for she left London on 16 December 1830 and travelled via Pernambuco and Cape of Good Hope arriving at Sydney on 13 May 1831. Her owners had tried to sell her in Cape Town while on the way out but sufficient money could not be raised, so the little ship continued on to Australia. She ran on the Hawkesbury river for many years until 1841 when she worked between the south west ports and Sydney, returning to the river in 1844. Shortly afterwards she was scrapped and her engines put into another vessel.

The first serious attempts at operating steam passenger-carrying ships were made by the British & American Steam Navigation Company and the Great Western Steam Ship Company. Both companies effected their first crossing of the Atlantic in 1838. The former company was registered in 1835 and the following year placed an order with Curling & Young of

SOPHIA JANE
256 tons
126 x 20 feet
Barnes & Miller
1827

GREAT WESTERN
1,340 tons
212 x 35 feet
Leaving Avonmouth
in 1846

London for a wooden paddle-steamer of about 1,900 tons. The Great Western Steam Ship Company was formed in 1836 and an order was placed with William Patterson of Bristol for a 1,340 ton wooden paddle-steamship to be called the GREAT WESTERN.

The British & American Steam Navigation Company's ship, which was to be called the ROYAL VICTORIA, was delayed in construction by the bank-ruptcy of the Scottish company who were supplying the engines. When this happened it appeared obvious that the GREAT WESTERN would be ready to sail first, and so as not to be outdone British & American Steam Navigation decided to charter from the St George Steam Packet Company a much smaller vessel of 700 tons called the SIRIUS which had been built the previous year by Menzies of Glasgow. The SIRIUS left London on 28 March 1838 and called at Cork to take on passengers and mail and replenish bunker coal before sailing for New York on 4 April with 40 passengers, 450 tons of coal and 20 tons of fresh water, as well

SIRIUS
700 tons
British & American
Steam Navigation Co.
1838

as a small cargo. She was very low in the water much to the consternation of the crew who wanted to turn back when rough weather was encountered shortly after leaving Cork. However the commander Lieutenant Roberts continued and finally reached New York on 23 April a few hours before the GREAT WESTERN, after a journey of $18\frac{1}{2}$ days.

SIRIUS returned to Falmouth (England) and did one more return trip to New York before being returned to her owners. Much of her success was due to condensing the exhaust steam and reusing the water, a practice that was adopted in all steamships thereafter and avoided cleaning the boiler of salt every few days.

The GREAT WESTERN was launched at William Patterson's yard in 1837 and taken by tug to London to have her engines fitted. These had been built by Maudsley, Sons & Field to the design of I. K. Brunel who was the company's chief engineer, as well as being engineer to the Great Western Railway.

The GREAT WESTERN was a good deal bigger than SIRIUS weighing 1,340 tons and was 212 feet long by 35 feet beam. Her hull was of timber construction and propelled by paddles driven by a two-cylinder side-lever engine. There was an obvious rush to prepare her for her maiden voyage in competition with SIRIUS and she sailed from Bristol for New York on 8 April 1838 with only 7 passengers on board, reaching New York on

23 April a few hours after SIRIUS. The British & American Steam Navigation Company just won the day, albeit with a chartered ship which had not been designed to work the Atlantic route, whereas the GREAT WESTERN had been purpose-built and continued in this service until her sale to another company in 1847.

In 1837–38 a 617 ton wooden paddle-steamer, the ROYAL WILLIAM, was built by Wilson for the City of Dublin Steam Packet Company. She was 175 x 27 feet, with a two-cylinder side-lever engine. She commenced her maiden voyage from Liverpool to New York on 5 July 1838. Subsequently she was chartered by the Transatlantic Steam Ship Company to operate the same route and did two more return trips to New York, the last commencing 15 December 1838. She then returned to her owners for operations in the Irish Sea. She was the first steamer to have watertight compartments.

The Transatlantic Steam Ship Company, who had hired the ROYAL WILLIAM, had a steamship of their own being built by Humble & Milcrest of Liverpool which was named the LIVERPOOL. She was a little larger than the ROYAL WILLIAM being 1,150 tons with a length of 223 feet by 31 feet beam. She was of wooden construction with a two-cylinder side-lever engine. As the name of the company implied, it was only interested in transatlantic service and she left Liverpool for New York on 20 October 1838. After encountering very rough weather in the Irish Sea, she

ROYAL WILLIAM
in a storm
1838

BRITISH QUEEN
1,862 tons
245 x 41 feet
British & American
Steam Navigation Co.
1839

put into Cork for more coal and then took 20 days to reach her destination. In all she made seven return trips to America and started her last voyage in December 1839. The company then ceased to trade and in 1840 sold the LIVERPOOL to P & O who renamed her the GREAT LIVERPOOL. A similar vessel to LIVERPOOL was also sold to P & O and became the ORIENT. The LIVERPOOL was the first steamer to have two funnels

and warm and cold baths for the passengers. As the GREAT LIVERPOOL with P & O she sailed to the Orient. On 24 February 1846 she was wrecked off Cape Finisterre (Spain) while on a voyage back to England, and though there were 145 passengers on board, only two lives were lost. *The Illustrated London News* of 14 March reported that 'on the 27th the ship went entirely to pieces. A great portion of the cabin luggage and cargo was lost and the Spaniards along the shore behaved ill, plundering all they could lay hands on.'

In 1839 the British & American Steam Navigation Company's ROYAL VICTORIA was completed and sailed round from London to the Clyde to have her engines fitted by Robert Napier & Co. of Glasgow. She was renamed the BRITISH QUEEN prior to being put on show at Liverpool in 1839 and created great interest as the then largest steamship in the world with a finished weight of 1,862 tons, 254 feet in length and 41 feet beam. The BRITISH QUEEN left London on 11 June 1839 for her maiden voyage to New York with 220 passengers, 80 tons of cargo and mail and 600 tons of bunker coal. After calling at Portsmouth she had an uneventful run to New York in 15 days. The BRITISH QUEEN continued on the North Atlantic route, working three round trips to New York in 1839 and five in 1840. In 1841 she was sold to the Belgian Government and made three round voyages, Antwerp––Southampton–New York, under the Belgian flag. She was subsequently laid up in Amsterdam until 1844 when she was sold for scrap.

The British & American Steam Navigation Company had one more steamship on the stocks, the PRESIDENT. Yet again this ship was built by Curling &

Young of Glasgow and was launched at the end of 1839 and moved down to Liverpool. She was a good deal heavier than the BRITISH QUEEN, being 2,366 tons with a wooden hull, length of 243 feet and 41 feet beam. She made her maiden voyage from Liverpool to New York sailing on 1 August 1840. After completing four voyages, two outward and two return, she was laid up until February 1841 when she sailed to New York. The return trip started on 11 March 1841 but she was unfortunately lost with all hands, probably due to rough weather. (Without radio no one knew what happened to a ship in difficulties, they just did not arrive.) 136 lives were lost.

1840–1850

In the meantime, the GREAT WESTERN was running a regular service from Liverpool to New York and back, except during the months of December to March. In the autumn of 1842 the GREAT WESTERN was laid up and unsuccessfully put up for sale. She was then put back on the Liverpool–New York service until 1846. A year later she was sold to the Royal Mail Steam Packet Company who kept her for 10 years.

PRESIDENT
2,366 tons
243 x 41 feet
British & American
Steam Navigation Co.
1840

BRITANNIA
1,135 tons
207 × 34 feet
Cunard
1840

Meanwhile in 1840, a certain Samuel Cunard of Nova Scotia had entered the field, and formed the British & North American Royal Mail Steam Packet Company. However, because of the rather cumbersome title of the company, it was soon unofficially known as the Cunard Line after its founder and major shareholder. Orders were immediately placed for four steam-propelled wooden-hulled paddle vessels all of about the same size. BRITANNIA, 207 × 34 feet, was the first off the stocks and was launched in February 1840 with engines fitted by Robert Napier, who had the contract for all four of these early vessels. BRITANNIA sailed on her maiden voyage from Liverpool to Halifax on 4 July 1840, making the journey in 12 days 10 hours. A month later the second steamer ACADIA sailed on 4 August. The third, CALEDONIA, sailed on 19 September and finally the COLUMBIA on 5 January 1841. These four ships operated a twice monthly sailing from Liverpool on the 4 and 19 of each month (except when this fell on

a Sunday when the sailing was one day later) apart from November, December, January and February when there was only one sailing on the 4th. Whilst a regular service was maintained, the venture was unprofitable despite the £60,000 per annum paid by the Admiralty for the carriage of mail across the Atlantic. Accordingly a revised contract was negotiated with the Admiralty raising the annual payment to £81,000 provided a fifth steamship was built. As a result a contract was placed with Robert Steele of Greenock who had built the COLUMBIA. This new steamer was a little larger than the first four, at 1,423 tons and 219 × 35 feet, against the earlier vessels' 1,135–1,175 tons and lengths of 207 feet and beam of 34 feet. She was named the HIBERNIA and made her maiden voyage from Liverpool to Halifax in April 1843. Only three months later the COLUMBIA was wrecked on Cape Sable, the southernmost tip of Nova Scotia, while on a voyage between Halifax and Boston, but without loss of life.

While such expansion was taking place on the North Atlantic route, developments were also occurring on ocean routes to other parts of the world.

In 1845 a 400 ton wooden screw-steamer, the MARMORA, was built in the USA for the Turkish government. After a trial voyage from New York to New Orleans, she sailed across the Atlantic to Liverpool, leaving on 2 September 1845 and reaching the Mersey on 26 September at 10.00 am after a voyage of $23\frac{1}{2}$ days, under the command of Captain Page. She was 145 feet long and $24\frac{1}{2}$ feet beam. The MARMORA was a very trim ship with exceedingly tall masts. She was fitted with Ericsson's propellers similar to that of the GREAT BRITAIN (see next chapter). 'The entire steam fixtures, boilers, engines, coal bins and all do not cover a space of more than 16 square feet' (*The Illustrated London News*, 4 October 1845). The main and upper decks had a clean sweep unencumbered by coal or steam machinery of any, description. Her cabins were comfortable and airy, and, fitted out with a great deal of taste and neatness, they provided accommodation for 43 passengers. The MARMORA was the first American steamer to cross the Atlantic to England since the SAVANNAH in 1819. She left Liverpool for Constantinople (Istanbul) at the end of October to be employed by the Turkish Government to ply between Constantinople and Paris (*The Illustrated London News*, 4 October 1845).

MASSACHUSETTS
770 tons
161 x 31.75 feet
R. B. Forbes
1845

Another timber-hulled steamship crossed the Atlantic from west to east and arrived at Liverpool just seven days after the MARMORA. This was a much larger American vessel, the auxillary steam packet ship the MASSACHUSETTS of 770 tons, 161 feet in length and $31\frac{3}{4}$ feet in beam. She had left New York on 15 September 1845. The MASSACHUSETTS was described in a contemporary publication as presenting a novel combination of sailing and steam power. In other words, she was fitted with an Ericsson screw propeller, which could be shifted whenever the wind rendered it desirable to take advantage of the sailing qualities of the vessel, hence the term 'auxiliary steam'. Under the ownership of R. B. Forbes of Boston, two return trips were made by the MASSACHUSETTS from New York to Liverpool before being sold to the American government in 1846 and renamed the FARRALONES.

A large steamship built for the East India Company by Fletcher of Limehouse (London) was launched on 24 January 1846 and named the MOOZOFFER. She was a handsome craft, with a length of 256 feet, a weight of 1,440 tons and two engines of 500 hp each driving side paddles. Her completed cost was £100,000.

June 1847 saw the maiden voyage from New York to Southampton and Bremen of the first steamer of the Ocean Steam Navigation Company (United States). The WASHINGTON, built by Westervelt & McKay of New York, was a wooden-hulled paddle-steamer of 1,640

MARMORA
400 tons
145 x 24.5 feet
Turkish Government
1845

MOOZOFFER
1,440 tons
256 feet
East India Co.
1846

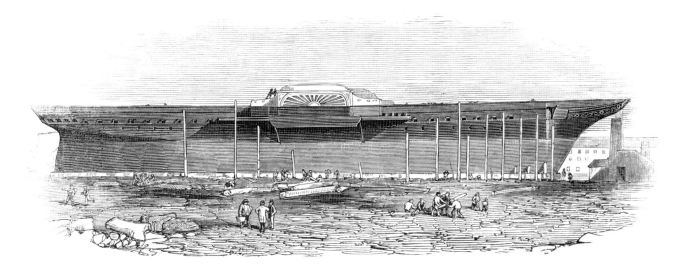

tons and 230 feet in length with a two-cylinder side-lever engine and a service speed of 9 knots. Her first voyage was an unofficial race with the BRITANNIA, which the latter won by two days. *The New York Herald* reported: 'The delay on the passage is stated to have been occasioned by the steam machinery of the WASHINGTON giving way; besides which, she proved a slow goer, and is pronounced by our critics as "any-thing but a handsome steamer".' Accommodation was for 40 first class passengers and 44 second class.

A sister ship named the HERMANN was ordered at the same time from the same builder and made her maiden voyage nine months later. Both ships were sold in 1858 and were used in the Pacific. In 1863, the WASHINGTON was scrapped and the HERMANN was wrecked a year later.

WASHINGTON
1,640 tons
Ocean Steam
Navigation Co.
1847

GREAT BRITAIN
3,500 tons
322 x 50 feet
Great Western Ship Co.
1845

ATLANTIC
2,860 tons
282 x 45 feet
Collins Line
1850

1850–1858

In 1850 a new contender entered the field of North Atlantic travel under the flag of the New York & Liverpool United States Mail Steamship Company, often referred to as 'The Collins Line'. On obtaining the United States contract to carry North Atlantic mail, they placed an order for four similar vessels with James Brown, later Brown & Bell, of New York. The four steamships in order of completion were named the ATLANTIC, the PACIFIC, the ARCTIC and the BALTIC. All were of similar specification, weighing 2,860 tons, being 282 feet long by 45 feet beam, and with wooden hulls with two-cylinder side-lever engines driving paddle-wheels. The ATLANTIC left New York on 27 April 1850 for her maiden voyage to Liverpool

arriving in the Mersey on 10 May. At that time she was the second largest steamship in existence, exceeded only by the GREAT BRITAIN. Her appointments were of a very high standard and were described as follows in *The Illustrated London News* of 25 May 1850:

'It would occupy more space than we can spare to detail the magnificence of the furniture of the ATLANTIC. The carpets are of the richest description; the table slabs are of Brocatelli marble. The stained glass ventilators are let down into the saloon from the deck in the form of chimneys and protected by lattice-work of brass. These ventilators are so constructed that they serve the double purpose of admitting the light and air. They are covered on top with crowns of clear transparent glass, to let down light and keep out the rain, while immediately underneath them are all around apertures which can be opened or closed at pleasure to admit the air. When they are illuminated at night with lamps suspended inside, the effect is very brilliant indeed. The steam heaters are covered marble slabs presenting the appearance of handsome tables. Each stateroom has an elegant sofa, two handsome glasses – one of them so constructed on a pivot that it can be turned in any direction. The berths are of satin-wood and curtains of rich damask.'

The description continues with a report of the maiden voyage:

'The ATLANTIC left New York on the 27th. ult. bringing nearly a hundred passengers and a valuable cargo, under the command of Captain West. Shortly after leaving Sandy Hook (New York), she got entangled amongst some drift ice which did considerable damage to her floats or "buckets" as the Americans term them. This mishap was a serious drawback to her, inasmuch as the engines had to be worked at a reduced rate to prevent the floats from being torn from the wheels altogether, and the weather was too boisterous to admit them being repaired. During the five succeeding days the noble vessel continued to prosecute her voyage to the satisfaction of her Captain and all on board. On the 3rd. instant, however, an accident of a more formidable nature occurred, one of her condensers giving way. After a fruitless

attempt to adjust the machinery, the vessel having been hove to forty hours, Captain West decided to pursue his course, the steam being kept at a low point in consequence, which considerably retarded the vessel's progress during the remainder of her passage.'

The Illustrated London News also noted:

'The ATLANTIC, as well as other vessels building for the same line, are so constructed as to be converted into vessels of war in a few days, should necessity require.'

The ATLANTIC completed her last voyage from Liverpool to New York on 23 December 1857. She was laid up in 1858–59 and in 1860 did one round trip for the North Atlantic Steamship Company before being taken over the following year by the Federal Government as a transport. In 1866 she was purchased by North American Lloyd which had been founded in 1865 by Roger Brothers of New York. After making several voyages in 1866 she was transferred to the New York & Bremen Steamship Company which was another Roger Brothers enterprise. She completed her first voyage for her new owners in February 1867 (New York–Southampton–Bremen) and did six further round trips finishing in New York on 27 November 1867. The ATLANTIC was finally scrapped in 1871.

The interior of the ATLANTIC

The PACIFIC completed her maiden voyage on 25 May 1850 and ran with the company until January 1856 when she was lost without trace on a voyage from Liverpool to New York with 240 drowned.

The ARCTIC began her maiden voyage on 27 October 1850. On 27 September 1854 she was involved in a collision with the French VESTA off Cape Race (Newfoundland) in foggy weather on a voyage from Liverpool to New York with a loss of 322 lives.

The BALTIC's maiden voyage from New York to Liverpool was completed on 16 November 1850. Her last voyage with her original company was Liverpool to New York, completed on 3 February 1858. She was laid up in New York from 1858 to 1861 when, like her sister ship the ATLANTIC, she was taken over by the Federal Government as a Civil War transport. In 1866 she sailed under the flag of North American Lloyd and the following year was transferred to New York & Bremen Steamship Company in company with the ATLANTIC. Her engines were removed in 1870 and she was scrapped in 1880.

Two of the last wooden-hulled steamships built for the Cunard Line were the ASIA and the AFRICA. Both were built in 1850 by Robert Steel & Son of Greenock with two-cylinder side-lever engines built by Robert Napier and a similar specification of 2,226 tons, 266 feet long and 40 feet beam. They remained in service until 1867 when they were sold. When the ASIA was

AFRICA
2,226 tons
266 x 40 feet
Cunard
1850

built she was the largest steamship to be built on the Clyde.

In 1850 an Irish Channel wooden paddle-steamer of 800 tons was taken over by what was to become the New York & Galway Steam Ship Company. Named the VICEROY, she was rather small for the job at only 800 tons but nevertheless sailed for Halifax and New York from Galway on 1 June 1850, arriving in Halifax on 11 June. On the return voyage she left New York on 22 June but ran aground near Cape Sable (Nova Scotia) on 24 June. Fortunately all the passengers, crew and baggage were saved, but the VICEROY was a total loss.

In June 1851 what was described as the largest timber-built steamship ever to be constructed in England was launched at Blackwall, London for the Royal Mail Steam Packet Company and named the AMAZON. She was 3,000 tons, 310 feet long with a beam of 42 feet and 72 feet over the paddle-boxes and was built by R. & H. Green of Blackwall. The 800 horse-power engines were built by Seaward & Capel of Millwall, London, and were fitted in an independant framework to reduce vibration. As with many ships built at this time, she was so constructed as to be easily converted for naval use. She was surveyed and considered capable of carrying 14 twenty-two pounders and two 10 inch pivot guns on her main deck and of accommodating 360 troops. The interior was fitted out in a very elegant style and the cost of the vessel was stated as upwards of £100,000. She arrived at Southampton from the Thames on 16 December 1851 and prepared for her

ASIA
2,226 tons
266 x 40 feet
Cunard
1850

AMAZON
3,000 tons
310 x 42 feet
Royal Mail Line
1851

midnight to allow overheated bearings to cool and again on the following night (Saturday 3 January) for $2\frac{1}{2}$ hours. Early on the Sunday morning when about 110 miles west-south-west of the Scilly Isles, an uncontrollable fire broke out and it was decided to abandon ship. Trouble was encountered in lowering the boats and loss of life was heavy; out of a total of 161 crew and passengers only 21 were saved.

Only a month after the loss of the AMAZON, another new Royal Mail steamship left Southampton for Chagres on her maiden voyage. Built by W. Pitcher at Northfleet (London) with engines by Maudsley, Sons & Field, she was 270 × 42 feet. As a result of the AMAZON disaster she had modified lifeboat apparatus and a weight of 2,250 tons. She was named the ORINOCO and was commanded by Captain Chapman who should have had charge of the AMAZON.

1853 started with the maiden voyage on Saturday 1 January of the last wooden-hulled steamship built for the Cunard Line. She was one of a pair of twin ships and originally was destined to be named the PERSIA. However, her sister which should have been the ARABIA was sold to the Royal West India Company and named LA PLATA, and the PERSIA became the ARABIA. It is not known whether the sale was the result of a conscious decision by Cunard not to have any more wooden ships driven by paddle-wheel. The ARABIA was built by Napier of Glasgow. She was 285 feet long with a beam of 41 feet and weighed 2,393

maiden voyage to the West Indies. She was the first of the new 'direct line' steamships intended to run every two weeks between Southampton and Chagres (Panama). In spite of very glowing reports on the magnificence of her engines, shortly after leaving Southampton on 2 January 1852 on her maiden voyage, she had to stop off Portland Bill between 8.00 pm and

ORINOCO
2,250 tons
270 x 42 feet
Royal Mail Line
1851

ARABIA
2,393 tons
285 × 41 feet
Cunard
1853

the mail. She plied the Atlantic for a year before being taken over as a Crimean War transport. After she had returned to the North Atlantic route, she was involved in a collision with another of the company's vessels, the EUROPA, off Cape Race (Newfoundland) in which both were damaged but repaired. From 1859 onwards she transferred to the Liverpool–Halifax–Boston run until her last voyage on 3 September 1864, when she had her engines removed and was sold.

The EUROPA was one of the early Cunard wooden paddle-steamers of 1,834 tons and 251 × 38 feet which had been built by John Wood of Glasgow in 1848 and had served on the Liverpool–Boston–New York service. She was requisitioned by the government in 1854 for the conveyance of troops to the Crimea. On 18 November 1854 she took on 155 men of the Royal Artillery and a detachment of infantry at Liverpool, before sailing for Dublin to pick up men of the 90th Light Infantry and leaving the next morning for the Crimea.

1853 had seen Cunard's last wooden-hulled paddle-steamer, but it was another three years before the last and at the same time the largest wooden paddle-steamer was built for the Collins Line. The ADRIATIC, built by George Steers of New York and launched on 7 April 1856, had engines by the New York Novelty Works which were said to be the two largest oscillating

tons. Her engines were stated to be the largest and most powerful ever put into a ship at that time, with a 9 foot stroke and an 8 foot 5 inch bore driving a 36 foot paddle-wheel. They were supplied with steam from a tubular boiler placed amid-ship. Her fitting out was luxurious and she had accommodation for 180 passengers as well as 1,200 tons of coal and a full cargo and

EUROPA
1,834 tons
251 × 38 feet
Cunard
1848

ADRIATIC
3,670 tons
355 x 30 feet
Collins Line
1856

engines ever constructed. She was 355 feet long with a beam of 50 feet. Her paddle-wheels were 40 feet in diameter and her total weight was 3,670 tons. She sailed from New York on her maiden voyage to England on 23 November 1857 and reached Point Lynas at 9.00 pm on Thursday 3 December after a run of ten days and four hours. It was estimated that had she run direct to Liverpool she would have made that port in ten days and eight hours. The massive engines were rated at 1,500 horsepower, but were considered to be capable of an output of 2,800 horsepower with two cylinders, each 100 inches in diameter, and a stroke of 120 inches. She had accommodation for about 400 passengers, 300 of them being First Class. She had a crew of 183 made up as shown below.

In 1858, the Collins Line ceased to operate and the ADRIATIC was laid up after completing only one return voyage for her owners. She was then operated for five round voyages between New York and Southampton by the North Atlantic Steamship Company, making her final trip in March 1861. The ADRIATIC was purchased in 1861 by the Atlantic Royal Mail Steam Navigation Company (the Galway Line), and sailed on her first voyage for her new owner from Galway on 23 April 1861 for St. Johns (Newfoundland) and New York. Soon after her acquisition, the Galway Line had to suspend operations, due to a change in the Mail contract, and it was 1863 before sailings were resumed. However, the end of the year also saw the end of the company and the ADRIATIC made her last voyage under the Galway flag on 18 December 1863 from Liverpool to New York. It would appear that this great ship only made seven return voyages between America and Europe before losing her engines in 1869 and being converted to sail. In 1873 she became a hulk at Bonny near Port Harcour in Nigeria.

CREW OF THE ADRIATIC			
1 Commander	1 Engineer	1 Steward	1 Chief Cook
4 Mates	3 Assistant Engineers	3 Assistant Stewards	1 Assistant Cook
1 Surgeon	6 Superintendants of	36 Waiters	1 Baker
1 Purser	Fires and Boilers	3 Stewardesses	2 Pastry Cooks
4 Quatermasters	4 Oilers	2 Storekeepers	2 Engineers Messmen
2 Carpenters	2 Engineer Storekeepers	1 Bar-keeper	2 Keepers of Lamps
1 Boatswain	24 Firemen (Stokers)	1 Barber	and Oil
36 Seamen	36 Coal-Persons		1 Hose-keeper

CHAPTER 3

The Iron Age 1838−1881

After the success of the steamship GREAT WESTERN, Isambard Kingdom Brunel and his co-directors of the Great Western Steam Ship Company decided that a ship of at least 2,000 tons to be called the MAMMOTH was needed for the expected improved demand for passages across the Atlantic. In 1838, shortly after the GREAT WESTERN had completed her second voyage to America and back, Brunel observed a small steamship with an iron hull named the RAINBOW, which was in the Port of Bristol. She was

taking on a cargo for Antwerp, and Brunel suggested to his friend Christopher Claxton, a retired naval Captain, and William Patterson, a shipbuilder of Bristol, that they sail on the RAINBOW to Antwerp and observe her performance. Their reports were favourable, so the directors of the Great Western Steam Ship Company decided to build in iron. Ultimately designs for a mammoth 3,000 ton vessel were approved and the keel was laid down in July 1839. It had initially been proposed to use paddle-wheels for propulsion, but difficulties had

THE ARCHIMEDES, STEAMER.

ARCHIMEDES
237 tons
Ship Propeller Co.
1838

been encountered with the very heavy forging required to make the drive shaft.

Again fate intervened, for in May 1840, an unusual steamship named the ARCHIMEDES entered the Port of Bristol, being a vessel of 237 tons, which had been launched at Millwall in 1838. She was very aptly named as she was propelled, not by paddle-wheels, but by a screw propeller and was the first sea-going steamship in the world to be fitted with a 'screw'. Richard Guppy, a wealthy sugar merchant-cum-engineer and one of Brunel's colleagues in the Great Western Railway, took a trip on the ARCHIMEDES to Liverpool and reported very favourably to Brunel. As a result it was decided to give consideration to using a 'screw' on the GREAT BRITAIN instead of paddles. To this end the company chartered the ARCHIMEDES for six months to carry out tests, with a resulting change in design and abandonment of the partly completed paddle engines.

This new engine designed to drive a screw had four cylinders 7 foot 4 inches in diameter and a stroke of 6 feet in the form of two inverted 'Vs' with a one to three multiple chain drive to the propeller shaft. The boiler supplied steam at 15lbs per square inch and with engines running at 18 revolutions per minute, a propeller shaft speed of 54 revolutions per minute was attained. Built by the Great Western Company, the iron hull was 322 × 50 feet 6 inches and she weighed 3,500 tons. The GREAT BRITAIN was launched in July 1843 by HRH Prince Albert and taken out of her dock and

into the River Avon in December. On 23 January 1845 she sailed for London to complete her fitting out. According to an advertisement in *The Times* of 22 August 1845, she had accommodation for 360 passengers with a crew of 130 and carried 1,100 tons of coal in her bunkers plus a hold for cargo. The GREAT BRITAIN steamed out of Liverpool on 26 July 1845 to start her maiden voyage to New York. The journey was completed in 14 days and 21 hours and the return in 15 days and 12 hours, these times being rather disappointing. She did one more return trip in 1845, breaking her propeller on the return voyage and having to complete the journey by sail. The ship was laid up at the end of the 1845 season and during the winter a number of modifications were carried out.

The 1846 season started well, but disaster struck the GREAT BRITAIN on 22 September 1846. She left Liverpool with 180 passengers (the largest number of passengers ever embarked on an Atlantic crossing) but during the night of 22/23 September she ran aground in Dundrum Bay between Belfast and Dundalk on the east coast of Ireland and all the passengers had to be taken off. After consultation with Brunel, arrangements were made for her winter protection, and she was refloated in August 1847 and towed to Liverpool for repair.

This unfortunate disaster ruined the Great Western Steam Ship Company, and after repair the GREAT BRITAIN was sold in 1850 to Gibbs, Bright & Company. They changed the engines to one of half the power and

STEAM FROM LIVERPOOL TO AUSTRALIA,

FORMING PART OF

THE LIVERPOOL "EAGLE LINE" OF PACKETS.

A Steamboat will leave the Old Seacombe Slip Prince's Dock, on Saturday Morning, 21st August, at 10 a.m., and 12 noon, taking off Passengers and their hat-boxes and carpet-bags only.

None but Passengers having tickets, will be allowed on board the "GREAT BRITAIN" on 21st Aug.

THE GREAT BRITAIN

IRON SCREW STEAMER, 3,500 TONS, & 500 HORSE POWER,

B. R. MATHEWS, COMMANDER,

WILL BE

DESPATCHED FROM THE RIVER MERSEY FOR

MELBOURNE, PORT PHILIP; AND SYDNEY, NEW SOUTH WALES,

CALLING AT THE CAPE OF GOOD HOPE FOR COALS, WATER, AND FRESH PROVISIONS.

On SATURDAY, August the 21st, at One o'Clock, p.m.

THE VESSEL WILL LEAVE THE DOCK THE PREVIOUS DAY.

This magnificent Ship, fitted up with every possible convenience, has just performed her Trial Voyage to New York in the most satisfactory manner, and with remarkable rapidity. Fully equipped for sailing, she combines all the advantages of a Clipper-ship with those of a powerful Steamer, adapting her in a peculiar manner for a long voyage, and securing its being made in the shortest possible time.

FARES:

To MELBOURNE :

After-Saloon, 70—72—73—80 Guineas,	Including Provisions, Live Stock, Luxuries and Delicacies.
Fore-Saloon, 40—41—42—50 "	Including all articles of food of the best quality necessary to provide a plain substantial table, and attendance.
Second Cabin, 30—35 "	Including food of the best quality, as per Scale, and attendance.

To SYDNEY, 5 Guineas extra will be charged.
To the CAPE OF GOOD HOPE,—After Saloon 50 Guineas.

CHILDREN, FROM 1 TO 14, HALF-PRICE.

Including Stewards' Fees, the attendance of an experienced Surgeon, and all Provisions of the best quality, except Wines, Spirits, and Malt Liquors, which will be supplied at very moderate prices on board.

In the After and Fore-Saloon State Rooms every requisite will be provided, including Beds, Berths, Plate, Bedding, Linen.

In the Second Cabin the Passengers will have to supply themselves with Bed, Bedding, and Linen, which may be purchased at Silver & Co.'s St. George's Crescent, Liverpool. The berths are 6 feet by 20 inches.

The AFTER-SALOON is fitted with Ladies' Boudoirs, Music, and Smoking Rooms, Baths, &c.

DECK.—The Poop aft is appropriated to the After Saloon Passengers alone. The Spar deck amidships to the After and Fore-Saloon Passengers, and forward to the Second Cabin Passengers.

No Passenger can be accommodated in a State Room by himself, so long as he can be placed with other Passengers, unless the State-Room is specially arranged for; and Berths may be changed before sailing, if necessary, unless a whole State-Room is secured.

Poster advertising one of the GREAT BRITAIN's trips to Australia

---

112   THE ILLUSTRATED LONDON NEWS.   [FEBRUARY 15, 1845.

INTERIOR OF "THE GREAT BRITAIN" STEAM-SHIP.

This stupendous steam-ship has been inspected by crowds of visitors during the past week. She continues moored off Blackwall, close to the terminus of the Railway, of which economical access thousands have availed themselves.

Although we have already illustrated the construction of this "interesting monster" (see Nos. 63 and 138 of our Journal), there remain to be described her interior fittings. Their style partakes of that plainness and simplicity which characterises the entire vessel. In this respect, consists her claim to admiration, as well as in the vastness of her proportions, and the rigid utilitarianism with which not one inch of space is thrown away. In illustration of the latter, we annex two engravings, in which the situation of the machinery, and the general interior accommodation, are clearly seen at one view.

SECTION OF "THE GREAT BRITAIN."

UPPER DECK OF "THE GREAT BRITAIN."

The next illustration shows the Upper Deck of "The Great Britain." The third Engraving shows the Promenade Deck of "The Great Britain." The most noticeable peculiarity here, is the range of "lights" on each side of the vast apartment : these, in form, resemble "cucumber frames," and like them, are glazed, and admit the light to the Saloon and Cabins beneath. This Promenade is sheltered by the upper deck from the air, and will, accordingly, prove a very convenient resort for the passengers during inclement weather.

The fourth illustration shows the Saloon of "The Great Britain." In this vast apartment, which is the main room, 360 persons can dine. There is little by way of ornament either in this Saloon, or in the Promenade. In both, the sides, roof, and supporting columns, are imitative wainscot with a slight moulding around the tablets, on which are neat allegorical figures.

Probably, we cannot better conclude than by the following passage from a very able précis of the structural merits of "The Great Britain," in the Athenæum :—

"But we must descend from our promenade on the deck into the huge caverns, the cauldrons below. The first peculiarity noticed, is the engine and the enormous chain and chain-wheel for driving the screw. Four separate steam-engines drive round the axis of this monstrous wheel—two at one end of the axle, two at the other—the wheel between. The cylinders are placed apart at the bottom of the vessel, and the piston rods, which issue out of them, converge to the end of the cranks of this wheel. Each pair of engines works one crank, and the two cranks are placed at right angles; but the chain is the extraordinary thing; there are grooves on the wheel—at the end of each link of this huge chain there are teeth projecting into these grooves, so that as the wheel revolves the chain is compelled to revolve with it; at the bottom of the vessel, immediately below the great wheel, lies a little wheel or pinion, having grooves cut in its circumference of the same size, and at the same distance from each other, though less in number than those of the large wheel. The same chain passes round both wheels, and while the large wheel revolves by the power of the engines once, the small one revolves as much oftener as it is smaller. The small wheel has for its axis, the axis of the Archimedes Screw, which is attached to the after end of the axis, and protrudes through an aperture at the stern into the water. Its revolutions give motion to the vessel by their reaction on the water. Such is the Vital Principle of this Monster of the Deep."

PROMENADE DECK OF THE "GREAT BRITAIN."

THE SALOON OF "THE GREAT BRITAIN."

LONDON : Printed and Published at the Office, 198, Strand, in the Parish of St. Clement Danes, in the County of Middlesex, by WILLIAM LITTLE, 198, Strand, aforesaid.—SATURDAY, FEBRUARY 15, 1845.

Cross section, upper deck and interior of the GREAT BRITAIN

---

redesigned the screw, while outwardly giving her two funnels instead of one. In 1852 she sailed from Liverpool on her first voyage to Australia. During the next 23 years she made 32 round trips to Australia, and in 1875 she was put up for sale and bought by A. Gibbs of London in 1882, who removed her engine and converted her to a three-masted sailing ship. In 1886 she was severely damaged in a gale off Cape Horn and made for the shelter of the Falkland Islands, where she was condemned as unseaworthy and sold to the Falkland Islands Company who used her as a store for coal and wool until 1933. In 1937 she was beached at Sparrow Cove (Falkland Islands) until rescued in 1970 and brought back to Bristol for preservation in the same

CAPRI
600 tons
Neapolitan Steam
Navigation Co.
1846

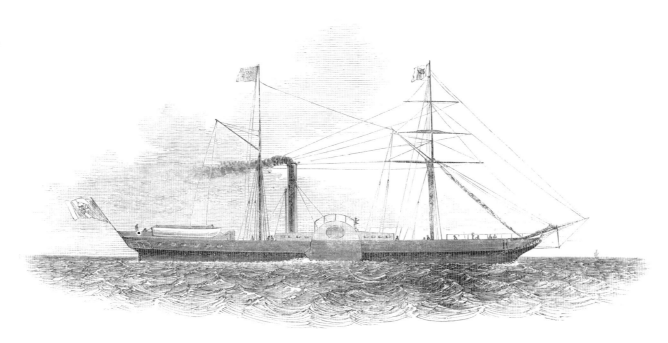

dock in which she had been built and where she may still be seen.

In 1846 two iron ships were built by Ditchburn & Mare of London for the Neapolitan Steam Navigation Company for 'cruising' in the Mediterranean. They were named VESUVIO and CAPRI and were paddle-steamers of 600 tons and approximately 150 feet in length, with 220 horsepower twin-cylinder engines supplied by Maudsley & Field. They had sleeping accommodation for 180 passengers and were fitted out in the most elegant and commodious manner. The saloon resembled a drawing-room more than a cabin on board ship. The panels were of maplewood and the mouldings were of carved mahogany, the sofas were covered with crimson-figured velvet and all the furniture was either maple or mahogany.

ship. The object was to sail from Hamburg to America direct. The HELENA SLOMAN made her maiden voyage from Hamburg on 9 June 1850 with 400 passengers. On 26 October 1850 she left Hamburg on her third voyage to America with 110 passengers and picked up a further 40 at Southampton leaving on 1 November. She ran into trouble towards the end of November, but although 141 of her passengers were rescued, the HELENA SLOMAN was left in a sinking condition. The company then abandoned all further steamship projects.

In 1851 a very handsome screw steamship named ARNO was built by Reid & Wood of Glasgow for work in the Mediterranean. She was not a large vessel being only 700 tons with a length of 200 feet and a beam of

HELENA SLOMAN
800 tons
Robert M. Sloman
1850

1850–1859

In 1850 the German firm of Robert M. Sloman of Hamburg purchased an 800 ton iron-hulled screw steamship from T. & W. Pim of Hull. At that time she was the largest steamship built on the River Humber and was named HELENA SLOMAN. She was the first of what was to have been a line of steamers designed for conveying emigrants from Germany to the United States of America. Their route had previously been from Hamburg to Hull and thence by rail to Liverpool where they embarked in either an English or American

BOSPHORUS
General Screw
Steamship Co.
1850

28 feet. She was described by a contemporary publication as a beautiful specimen of Clyde shipbuilding, the finest screw steamship, in appearance, size and speed that had ever appeared at Liverpool. She was built for John Bibby & Sons and other parties in Liverpool, under the title of the Liverpool & Mediterranean Screw Steamship Company.

1850 saw the commencement of steam passages to Cape Town by the General Screw Steamship Company, who already ran services to India and the Far East. The first Admiralty contract for the regular carriage of mails to South Africa was placed with this company in 1851, and the first return voyage was carried out by the screw steamship BOSPHORUS. This vessel left Plymouth on 18 December 1850 with a full compliment of passengers, and after calling at Madiera and Porto Grande in St. Vincent (one of the Cape Verde Islands) reached Sierra Leone in 16 days. A contemporary newspaper said that: 'No vessel has ever accomplished this in so short a time, even making a direct passage, whereas St Vincent is 900 miles out of the track. Leaving Sierra Leone on 4 January 1851, the BOSPHORUS reached Cape Town on the 27, and though the South-East trade wind was particularly adverse, she thus completed the passage in 40 days. This was the quickest voyage to Cape Town, even by the fastest vessels, steam or sailing, going direct. Her almost unexpected arrival at the Cape was greeted with heartfelt delight and the commencement of the line is considered a great boon to the colony. Many of the elite of the inhabitants of Cape Town and its environs visited the BOSPHORUS during

her short stay in Table Bay, and returned highly pleased with their reception and the odour and cleanliness of the vessel.'

In 1850 the Liverpool & Philadelphia Steam Ship Company was formed by two brothers Richard and William Inman. The first ship they acquired was the 1,609 ton CITY OF GLASGOW from her builders Tod & McGregor of Kelvin Dock Glasgow, who had themselves sailed her on four return voyages between Glasgow and New York, before she was taken over to run her first voyage for her new owners in December 1850. The CITY OF GLASGOW was 227 feet with a 34 feet beam and was of iron construction with screw propulsion driven by a two-cylinder geared beam engine. She was quickly followed by a slightly larger ship, also built by Tod & McGregor, the CITY OF MANCHESTER. This new ship was 1,892 tons, also with an iron hull and screw propulsion driven by a similar geared beam engine. She was launched on 14 June 1851 at the Tod & McGregor yard and was completed and ready to go to sea in three weeks. In fact, the three boilers each weighing 30 tons were all got aboard and fixed in their places on the evening of the same day as the launch. The CITY OF MANCHESTER, with a length of 262 feet and a beam of 36 feet, was at the time the largest screw-steamer built on the Clyde. She sailed from Liverpool on her maiden voyage to Philadelphia on 26 July 1851, just 42 days after being launched, which must have been something of a record. Between 1854 and 1856 she became a Crimean War transport, and after a refit and modification which increased her

CITY OF MANCHESTER
1,892 tons
262 x 36 feet
Liverpool & Philadephia
Steamship Co.

tonnage to 2,109, she went back onto the Liverpool –Philadelphia service. A year later she acted as a transport to India during the Mutiny and then returned to the North Atlantic.

In the meantime, two disasters struck the company in 1854. On 1 March 1854 the CITY OF GLASGOW sailed from Liverpool to Philadelphia with 480 passengers and crew on board and was never heard of again. In September, the CITY OF PHILADELPHIA, a brand new and slightly larger vessel (2,168 tons and 294 × 39 feet) set off from Liverpool on 9 September for her maiden voyage to Philadelphia and ten days later was wrecked off Cape Race, Newfoundland, fortunately without loss of life. The CITY OF MANCHESTER continued with the Liverpool to Philadelphia service until 1871 when she was sold and her engines removed. Presumably she saw service as a sailing vessel until she was wrecked in 1876.

Following the success of the BOSPHORUS, the General Screw Steamship Company took delivery in 1852 of a new vessel the QUEEN OF THE SOUTH, built by J. C. Mare & Co. of Blackwall, London. She was 240 feet with a beam of 39 feet and weighed 1,777 tons (some authorities say 2,221 tons). The engines were built by Maudsley, had a direct drive to the screw and ran at 60 revolutions per minute, a high speed for those days. The blades of the propeller were of novel design and when required could be feathered and thrown in line with the keel, so as not to impede the ship when under sail. When the company ran into financial difficulties, the QUEEN OF THE SOUTH

became a Crimean War transport until 1857, when she was purchased together with seven other vessels by the European & American Steam Shipping Company. Under her new owners she was on the Bremen, Southampton and New York route and commenced her first voyage in this service on 25 April 1857. In 1859 she was transferred to the Anglo-Luso-Brazilian Royal Mail Steam Navigation Company and was renamed the MILFORD HAVEN. Two years later she again changed her flag and came into the ownership of the East India & London Shipping Company, regaining her original name QUEEN OF THE SOUTH.

QUEEN OF THE SOUTH
1,777 tons
240 x 39 feet
General Screw
Steamship Co.
1852

CLEOPATRA
1,500 tons
235 × 37 feet
McKean, M'Clarty & Co.
1852

In early September 1852 a new ship started on her maiden voyage to Australia. Her name was the CLEOPATRA and she was owned by McKean, McClarty & Co. of Liverpool. With an iron hull and a clipper bow, she weighed 1,500 tons and was built by Alexander Denny & Brothers of Dumbarton. She was 235 feet long x 37 feet beam and had screw propulsion. Her accommodation was for 130 First and 120 Second Class passengers and 60 Third Class for emigrants only who were required to supply their own beds and bedding. The cost of a passage of approximately 60 days varied from £65–80 for First Class passengers to £40 for Second Class and £25 for Third Class. The CLEOPATRA was fitted with an artificial refrigerator calculated to preserve fresh meat for three to four weeks and condensing equipment capable of producing 1,000 gallons of fresh water per day. She had stowage for 600 tons of cargo and 600 tons of coal. She sailed from the Thames on her maiden voyage on 4 September 1852 for Sydney and Melbourne via Cape Town. In 1853 she was sold to the Canadian Steam Navigation Company and made her first voyage from Liverpool to Quebec and Montreal on 14 July 1853. After seven return voyages the CLEOPATRA became a Crimean War transport between 1854 and 1855. In 1856 she was sold to the African Steam Ship Company, and six years later she was wrecked off the coast of Sierra Leone.

In 1852 the African Steam Ship Company had ordered five iron-hulled screw steamships to be built by Macgregor Laird of Birkenhead. The first of these ships was named the FORERUNNER. A handsome ship with clipper bow, she weighed 381 tons and was 160 feet by 22 feet. She left Plymouth on 24 September 1852 on her maiden voyage to Sierra Leone calling at Madiera,

Teneriffe, Goree and Bathurst in the Gambia on her way, and arriving back in Plymouth on 22 November. Her four sisters the FAITH, the HOPE, the CHARITY and the NORTHERN LIGHT were all much larger at 1,200 tons. The African Steam Ship Company was managed by Elder, Dempster & Company who gained control of them in the 1890s.

In 1852 the Australian Royal Mail Steam Navigation Company ordered two vessels for carrying mails between England and Sydney. Named the ADELAIDE and the VICTORIA, these steamships were built by Scott Russell & Company of Millwall, London under the direction of I. K. Brunel, who framed the specification on which they were constructed, but did not design them. Brunel, always one for original ideas, advised upon ships of 5,000 to 6,000 tons which would only have to call for coal at Cape Town. However this recommendation must have frightened the directors out of their wits and in the event the vessels had a weight of 1,822 tons, and were 288 × 38 feet. The keel of the ADELAIDE was laid down on 26 May 1852 and she was launched on 12 November the same year, with her masts, yards and rigging complete and her engines and boilers fitted ready for sea. In her trial trip on 20 November she attained a speed of $12\frac{1}{2}$ knots and the Admiralty inspectors confirmed the results which were the best that had been obtained at that time from a screw propeller. Accommodation was provided for 80 First and 120 Second Class passengers. The ADELAIDE left England on her maiden voyage to Sydney on 9

FORERUNNER
381 tons
160 × 22 feet
African Steamship Co.
1852

ADELAIDE
1,822 tons
288 × 38 feet
Australian Royal Mail Steam
Navigation Co.

December 1852 and reached Adelaide in 60 days, thereby winning a prize of £500 offered by the Australian colonies. Her sister ship sailed two months later. However after this success, these ships proved very unreliable in performance and they were often outstripped by weeks by the sailing clipper-ships over a return voyage. As a result, they were unprofitable and the service closed at the end of the year. The further history of these two ships is hard to find, but the ADELAIDE was chartered in April 1859 by the Galway Line and made two return voyages from Galway to New York.

The steamship SYDNEY was built by William Denny & Brothers of Dumbarton in 1852 for the Australian Royal Mail Steam Navigation Company. An iron-hulled vessel of 1,500 tons and 216 × 34 feet, she had a clipper bow and screw propulsion. The SYDNEY left London on 31 July 1852 on her maiden voyage to Australia, calling at Plymouth, St Vincent and the Cape of Good Hope on the way and arriving in Sydney on 16 November, having made further coastal stops in Australia. Her return voyage created considerable interest because of the very valuable cargo she carried – £800,000 in gold – in addition to 122 adult passengers and 17 children, and a further £2,000 in fares obtained from intermediate passengers en route.

A timetable of her journey makes interesting reading. Having sailed from Sydney on 4 December 1852 she arrived at Port Phillip (Melbourne) in 89 hours and remained there 3 days and 7 hours. On 11 December she sailed for Adelaide where she arrived on the 14th in

$61\frac{3}{4}$ hours, and remained 3 days and 9 hours taking on passengers and the gold. The SYDNEY sailed from Adelaide on 17 December and arrived at King George's Sound (the southern tip of South-West Australia) on 23 December having taken 6 days. She remained 9 days $3\frac{1}{2}$ hours taking on coal and sailed on 1 January 1853 for the Cape of Good Hope where she arrived on 1 February after a voyage of 30 days and 23 hours. She then remained at the Cape for 4 days and $12\frac{1}{2}$ hours taking on coal and sailed on 6 February for St. Vincent where she arrived on 26 February after a voyage of 20 days $13\frac{1}{2}$ hours. She remained coaling for 3 days 21 hours and sailed on 2 March, arriving at Plymouth in 14 days 3 hours on 16 March 1853. It would seem that subsequently the SYDNEY came under the flag of the

SYDNEY
1,500 tons
216 × 34 feet
Australian Royal Mail Steam
Navigation Co.

ANTELOPE
1,200 tons
214 feet long
Millers & Thompson
1853

later in the year, when she sailed for Australia and arrived at Sydney on the 27 January 1854. Her owners intended to sell her in Australia for use on coastal services, but it is not clear if this was ever done, because three years later it would appear that she was chartered by the North Atlantic Steam Navigation Company for one return voyage from Liverpool to St. John's, Halifax and Portland, before presumably returning to Australian waters.

On 17 May 1853 the iron paddle-steamer ATRATO, which was described as the largest ship in the world was launched at the Greenock yard of Caird & Co. Her overall length was 350 feet with a beam of 42 feet. She was the first iron-hulled paddle-steamer built for the Royal Mail Steam Packet Company (Royal Mail Lines). The ATRATO's weight was 3,466 tons, 30 less than the GREAT BRITAIN but she was 40 feet longer and provided accommodation for 224 First Class passengers. After many years sailing under the Royal Mail flag, she was sold in 1880 to the Adamson & Ronaldson Line and, having been renamed the ROCHESTER, she was used on the London to Boston service. In 1882 she was transferred to the South American trade as a sailing vessel with auxiliary screw. She was wrecked in 1884.

Melbourne Steamship Company, which had been formed in the 1860s. She was renamed the MELUSIA and was later sold to an Eastern company by Burns & Phillips who had been her last owners.

The ANTELOPE was built in 1845 as a sailing ship and had a very successful life under sail, in one instance having made Rio de Janiero in 27 days, the quickest time on record at that date, as well as having sailed round Cape Horn to California. Her owners Millers & Thompson of Liverpool, who had eyes on the trade with the Antipodes, decided to have her lengthened and engines installed with a screw propeller. For this purpose she was placed in the hands of John Laird of Birkenhead. She was lengthened to 214 feet and her new weight was stated as 1,200 tons. This rebuild was put in hand in February 1853 and not completed until

The 'largest steamships in the world' seemed to come thick and fast from 1853 on! Soon after the launch of the ATRATO, came the HIMALAYA, a screw steamship built by Mare & Company of Blackwall (London) for the Peninsular and Orient Company (P & O). With a length of 340 feet and a beam of 46

ATRATO
3,466 tons
350 × 42 feet
Royal Mail Lines
1853

HIMALAYA
3,550 tons
340 x 46 feet
P & O
1854

increasing price of coal due to the Crimean War, P & O found her too expensive to run economically. She was purchased by the government for £130,000 and became a permanent troop-ship until 1894. The following year her engines were removed and she was laid up at Devonport and converted into a coal-hulk. In 1920 she was sold by the government to the Admiralty and moved to Portland where she lay until destroyed in an air-raid in 1940 when she was 87 years old.

On 10 July 1855 yet another 'largest steamship in the world' was launched. This time it was the PERSIA built by Robert Napier at Govan for the Cunard Line. She was 390 feet long with a beam of 45 feet and weighed 3,600 tons. It was to take another six months to complete this ship which was to be both the second last paddle-steamer built for Cunard and the pride of their fleet. Her maiden voyage from Liverpool to New York commenced on 26 January 1856. On this first crossing she had a minor collision with an iceberg which delayed her, but soon she was to hold the Blue Riband for the fastest eastbound Atlantic crossing from May 1856 until December 1863, improving her time from 9 days 12 hours 7 minutes to 9 days 5 hours during this period. Later she was chartered by the government to carry troops to Canada and just reached Quebec before the St. Lawrence froze. In 1868 she was sold to another ship owner who removed her engines.

The origins of the Blue Riband are somewhat obscure and no one seems clear just when and how it began. Recording steamship times for transatlantic

feet, she weighed 3,550 tons, which was 300 tons more than the GREAT BRITAIN. The 700 horse-power engines were built by John Penn & Son. Fitting out was completed early in 1854 and on 20 January she left Southampton on a trial maiden voyage to Alexandria. A contemporary publication said that: 'The possession of such a stupendous steam-ship as the HIMALAYA must be a matter not merely of local but of national interest. If, unhappily, the threatened war should break out, there is no telling the uses to which this vessel might not be applied.' (Shades of the CANBERRA.) HIMALAYA made one more voyage under the P & O flag as a troop carrier to the Crimea. However, with the

PERSIA
3,600 tons
390 x 45 feet
Cunard
1855

ROYAL CHARTER
2,720 tons
335 x 41 feet
Liverpool & Australian
Navigation Co.
1856

voyages started in 1838 and has continued to the present day. There has always been interest in England and America as to who held the current record. An actual 'Blue Riband' does not seem to exist although in 1935 H. K. Hales, MP, presented a silver cup to be held by the fastest passenger-carrying ship between the fastnet and Ambrose lighthouses.

On 17 January 1856 the Liverpool & Australian Navigation Company's steam clipper the ROYAL CHARTER left Liverpool on her maiden voyage to Melbourne. As previously mentioned, there was considerable doubt in the minds of those companies operating between England and Australia via the Cape, as to which was the best method of propulsion – steam or sail. The ROYAL CHARTER was built by William Patterson at Bristol, who had previously built the GREAT BRITAIN. She was 335 × 41 feet and weighed 2,720 tons. She could carry a spread of 15,000 square feet of canvas as well as having a 200 horse-power engine which had been built by Penn of Greenwich for working the auxiliary screw. The screw was so arranged that when not wanted, it could be completely lifted out of the water and if necessary placed on the deck. The Liverpool & Australian Navigation Company had become convinced that neither steamers relying entirely on their engines, nor sailing vessels trusting only to

sails, could make the passage with regularity and despatch. The steamer would either need to carry coal for the whole voyage and thus lose much valuable space, or it would require stops at coaling stations and thereby lose valuable time. The ROYAL CHARTER operated on the Liverpool to Melbourne service for nearly five years and an average voyage took 59 days.

When she sailed from Melbourne on 26 August 1859, in addition to over 400 passengers she was carrying 68,397 ounces of gold and £48,000 in gold sovereigns, and with passengers' valuables had a cargo worth nearly £400,000. Having had a trouble-free voyage as far as the Irish Sea, 13 passengers and the mail were taken off by the pilot-boat at Queenstown before proceeding to Liverpool. It happened that the GREAT EASTERN was at Holyhead, and the Captain was asked to sail in-shore to give his passengers a good view of the mammoth ship. When doing this a storm blew up with disastrous results. After a night of terror the ROYAL CHARTER was driven onto the rocks at Moelfre Bay, Anglesey. The ship was a total loss and 459 passengers and crew died on 26 October 1859.

On 30 December 1855 the latest addition to P & O's fleet had her sea trials. Bearing the name PERA, she was the largest vessel owned by the company (the HIMALAYA had been larger but had been sold to the

Menu from the PERA
1869

government). She was 2,630 tons and 303 × 42 feet and was built by Mare & Company. Although smaller than the HIMALAYA she had almost as much accommodation. She had compound engines with a one to two ratio gear to the propeller shaft drive. However she was not a very successful ship; in the first three years she twice broke her main shaft and on two occasions was almost completely destroyed by fire. In August 1858 she was used to take a party of Members of the British House of Commons from Southampton to the Cherbourg Fetes. The PERA was sold at the end of the 1870s to another British shipowner.

The GENOVA was also built by Mare & Company in 1856 for the Italian Transatlantica Company. With a weight of 1,950 tons, she was 286 × 38 feet and had an iron hull with clipper bow. Engines supplied by Maudsley provided the power to drive the screw. Two months later her sister ship, the TORINO, was launched from the same yard. The purpose of these two ships was to establish a service between Genoa and New York in addition to their South American business. After the Crimean War, trade was bad and in 1859 the Genoese

PERA
2,630 tons
303 × 42 feet
P & O
1855

TORINO
2,000 tons
263 × 38 feet
Italian Transatlantica Co.
1856

Transatlantica Company was dissolved and the ships sold off. Thereafter they only had a short life. The GENOVA was destroyed by fire at Malaga, and the TORINO was lost in 1860.

In October 1857 the European & Australian Royal Mail Company took delivery from J. & G. Thomson of Glasgow of a new ship called the AUSTRALASIAN. She was 2,750 tons, 322 × 42 feet and had an iron hull with a clipper bow. When built she was supposed to be the most powerful steamship afloat, as well as having accommodation for 200 Cabin Class passengers and 1,200 tons of cargo. She left Southampton on 12 October 1857 on her maiden voyage to Alexandria and, after returning to England, went out to Suez to work on the 'second leg' of the Australian service. In 1860 she was taken over by the Cunard Line from the then bankrupt European & Australian Royal Mail Company in settlement of unpaid charter fees. The AUSTRALASIAN started work for her new owners by sailing between Liverpool and New York. In December 1860, she made Cunard history by being the first screw steamer to carry the Liverpool to New York Mails. However, she was an unsatisfactory vessel, being too

light for the North Atlantic service and subject to excessive rolling. Most of the time she was kept as a reserve steamer for the New York service until 1869, when, having been renamed the CALABRIA and fitted with a new single expansion engines, she had accommodation for 80 saloon and 900 steerage passengers. Her first voyage after rebuilding was Liverpool to New York on 8 January 1870. Early in 1876 she was sold and became a cable-laying ship. She was eventually broken up in 1896.

In 1857 the North German Lloyd Line (Norddeutscher Lloyd) took delivery of two steamships from Palmer, Allport & Company of Jarrow-on-the-Tyne (England). The first to be delivered was the HUDSON, an iron screw steamship of 3,000 tons (although some sources say 2,226 tons, another 2,166) and 345 × 40 feet. The nominal horsepower of her engines was 750 and steam was supplied by four boilers each with six furnace holes. The ship had accommodation for 620 passengers. On 11 September 1858 she sailed from Bremen on her maiden voyage to New York. On her return she was badly damaged by fire at Bremerhaven on 2 November 1858, just before setting out on her

AUSTRALASIAN
2,750 tons
322 × 42 feet
European & Australian
Royal Mail Co.
1857

HUDSON
3,000 tons
345 × 40 feet
North German Lloyd
1857

PARAMATTA
3,500 tons
330 × 44 feet
Royal Mail Line
1858

second voyage. She was resold to her builders who repaired her at Jarrow. The repair work was so extensive that she was re-registered at Lloyds, and then sold to Fernie Brothers (the Guion Line) in 1862 and renamed the LOUISIANA.

Her first sailings for her new owners were in the Mediterranean and in 1863 she was moved to the Liverpool to New York service and was almost immediately transferred to the National Steam Navigation Company (the National Line). Being a new company, the LOUISIANA was their first ship, and she sailed between Liverpool, Queenstown and New York until she was laid up in 1867 for extensive alterations. She was lengthened to 395 feet and her weight increased to 3,847 tons; compound engines were also fitted, the first on a large vessel on the North Atlantic. At the same time her name was changed to the HOLLAND before she sailed from London to New York on 20 April 1870. In 1893 she was sold to France and broken up the following year.

The HUDSON's sister ship, the WESER, had identical dimensions. She left on her maiden voyage from Bremen to New York on 4 December 1858 but was damaged by heavy seas and put into Cork for repairs which were not completed until June 1859. Thereafter she only made three return voyages before being sold later in the year to a French company.

A new Royal Mail Line steamer, built by the

Thames Ironwork & Shipbuilding Company at Blackwall, was launched on 8 November 1858 and named the PARAMATTA. The iron-hulled paddle-steamer weighed 3,500 tons and was 330 feet × 44 feet. She sailed from Southampton in June on her maiden voyage. On 30 June 1859 she ran aground while travelling at full speed off Anegada in the Virgin Islands. Attempts to salvage her were not successful and she was broken up where she lay.

LY-EE-MOON
1,200 tons
270 × 27 feet
Alfred Dent
1857

The LY-EE-MOON, built by Thames Shipbuilders in 1857, was a vessel of 1,200 tons and 270 × 27 feet, with a 50 horsepower engine with oscillating cylinders driving paddles. This very beautiful steamer achieved the then remarkable speed of over 17 knots, which was reported as being the fastest speed attained by an English-built vessel. She started life as a blockade-runner in the American Civil War, after which she returned to her builders in July 1860 for a refit, having been purchased by Alfred Dent of Hong Kong. On the voyage out she used sail only, her paddles having been removed and stowed on board.

Once in the East it is said that she was used to meet the English mail boats at an early port of call and take on the mail for her owners and other merchants. With her high speed she could reach Hong Kong before the official mail boat, so giving advance information on the markets to a favoured few. It was also said that she was used for somewhat shady work in the opium trade in the China Sea. In 1872 she was rammed and sunk in Hong Kong harbour, but salvaged and taken to England for a refit, when the paddles were replaced by a screw. When completed she made several fast voyages between England and Singapore, and one trip to Australia with tea from China. In 1878 she was purchased by the Australian Steam Navigation Company. On arrival at Sydney she created a lot of interest because of her reputation for speed and also because of the fine accommodation and decoration of the passenger quarters. Regrettably she caught fire and had to be refitted yet again. She was then used on the Melbourne to Sydney service until wrecked in May 1886 off Cape Green, with the loss of 19 passengers and some of the crew. 15 passengers were saved.

1860–1869

The first 2,000 ton steamship built for the P & O Line was the MOOLTAN. In 1859 the company had bought a slightly larger 2,350 ton ship from the Orient Line, which had been built in 1855. However, it was not successful and was quickly disposed of. The MOOLTAN, delivered in 1861 from the yards of the Thames Iron Company, was 2,250 tons and 350 feet × 39 feet, with compound engines driving a single screw. She had accommodation for 112 First and 37 Second Class passengers. She was built to run between Southampton and Alexandria and she left Southampton on her maiden voyage at the beginning of August 1861. She did not prove very reliable and after an uneventful life was sold in 1881, had her engines removed and was converted to a four-masted barque renamed the ELEANOR MARGARET.

MOOLTAN
2,250 tons
350 × 39 feet
P & O
1861

CITY OF NEW YORK
2,550 tons
335 x 40 feet
Inman Line
1861

length, and was re-engined. In 1879 she was sold to the Thistle Line and compound engines were fitted in 1881. In November of that year she was lost at sea without trace.

The South African trade was one of the last to get established on a commercial footing. In 1851 the General Screw Steamship Company had received the first Admiralty contract for mail carriage to South Africa and in 1857 the British government awarded the contract to the Union Steam Ship Company Limited (the first ocean mail company to be registered as a limited liability company under the Companies Act of 1856). The company had been founded as the Union Steam Collier Company, which then diversified into carrying mails and passengers. Their ships were comparatively small. The BRITON was the third steamer they had built and was of structural interest, as she was designed to be unsinkable and incombustible. The idea patented by a Mr Charles Lungley was to divide the hull with horizontal, rather than vertical, bulkheads at deck levels, so that if the hull was holed it would take water but remain on an even keel. The BRITON was 1,150 tons and 248 × 31 feet, with 120 horsepower engines supplied by Day & Co. Under Admiralty test she made 11 knots. She had accommodation for 60 First and 40 Second Class passengers. The mail contract stipulated a departure from Southampton once a month and were permitted a maximum voyage time of 42 days. In the event, passages usually took about 34 days. In 1873 the BRITON was sold to the British Government and became the troop-ship the DROMEDARY.

In October 1861 the Liverpool, New York & Philadelphia Steam Ship Company (the Inman Line) took delivery from Tod & McGregor of Glasgow of the first ship they were to own called the CITY OF NEW YORK (they had two more of this name during the next twenty-seven years). She was 2,550 tons and 335 × 40 feet, with a two-cylinder engine driving a single screw. Her iron hull had a clipper bow. The CITY OF NEW YORK sailed from Liverpool on 11 September 1861 on her maiden voyage to New York. At the time of her building she was the largest Inman steamer and, with her sister ship the CITY OF LONDON, was the fastest of their fleet for at least five years. The CITY OF NEW YORK was wrecked outside Queenstown on 29 March 1864, with no loss of life.

The CITY OF LONDON, also by Tod & McGregor, was 2,560 tons and 336 × 40 feet. She made her maiden voyage from Liverpool to New York in July 1863. In 1869 she was enlarged to 2,765 tons and 374 feet in

In March 1862, a very fine vessel was completed at the yard of Robert Napier & Sons of Glasgow. She was the SCOTIA built for the Cunard Line and, apart from the GREAT EASTERN, she was the largest paddle-steamer ever built. Weighing 3,850 tons, she was 379 × 48 feet and was driven by two side-lever engines of 100 inch bore by a stroke of twelve feet with an estimated output of 1,000 horsepower. She had accommodation

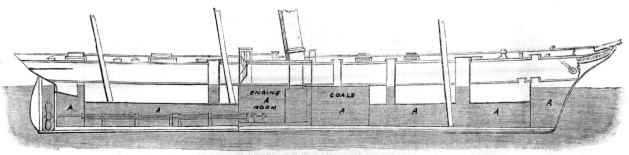

A. A. are the parts in which, if the bottom of the vessel be torn out, the water will take the place of ballast, the ship being as safe as before.
PLAN OF ONE OF LUNGLEY'S UNSINKABLE SHIPS.

BRITON
1,150 tons
248 x 31 feet
Union Steamship Co.
1861

SCOTIA
3,850 tons
279 x 48 feet
Cunard
1862

for 573 First Class passengers, and her internal arrangements could be altered in a day to accommodate 1,500 troops. She sailed from Liverpool on 10 May 1862 on her maiden voyage to New York. In December 1863 she gained the eastbound 'Blue Riband' with a crossing time of 8 days 3 hours, a record she held until July 1869 when she lost it to the RUSSIA, another Cunarder. In July 1866 she gained the westbound record with a time of 8 days 4 hours 35 minutes, which record she held until broken by the White Star Line's ADRIATIC in May 1872. The SCOTIA was also the Cunard Line's last paddle-steamer, becoming part of the Cunard reserve fleet in 1876. She was sold two years later and, after being converted to twin screw, became a cable-laying steamer, retaining her name SCOTIA. In 1904 she was wrecked in the Pacific.

At the same time as Robert Napier were building the SCOTIA, they were also building another ship for Cunard, the CHINA. While the SCOTIA was the last Cunard paddler, the CHINA was their first screw steamer. Not as large as the SCOTIA, the CHINA was 2,550 tons and 326 × 40 feet. She was powered by two oscillating engines with a combined output of 560

horsepower, and provided accommodation for 268 First and 771 Second Class passengers. While not being quite as fast as the SCOTIA she was much more economical. On an average voyage she burned 82 tons of coal a day while carrying 1,400 tons of cargo, whereas the SCOTIA burned 164 tons of coal in similar circumstances and only carried 1,050 tons of cargo. The comparison of these two ships definitely proved the superiority of screw propulsion. In 1873 she had compound engines fitted, and in 1878 made her last Atlantic crossing for Cunard, before being sold two years later to a Spanish ship owner who renamed her the MAGALANES. In 1889 she became the German barque the THEODOR having had her engines removed. Finally, in 1906 she disappeared at sea, lost without trace.

The French company Chantier de l'Atlantique of St. Nazaire was the first French company to build ships for their own shipping line the Compagnie Générale Transatlantique (CGT). In 1864 they built three iron-hulled vessels of 3,200 tons and 355 × 44 feet, with paddles driven by two-cylinder side-lever engines. The first was named the IMPERATRICE EUGENIE and made her

CHINA
2,550 tons
326 × 40 feet
Cunard
1862

undertaking her first voyage, under this name, from Le Havre to New York on 16 January 1874. On the return journey she ran into trouble about 100 miles west of Brest on 14 April when she had 83 passengers and 152 crew on board. Encountering a violent storm, she was in apparent danger of sinking, and after three vessels came to her aid to take off passengers and crew, the AMERIQUE was abandoned. A British ship was sent out from Plymouth to look for her and, finding her still afloat, towed her into Plymouth. There she was found to be sound and after being pumped dry, was refloated and taken back to Le Havre. Shortly after this she returned to service. In 1877 the AMERIQUE ran aground off New Jersey, was refloated three months later and after repairs returned to duty. In 1888, she was fitted with electric light and four years later triple expansion engines were installed. She was finally wrecked at Savanilla in January 1895.

In the mid-1860s two new sister mail steamers were built for the Cunard Line, the CUBA in 1864 by Tod & McGregor of Glasgow and the JAVA in 1865 by J. & G. Thomson, also of Glasgow. Both were 2,700 tons, 338 × 42 feet and were fitted with geared oscillating engines driving a single screw. Accommodation was provided for 160 Cabin and 800 Third Class passengers. The CUBA sailed on 3 December 1864 from Liverpool on her maiden voyage to New York. She remained on the North Atlantic all her life and made her final voyage

maiden voyage on 16 February 1865 from St Nazaire to Vera Cruz. She generally operated on the West Indies and Central American service with her sister ships the FRANCE and the NOUVEAU MONDE.

In 1871, the IMPERATRICE EUGENIE was renamed the ATLANTIQUE and three years later was extensively rebuilt and enlarged. Her length was increased to 394 feet, her weight to 4,585 tons and she was converted to single screw with compound engines. After the rebuild she was again renamed, this time as the AMERIQUE,

IMPERATRICE EUGENIE
3,200 tons
355 × 44 feet
CGT
1864

CUBA
2,700 tons
338 x 42 feet
Cunard
1864

to New York on 17 April 1875. Later in the year, the CUBA was sold, her engines were removed and she was converted to a sailing ship. Her sister the JAVA had the same fate the following year. They were renamed the EARL OF BEACONSFIELD and the LORD SPENCER respectively. The EARL OF BEACONSFIELD was wrecked in 1887, and the LORD SPENCER was lost without trace in 1895.

December 1864 saw the delivery to the P & O Line of their last paddle-steamer, the NYANZA. The 327 × 36 feet vessel was built by the Thames Ironwork & Shipbuilding Company and was 2,100 tons, with oscillating engines driving the paddle-wheels. She had accommodation for 143 First and 34 Second Class passengers. The NYANZA left Southampton in December 1864 on her maiden voyage to Alexandria. However, with the opening of the Suez Canal, the Southampton to Alexandra service was stopped and ships for the Far

NYANZA
2,100 tons
327 x 36 feet
P & O
1864

(R) REGULATIONS FOR MAINTAINING DISCIPLINE,
SANCTIONED BY THE BOARD OF TRADE.

IN PURSUANCE OF THE MERCANTILE MARINE ACT, 13 & 14 VICT. c. 93, ss. 46, 79, 86.

THESE Regulations are distinct from, and in addition to, those contained in the Act, and are sanctioned, but not universally required, by Law. All or any of them may be adopted by agreement between a Master and his Crew, and thereupon the Offences specified in such of them as are so adopted will be legally punishable by the appropriate Fines or Punishments. These Regulations are all numbered, and the numbers of such of them as are adopted must be inserted in the space left for that purpose in the Agreement, and a copy of these Regulations must be made to correspond with the Agreement by erasing each of the Regulations as are not adopted, and must then be attached to, and kept with, the Agreement which the Master of the Ship takes to sea with him. If the Agreement is made before a Shipping Master, his signature or initials must be placed opposite such of the Regulations as are adopted

For the purpose of legally enforcing any of the following penalties, a statement of the Offence must, immediately after its commission, be entered in the Official Log Book by the direction of the Master, and must at the same time be attested to be true by the signature of the Mate, or, if there is no Mate, by the Carpenter, Boatswain, or one of the oldest members of the Crew. If the punishment is a Fine, this entry must, upon discharge of the Crew, be shown to the Shipping Master before whom the Crew is discharged, or, in the case of a Home Trade Ship, to some Shipping Master at or near the place where the Crew is discharged; and if he is satisfied that it has been properly and truly made and attested, the Fine must be deducted from the Offender's wages, and paid over to the Shipping Master.

If, in consequence of subsequent Good Conduct, the Master thinks fit to remit or reduce any Fine incurred by any Member of his Crew which has been entered in the Log, and signifies the same to the Shipping Master, the Fine shall be remitted or reduced accordingly. If Wages are contracted for by the Voyage or by Share, the amount of the Fines is to be ascertained in a manner in which the Amount of Forfeiture is ascertained in similar cases under 7 & 8 Vict., c. 112, s. 8.

	OFFENCE.	Amount of Fine or Punishment.	Shipping-Master's Signature or Initials.
1	Not being on Board at the time fixed by the Agreement	Two Days' Pay.	
2	Not returning on Board at the expiration of Leave	One Day's Pay.	
3	Insolence or contemptuous language or behaviour towards the Master or any Mate	One Day's Pay.	
4	Striking or assaulting any person on Board or belonging to the Ship	Two Days' Pay.	
5	Quarrelling or provoking to quarrel	One Day's Pay.	
6	Swearing or using improper language	One Day's Pay.	
7	Bringing or having on Board spirituous liquors	Three Days' Pay.	
8	Carrying a sheath knife	One Day's Pay.	
9	Drunkenness. First offence	Two Days' half allowance of Provisions.	
	Ditto. Second offence	Two Days' Pay.	
10	Neglect on the part of the Officer in charge of the Watch to place the look out properly	Two Days' Pay.	
11	Sleeping or gross negligence while on the look out	Two Days' Pay.	
12	Not extinguishing lights at the times ordered	One Day's Pay.	
13	Smoking below	One Day's Pay.	
14	Neglecting to bring up, open out, and air bedding, when ordered	Half a Day's Pay.	
15	(For the Cook)—Not having any Meal of the Crew ready at the appointed time	One Day's Pay.	
16	Not attending Divine Service on Sunday unless prevented by sickness or duty of the Ship	One Day's Pay.	
17	Interrupting Divine Service by indecorous conduct	One Day's Pay.	
18	Not being cleaned, shaved, and washed, on Sundays	One Day's Pay.	
19	Washing clothes on a Sunday	One Day's Pay.	
20	Secreting contraband goods on Board with intent to smuggle	One Month's Pay.	
21	Destroying or defacing the Copy of the Agreement which is made accessible to the Crew	One Day's Pay.	
22	If any Officer is guilty of any act or default which is made subject to a Fine, he shall be liable to a Fine of twice the number of Day's Pay which would be exacted for a like Act or Default from a Seaman, and such Fine shall be paid and applied in the same manner as other Fines.		

BY AUTHORITY: Printed for the Board of Trade, by James Truscott, Nelson Square, London.

Board of Trade
Regulations 1850

ADMIRALTY NOTICE respecting LIGHTS and FOG SIGNALS to be carried and used by Sea-going Vessels, to prevent Collision.

By the Commissioners for executing the Office of Lord High Admiral of the United Kingdom of Great Britain and Ireland, &c.

BY virtue of the power and authority vested in us, we hereby revoke, as from and after the thirtieth day of September, 1858, the regulations made and published by us on the first day of May, 1852, relating to the Lights to be carried by Sea-going Vessels to prevent collision: And we hereby make the following regulations, and require and direct that the same be strictly observed and carried into effect on and after the first day of October, 1858.

STEAM VESSELS.

All Sea-going Steam Vessels, when under Steam, shall, between sunset and sunrise, exhibit the following Lights

1. A bright White Light at the Foremast Head.
   A Green Light on the Starboard side.
   A Red Light on the Port side.

2. The Mast-head Light shall be so constructed as to be visible on a dark night, with a clear atmosphere, at a distance of at least 5 miles, and shall show an uniform and unbroken light over an arc of the horizon of 20 points of the compass, and it shall be so fixed as to throw the light 10 points on each side of the ship, viz.: from right ahead to 2 points abaft the beam on either side.

3. The Green Light on the Starboard side and the Red Light on the Port side shall be so constructed as to be visible on a dark night, with a clear atmosphere, at a distance of at least 2 miles, and show an uniform and unbroken light over an arc of the horizon of 10 points of the compass, and they shall be so fixed as to throw the light

[OVER.

Admiralty Notice
respecting lights
1858

RUAHINE
1,500 tons
265 × 34 feet
Panama, New Zealand &
Australia Royal Mail Co.
1865

Pacific. She was lost on the coast of Uruguay in January 1874.

The West India & Pacific Steamship Company were quick to take advantage of the increased demand for communications with Japan and the Far East. They sailed to Colon on the Isthmus of Panama and after travelling overland passengers had to be reshipped to continue their journey. In 1867 the company took delivery of a new steamship, the COLOMBIAN, which was built at West Hartlepool to look after the Pacific part of their trade. She was 1,991 tons and 307 × 38 feet, with unusual engines by Thomas Richardson with a 55 inch bore and only a 48 inch stroke driving a single screw. The COLOMBIAN was also one of the early steamships to have a straight stem. A footnote in a description of this vessel in a contemporary publication said that the vessels of the company had performed their numerous voyages entirely free from the dreadful scourge of yellow fever, which was a testimony to the care and attention paid to the ventilation of their ships.

Another steamer for the Far East trade was the LAMONT which was built in 1867 by Robert Napier & Sons of Glasgow for the old established firm of Jardine, Matheson & Co. of London and China. She was 1,390 tons and 240 × 35 feet, with a geared overhead beam engine, a type much favoured by American ship-builders, driving a single screw. Her iron hull had a straight stem. The accommodation was described as being of a very superior kind, the chief cabin was forward and the cabins for passengers, captain and officers were round the sides of the deck-saloon. There was a cabin aft for Chinese passengers.

East steamed straight through. In 1873 the NYANZA was laid up and sold the following year to the Union Steamship Company. Before the sale she had compound engines fitted to drive a single screw and had one funnel removed. The NYANZA started sailing to the Cape in early 1874, and held the record for the fastest voyage to Cape Town for several years. In 1880 she was transferred to the Cape Town to Zanzibar coastal trade until bought by the Sultan of Zanzibar to use as his private yacht – considerably bigger than the British Royal Yacht! Later the NYANZA was used commercially between Zanzibar and Bombay until broken up in 1904.

The short-lived Panama, New Zealand & Australia Royal Mail Company took delivery of four vessels when they commenced trade in 1866, namely the KAIKOURA, the RAKAIA, the RUAHINE and the MATAURA. The RUAHINE was the most interesting. She was built by J. & W. Dudgeon of Blackwall, London and was 1,500 tons and 265 × 34 feet, with compound engines driving twin screws. She had accommodation for 100 First, 40 Second Class and 65 Steerage passengers. RUAHINE was the first twin-screw ocean steamship used for general commercial purposes, a development which went almost unnoticed. The Panama, New Zealand & Australia Royal Mail Company went into liquidation in April 1869, and the Royal Mail Line took over three of the ships to clear mortgage debts. The RUAHINE was one of the ships taken over and she was renamed the LIFFEY and moved from the

COLOMBIAN
1,991 tons
307 × 38 feet
West India & Pacific
Steamship Co.
1867

LAMONT
1,390 tons
240 × 35 feet
Jardine, Matheson & Co.
1867

In 1868 the P & O Line purchased a steamer on the stocks at the builders William Denny & Bros of Dumbarton, which was given the name the DECCAN. She was 3,150 tons and 368 × 43 feet with 600 horse-power engines driving a single screw. Her accommodation provided for 85 First and 20 Second Class passengers. The DECCAN sailed from Southampton early in January 1869 on her maiden voyage to the Indian Ocean. For most of her life she worked from Suez to Calcutta, until the opening of the Suez Canal. Early on she also made some voyages from England to Australia via the Cape. The DECCAN had the distinc-

tion in 1875 of being one of the first ocean liners to be fitted with electric lighting in the saloon. She was sold in 1889.

1870–1881

A new mail service was started in 1873 between Antwerp and Valparaiso by the Ryde Line, who for this purpose acquired two new steamers, the LEOPOLD II and the SANTIAGO. The former was built by Barclay, Curle & Co. of Glasgow. She was 2,700 tons, 362 × 36 feet, with engines of a nominal

DECCAN
3,150 tons
368 × 43 feet
P & O
1868

LEOPOLD II
2,700 tons
362 × 36 feet
Ryde Line
1873

BOTHNIA
4,550 tons
422 x 42 feet
Cunard
1874

1874 they were sold to the Royal Mail Lines and the LEOPOLD II became the MONDEGO and the SANTIAGO, the MINHO. They both ran on their new owners' South American service until 1887, when the MINHO was sold to a Turkish owner and renamed the ASLAN and the MONDEGO was sold to a British company.

The BOTHNIA, built in 1874, was the first Cunarder to top the 4,000 ton mark. Built by J. & G. Thomson on Clydebank, she was 4,550 tons and 422 × 42 feet with compound engines driving a single screw. She had accommodation for 300 Cabin and 1,100 Third Class passengers. The BOTHNIA sailed from Liverpool on 8 August 1874 on her maiden voyage to New York. Neither the BOTHNIA nor her sister ship the SCYTHIA were a match for the White Star OCEANICS. In 1885 the BOTHNIA was switched to the Liverpool to Boston service and continued to run on that line until her last voyage in October 1896. Two years later she was sold to a French firm of ship-breakers.

450 horsepower driving a single screw. She had accommodation for 100 First Class passengers and 500 Steerage. She left Antwerp on 10 June 1873 on her maiden voyage to Valparaiso, which necessitated navigating the Magellan Strait. Because of this the officers' quarters were heated by steam from the engines – presumably the passengers just got cold! The LEOPOLD II was followed a month later by her sister, the SANTIAGO, built by Tod & Mac-Gregor. The service was not a success and was abandoned after one round voyage for each ship. In

In 1876, the Fairfield Shipbuilding & Engineering Company Ltd of Govan built the ZEALANDIA for Sir William Pearce, to be operated by the Pacific Mail Company. She was 2,730 tons and 376 × 37 feet, with compound engines driving a single screw. She and her sister ship the AUSTRALIA ran with two other steamers a monthly mail service Sydney–Auckland–Honolulu–San Francisco. Early in 1886 the American

ZEALANDIA
2,730 tons
376 x 37 feet
Pacific Mail Co.
1876

ORIENT
5,400 tons
446 × 46 feet
Orient Line
1877

The Orient Line was formed in 1877 to operate a service to Australia. In the first instance they chartered four steamers from the Pacific Steam Navigation Company and at the same time ordered a new ship, the ORIENT, from John Elder & Co. of Glasgow, which was completed in 1879. She was 5,400 tons and 446 × 46 feet, with compound engines driving a single screw. Accommodation was provided for 120 First, 130 Second Class and 300 Steerage passengers. The ORIENT was a very fine ship and was larger than any of the contemporary North Atlantic liners with the exception of the CITY OF BERLIN (see page 82). She was also the first liner built to Admiralty specifications for possible use as an armed merchant cruiser and had a bunker capacity which allowed her to reach Australia without refuelling. On her outward maiden voyage she reached Cape Town in the record time of 17 days and 21 hours, and Adelaide in 37 days and 22 hours. In 1898 the ORIENT underwent a heavy rebuild; a single funnel replaced the two originals, the second and third masts were removed and triple expansion engines were fitted to give her increased speed. Between 1899 and 1902, she did duty as a Boer

government bought the ZEALANDIA from Pearce and used her between San Francisco and Hawaii. Later in the year she was chartered to the American Oceanic Company to sail on the San Francisco to Sydney route. She made her last voyage from Sydney to San Francisco in 1890.

Interior of the QUETTA
3,300 tons
380 × 40 feet
British India Steam
Navigation Co.
1881

British India Steam
Navigation Co.
Handbook
1890s

British India baggage
tickets

War transport, before returning to the Australian service until being sold in 1909 for £12,000.

The QUETTA built by William Denny of Dumbarton in 1881 for the British India Steam Navigation Company was their first steamship. She was 3,300 tons and 380 × 40 feet, with compound engines driving a single screw. She had accommodation for 80 First and 35 Second Class passengers. She sailed in June 1881 from London on her maiden voyage, carrying mails under contract to the Queensland Government. Her route was via Suez, India, Ceylon, through the Torres Straits between New Guinea and Australia, followed by seven ports of call between Thursday Island and Brisbane. In February 1890, the QUETTA left Brisbane with a full compliment of crew and passengers. On 28 February, on a moonlight night when travelling at full speed she hit an uncharted rock, which tore out her bottom and she sank in three minutes with the loss of 134 lives. Two women were saved after being in the water for many hours.

CHAPTER 4

The Great Eastern 1854−1887

The Pacific Ocean trade was very slow to develop compared with the transatlantic South African trade – in addition to which distances were considerably greater. All this meant that as far as the steamships were concerned they did not have the same advantages over sail that they did on other routes. The greater distances of the Pacific meant that coaling points were a major problem, because coal had to be transported many thousands of miles by sailing ships, often in unsuitable weather, in order to supply the steamers' bunkers. Supplies of locally-mined coal in South Africa and Australia were not available for many years. Indeed, it was some considerable time before a ship was built that could steam to Australia without the assistance of sail and, before the opening of the Suez Canal, ships to Australia used steam only as an auxiliary power to sail.

Isambard Kingdom Brunel seems first to have envisaged his 'Leviathan' steamship in 1852, for there is a rough sketch of a giant ship in his notebook dated 25 March of that year. (These sketches and notebooks are in the custody of Bristol University.) It was always

Brunel's vision that a giant ship would be required to steam successfully and economically to the East Indies and Australia, one of the main criteria being the ability to steam from England to Australia and back on the coal she carried with her. The problem was building a ship large enough to carry 15,000 tons of coal, all the machinery to propel her as well as providing enough space for passengers, provisions and sufficient cargo to make such a vessel economically viable. One early jotting in his notebook suggests that he felt 700×67 feet would be adequate: 'As far as it affects speed through smooth water, I think these proportions will bear a considerable increase of beam – the question is rather one of comparative advantage of extreme steadiness obtained by great length and narrow proportional beam.' These notes are interesting as the dimensions of the GREAT EASTERN when built were 680×83 feet.

After much negotiation, the formation of the Eastern Steam Navigation Company and the raising of the necessary capital, it was two years before contracts were let and work commenced on 5 February 1854.

The Great Ship Co. share certificate

The contract was won by John Scott Russell, whose yard was at Millwall on the north side of the River Thames below London Bridge. The contractor was to 'provide for the construction, trial, launch and delivery of an iron ship of the general dimensions of 680 feet between perpendiculars, 83 feet beam and 58 feet deep according to the drawings signed by the engineer I. K. Brunel.' Her tonnage was to be 18,915 tons.

Other stipulations and requirements were: 'All vertical joints to be butt joints and to be double-rivetted wherever required by the engineer. Bulkheads to be at 60 foot intervals. No cast-iron to be used anywhere except for slide-valves and cocks without the special permission of the engineer. The water-tightness of every part to be tested before launching, the several compartments to be filled one at a time up to the level of the lower deck.' In addition: 'After the launch such trials and trial trips at sea will be made with engines and probably under sail as in the opinion of the engineer may be necessary to ascertain the efficiency of the work. Any defects then discovered in workmanship or quality of materials to be forthwith remedied, or at the expense of the contractor to the satisfaction of the engineer . . . All calculations, drawings, models, templates which the contractor may prepare shall from time to time be submitted to the engineer for his revision, alteration or approval. The engineer to have entire control over the proceedings and the workmanship.'

The quotation for this project must have been very much of a 'guesstimate'. Brunel had made tentative enquiries at various yards and imagined a total cost of about £500,000. In the event, John Scott Russell put in a price of £377,200, made up of £275,200 for the hull, £60,000 for the screw engines and boilers and £42,000 for the paddle engines and boilers (the great ship had been designed to have both paddles and screw). It is surprising that Brunel with all his practical experience accepted such a low estimate, while Russell may have been tempted by the publicity of building the world's largest ship.

The keel of the great ship was laid at Scott Russell's yard on 1 May 1854. Because of the size of the hull it had to be built on stocks sideways on to the river, and eventually would also have to be launched sideways. Construction proceeded slowly as nothing this size had been built before. The vessel had a double-skinned hull from the keel to a point six feet above the water-line, the inner and outer skins being 2 foot 8 inches apart, and it had nine transverse watertight bulkheads. The iron plates used in construction were 1 inch or $\frac{9}{4}$ inch thick according to their place on the ship, and they measured 10 feet by 2 feet 9 inches, this being the largest size which could be rolled at that time.

It was only eight months after laying-down that Scott Russell began to feel the financial pinch, as on 1 January 1855 he was asking for payment for work-in-progress and it was agreed by Brunel and Scott Russell's bankers that ten payments of £8,000 would be made on the basis of certificates from Brunel sanctioning that the work had been done. Finally the hull was completed, but not before Scott Russell had been made bankrupt and the construction work completed with direct labour by the Eastern Steam Navigation Company, at a final cost of £732,000 or nearly double the cost of the original estimate.

The completion and launch had to be hurried in order to vacate the site, occupancy of which was required by the yard owners by 5 October 1857. This date was exceeded and the first attempt to launch, which was also the day of the naming ceremony, was 3 November 1857. The ship was named the LEVIATHAN by Miss Hope, the daughter of the Chairman of the Eastern Steam Navigation Company. The launch, however, was not successful as Brunel had not had sufficient time to test the launching gear and it proved unequal to the task. A further delay occurred while more powerful hydraulic rams were procured and all prepared for the next spring tide. The LEVIATHAN was moved further down the slipway between 28 and 30 November, and after several further stages finally

Miss Hope naming the LEVIATHAN 3 November 1857

reached the water's edge by mid-January, whereupon a decision was reached by Brunel that she should be floated off her cradle on 30 or 31 January 1858. On 30 January, the high tide was lower than expected and the overall weather was unsuitable, but there was an improvement the next day, and the ship was eventually floated off her cradles at 1.42pm on Sunday 31 January 1858, before being moved over to Deptford by tugs for completion.

The Eastern Steam Navigation Company was insolvent with a partly completed ship on their hands. Moves to sell her by auction were fortunately over-ruled, and on 18 November 1858 a new company was formed, the Great Ship Company, which later in the same month purchased the LEVIATHAN for £165,000, renaming her the GREAT EASTERN.

At the time of the launch some of the machinery had been installed, but not all as Brunel had intended. James Watt & Company of Birmingham built the engines to drive the screw. The engines were supplied with steam at 25 pounds per square inch and had four horizontally-opposed cylinders of 84 × 48 inch stroke designed to operate at 45 revolutions per minute. The 58 foot paddle-wheels were driven by a four-cylinder oscillating engine with a 74 inch bore by $14\frac{1}{4}$ foot stroke to operate at 14 revolutions per minute. Various estimates of her possible performance were made by the press. *The Illustrated London News* put forward their view in the issue dated 23 May 1857. After describing both sets of engines, they continued:

'It is a question of much interest to determine what amount of speed this power will impart to the vessel. Messrs. James Watt & Co.'s anticipation is that the speed of the vessel will be about seventeen miles per hour; and from that to eighteen miles seems to be the limit engineers have hitherto predicted. But we believe that these anticipations fall very far short of what the real speed will be, and which we do not hesitate to predict will turn out to be between twenty-four and twenty-five miles per hour. No allowance has been made in the existing computations of the speed for the great size of the vessel; yet it is well known that large vessels are more easily propelled, relatively with their proportion of power, than small vessels, as is popularly manifested at every yacht race, where an allowance of time is made for the smallness of the vessels. It has been found that the velocities attained by similar vessels, but of different sizes vary as the square route of any linear dimension.'

Using calculations based on this theory, the GREAT EASTERN should have had a speed of 25 miles per hour. In the event on her maiden voyage from Southampton to New York, which commenced on 17 June 1860, she crossed the Atlantic in 11 days and $13\frac{1}{2}$ hours at an average speed of 11.36 knots ($13\frac{1}{4}$ miles per hour). On this voyage she carried only 40 passengers in what for

Diagrams of the
GREAT EASTERN

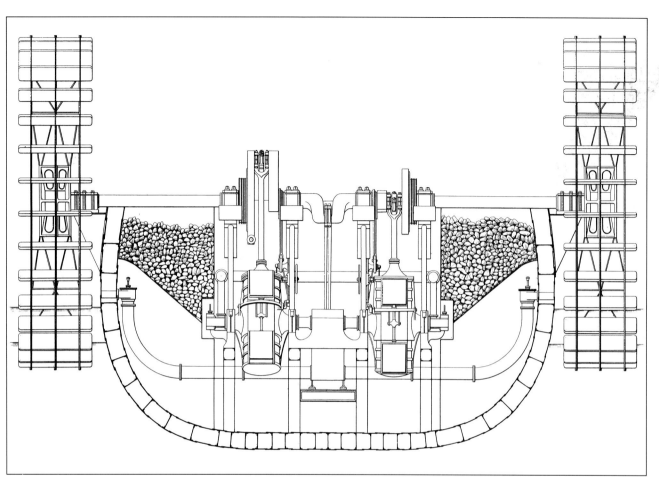

The screw engine-room

Longitudinal section

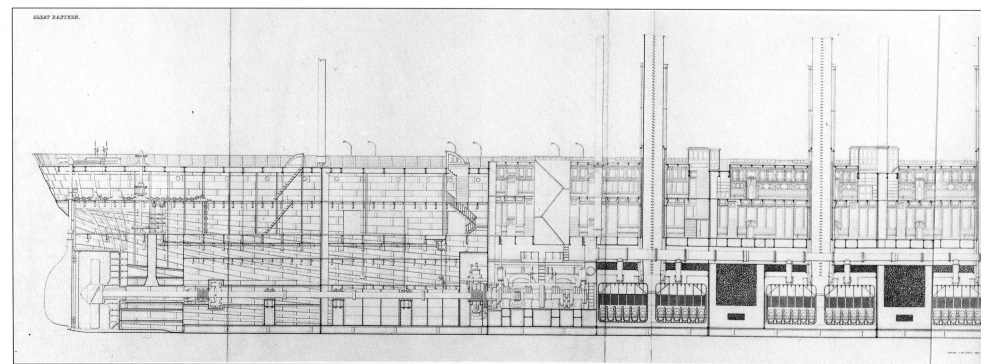

The paddle engine-room

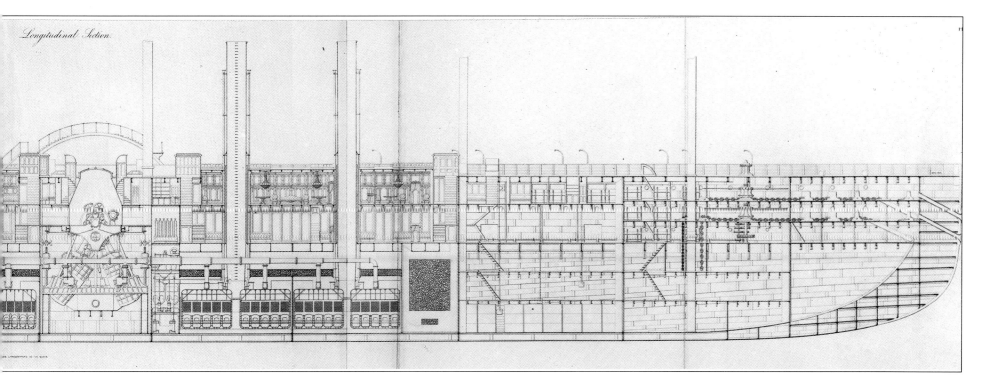

Longitudinal Section

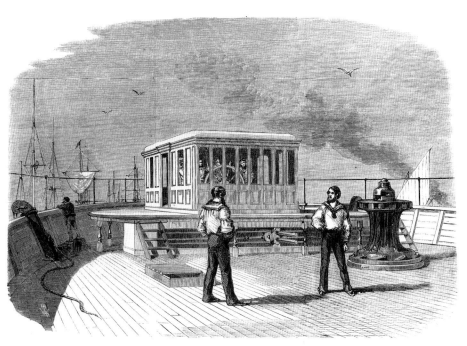

The wheelhouse

those days was considerable comfort, the chief saloon being particularly magnificent. All the cabinet work, upholstery and furniture for the three large dining rooms, which were aft of the Grand Saloon, and all First and Second Class cabins were furnished by Smee & Sons of Finsbury Pavement, London. These fittings were intended for the accommodation of more than a thousand passengers. The order for this fitting out had been placed on 2 July 1859 and nearly the whole order was delivered on 30 July and completed by 6 August 1859 – somewhat better than Scott Russell!

The operational aids of particular note were the compasses and the steering gear in the wheelhouse. The compasses, which were of the latest magnetic floating type were made and invented by Mr John Gray of Liverpool. The steering apparatus supplied by a Mr Langley was designed to overcome the difficulty in such a large ship of the Captain and the man at the wheel being so far apart. In a report in *The Illustrated London News* it was stated that the equipment 'works in a most satisfactory manner, and by its means the ship can be as easily steered as a ship of one thousand tons.' Also on the same platform was another piece of equipment which communicated with the engine room. Again a contemporary *Illustrated London News* report says: 'By this little instrument the engineer is told "ease her", "stop her", "run her ahead" or "astern" as the case may require; so that we find distance annihilated by mechanical science and the great steam giant of the ocean is as easily controlled as a fussy, noisy little dwarf of the Thames.'

After her return to Southampton from her maiden voyage, the GREAT EASTERN lay there until her next voyage from Milford Haven to New York which commenced on 1 May 1861. Her third voyage was under charter to the British Government to take troops to Canada. With nearly 1,500 on board, this was the greatest number she ever carried. On her fourth voyage she was to be less fortunate. Leaving Liverpool on 10 September 1861 with 400 passengers, on the second day out she ran into a heavy gale which put her steering gear out of action and damaged both paddle-wheels so that they were inoperable. For two days she was tossed about in the storm until temporary repairs were made to her steering gear and she was able to crawl back to Queenstown under the power of her screw. In 1862 she made three voyages to New York and in 1863 three more, but she was losing so much money that in December 1863 the Great Ship Company went into liquidation.

In February 1864 she was sold for £95,000 to the Great Eastern Company, who chartered her to the Telegraph Construction and Maintenance Company for Atlantic cable-laying. To this end she was moved from Liverpool to Sheerness in July 1864 to be fitted out for

The compass

The Grand Saloon

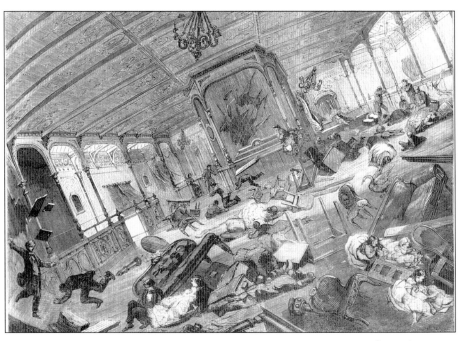

Storm damage to
The Grand Saloon

her new duties. On 4 June 1865 she left the Medway with 4,600 tons of cable and 7,000 tons of coal. After considerable trouble with faults in the cable and after laying over 1,000 miles, the project was abandoned and the GREAT EASTERN returned to Valentia (Ireland). A year later on the 13 July 1866 she set out again and reached Newfoundland in thirteen days having completed the job.

The following year she was chartered to a French company to bring passengers from New York to Brest for the Paris Exhibition of 1867. In 1869 the GREAT EASTERN did more cable-laying to America and also between Bombay and Aden. After this she was laid up at Milford Haven for many years. In 1886 she was rented by Lewis's of Liverpool, a large departmental store, as a floating exhibition at Liverpool and later at Dublin and Greenock. In October 1887 she was sold at auction for £26,000, but schemes for her use fell through and the next year she was again sold, this time for £16,000 to Henry Bath & Son, shipbreakers, of Birkenhead, where she was scrapped. A sad end for a great idea plagued by misfortune. Throughout the whole of her 30 year life she had remained the largest ship in the world.

GREAT EASTERN
being towed to
Queenstown, Cork

GREAT EASTERN
opposite Blackwall

GREAT EASTERN
leaving Sheerness with
French Atlantic cable

For the first 50 years all steamships on ocean routes carried sail as well, firstly, because steam was not 100% reliable and secondly, because on many routes if the wind was fair, the speed of the vessel under sail was greater than that which could be obtained by paddle or screw. However the end of this period was to see the final suppression of sail in favour of larger ships with more powerful engines.

Guion & Company, founded by Stephen Guion, originally acted as agent for Fernie Brothers, steamship operators, in 1863. However, the Fernie Brothers' line, commonly known as Guion & Co.'s Line, failed after less than a year. Of their three ships, two, the LUISIANNA and the VIRGINIA, were sold to the National Steam Navigation Company (National Line), while the third the GEORGIA was wrecked on Sable Island off Nova Scotia on 4 August 1863.

After the failure of Fernie Bros, Stephen Guion founded a new company in 1866, the Liverpool & Great Western Steamship Company Ltd, which operated under the name of the Guion Line. Their first two ships were similar, both built by Palmers of Newcastle-on-

Tyne. The first, the MANHATTAN, which made her maiden voyage from Liverpool to New York in August 1866, was registered as 2,866 tons with a length of 343 feet and a beam of 42 feet. She was fitted for the accommodation of 72 First and 800 Second Class passengers, in addition to carrying 1,000 tons of coal and 1,500 tons of cargo. The engines and hull were designed by John Jordan of Liverpool. She sailed from Liverpool on her maiden voyage to New York on 7 August 1866. Her iron hull had a clipper bow and her engines drove a single screw. In June 1875 she sailed on her last voyage for Guion.

When she arrived in Liverpool she was sold to the Warren Line who renamed her the MASSACHUSETTS. After refitting her with compound engines, she made her first voyage for her new owners from Liverpool to Boston (USA) at the beginning of 1876. In 1881 she again changed owners, having been purchased by W. H. Ross & Company of Liverpool and given the name CITY OF LINCOLN. Her new owners operated the Thistle Line of steamers and she first sailed under this flag from London to New York on 18 October 1881. After a refit and new engines she increased her gross tonnage to 3,185. In November 1881 and January 1882, the Thistle Line suffered two disasters; both the CITY OF LONDON and the CITY OF LIMERICK were lost at sea without trace. Fortunately loss of life was not too heavy as neither ship was carrying passengers and only the crews perished – even so a total of 84 lives were lost. As a result of this the Thistle Line abandoned business and sold their two remaining vessels, one of which was the CITY OF LINCOLN. She was purchased by a Spanish operator in 1884 and yet again renamed, this time the SOLIS. A year later she was bought by Cassels of Liverpool and her name was changed for the fourth time, reverting to the CITY OF LINCOLN. Cassels had her fitted with triple-expansion engines between 1885 and 1886. After a very varied life she was finally wrecked in August 1902 near Cape Town.

The second Guion Line ship was the CHICAGO. Her dimensions were the same as the MANHATTAN's and she made her maiden voyage from Liverpool to

Guion Line advertisement

MANHATTAN
2,866 tons
343 x 40 feet
Guion Line
1866

NEVA
2,998.5 tons
332 x 40 feet
Royal Mail Co.
1868

New York in December 1866. She was wrecked little over a year later off Queenstown in January 1868.

In 1868 *The Illustrated London News* reported as follows:

'It will be recalled by our readers that when the autumnal hurricane of 1867 passed over the West Indian Islands, causing such devestation amongst shipping in the harbour of St Thomas and neighbouring places, the Royal Mail Company were sufferers to a great extent, several of their fine vessels being much damaged and some totally wrecked. One of these was the large and powerful steamer RHONE, which about two years before had been built on the Thames by the Millwall Shipbuilding and Engineering Company. When the hurricane came on, RHONE, which was preparing to leave for England with mails, passengers and a general cargo, made for sea to out-live the storm, but was driven on shore and immediately became a total wreck. Only a very few out of all the crew and passengers of this ill-fated vessel were saved. When the news arrived in this country the utmost sympathy was expressed for the sufferers, and it was also felt that the loss to the Royal Mail Company was no ordinary one. They, however, took steps to repair their loss. They found a vessel suitable for their service then building at Greenock for the North German Lloyd Company. This was the screw steamship NEVA, which was, after some negotiations, eventually purchased by the Royal Mail Company, and arrangements were made with Messrs Caird and Co., the builders and engineers, for the internal fittings being rearranged for the West India mail and passenger service.

'The NEVA was launched at Greenock last February (1868), and, after being brought round to Southampton, was tried in Stokes's Bay on June 11th, when she attained a speed of $14\frac{1}{2}$ knots on the measured mile, and in every respect gave entire satisfaction to the Company, as well as to the Admiralty surveyors, Messrs Like and Steel, who were present on behalf of the Post Office authorities. She is a handsome-looking vessel of four decks, brig-rigged, and has a gross tonnage of $2,998\frac{1}{2}$ tons; her length is 332 feet overall, her breadth is 40 feet beam, and she is 33 feet 6 inches deep from floors to upper deck. She is fitted up for 289 first, 42 second, and 58 third class passengers. All that skill and experience could do for the comfort and convenience of the passengers has been brought to bear in making this ship suitable for the service. Her spacious saloon capable of dining at one time 160 persons, is fitted up with oak and walnut in the walls, white and gold in the ceilings, and cushions of the seats, sofas, and lounges in green morocco. The door-handles, finger-plates, lamps and glass-racks are electro-plated. The berths are fitted in a rich and substantial style. On the 2nd July she sailed for St. Thomas and Colon (Panama) with passengers, mails, and a general cargo, and she arrived at Colon some four days within the contract time, enabling the Australian passengers to leave Panama so much earlier, and thus reducing the length of their voyage considerably. On her return voyage, the distance between St. Thomas and Plymouth was accomplished in eleven days and seven hours steaming-time.'

The NEVA spent most of her life sailing to the River Plate until she was disposed of in 1890.

ABYSSYNIA
3,500 tons
363 x 42 feet
Cunard
1870

1870–1879

Delivery of a new steamship was made in 1870 to the Cunard Line from the yard of James & George Thomson of the Clyde Bank Foundry, Glasgow. This new ship was named the ABYSSINIA and was the first of three vessels ordered by Cunard to maintain the Royal Mail service to America; the other two being the ALGERIA, also built by Thomson, and the PARTHIA which was built by William Denny of Dumbarton. The latter vessel was slightly smaller (3,167 tons and 360 × 40 feet) but had compound engines, while the other two had twin-inverted single-expansion engines. The ABYSSINIA was 363 feet overall with a beam of 42 feet. Gross tonnage was 3,500 and she had an estimated speed of 13 knots. She had accommodation on the spar-deck for 120 First Class passengers, whose dining-saloons and sleeping-appartments were well heated and ventilated. Also on the spar-deck were the kitchens, sculleries, pantries, ice-houses, bakery, butchery, and the lavatories. The ABYSSINIA was provided with a male and female hospital. She had distilling apparatus which could produce 2,000 gallons of fresh water per day. On the main and lower decks was accommodation for about 1,000 third-class passengers, or if need be for two battalions of soldiers. She had holds for 80,000 cubic feet of cargo and 1,200 tons of coal. On the 24 May 1870 the ABYSSINIA sailed from Liverpool on her maiden voyage to New York.

She operated on this route with her sister ships for nearly ten years, her last voyage being in October 1880. She was sold to the Guion Line the following year and

worked for her new owners on the same North Atlantic route until 1885 when she was acquired by John Elder & Co. of Glasgow, shipbuilders. They fitted compound engines in 1887 and then chartered her to the Canadian Pacific Railway Company, together with two other ex-Cunarders, the PARTHIA and the BATAVIA, who were used in the Pacific to service their new railhead in British Columbia running between Vancouver, Yokohama, Shanghai and Hong Kong. In December 1891, the ABYSSINIA was destroyed by fire while at sea, without loss of life.

In contrast, the PARTHIA had a life of over 80 years. In 1892 after modernisation she went to Northern Pacific Steamship Lines and was renamed the VICTORIA. In 1898 she was sold to the United States government for use as a troop ship in the Spanish-American War, after which she eventually came into the ownership of the Alaska Steamship Company still with the name VICTORIA. In 1941 all her passenger accommodation was removed and she was used as a cargo vessel until she was finally laid-up in 1952, and sold two years later for conversion into a barge. The PARTHIA/VICTORIA was broken up in 1956, 86 years after launching.

The JOHN ELDER was the first of a class of six steamships built by John Elder & Company for the Pacific Steam Navigation Company. She was completed just after the death of John Elder and was thus named after him. She was built to operate her owner's Liverpool to Valparaiso (Chile) service via Cape Horn.

JOHN ELDER
3,900 tons
382 x 41 feet
Pacific Steam Navigation
Co.
1870

EGYPT
4,670 tons
450 × 44 feet
National Steamship Co.
1871

In December 1870 she sailed from Liverpool on her maiden voyage to call at Rio de Janeiro and Montevideo with the Brazil and River Plate mail. With a gross tonnage of 3,900 she was 382 × 41 feet with compound engines. However she was not altogether satisfactory and after a few months running she was lengthened to 406 feet with her weight increased to 4,150 tons. She was thereby converted to a 'long ship', and an additional boiler necessitated a second funnel. (Most ships had length to beam ratios of about 8:1. A 'long ship' was about 10:1.) Between 1879 and 1886, she sailed in conjunction with the Orient Line between England and Australia. In 1886 she returned to her original Liverpool to Valparaiso mail route until she was wrecked on 16 January 1892 off the coast of Chile.

In 1871 the National Steamship Company took delivery of a new vessel the EGYPT, which had been built by the Liverpool Shipbuilding Company and for a while was the largest steamship afloat apart from the GREAT EASTERN. She was 4,670 tons and 450 × 44 feet, with compound engines driving a single screw. The saloons, state-rooms, and officers' quarters were warmed by steam-pipes, which were far less dangerous than heat generated by stoves, especially when the ves-

sel was pitching in a heavy sea. The EGYPT left Liverpool on 9 November 1871 for her maiden voyage to New York. Basically a freighter with passenger accommodation for 120 Saloon Class passengers, the EGYPT fell short of mail ship standards, but she could when needed take 1,400 Steerage passengers. In 1879 she was used as a transport to South Africa for the Zulu War. At the time of a general refit in 1884 the passenger accommodation was improved so she could take 210 Cabin Class passengers and the Dining Saloon was extended right across the ship. On 19 July 1890 the EGYPT was destroyed in mid-Atlantic by a fire which started in a cargo of cotton. She had no passengers save 500 head of cattle who broke loose and jumped into the sea, threatening to damage the lifeboats in which the crew were escaping. Fortunately there was no loss of human life.

With the opening of the Suez Canal in 1869 the voyage to India was shortened by about 1,000 miles. The canal gave a great fillip to steampower, as sail was no use in the canal area, and as a result many more operators entered this market. In 1871 Robert Napier & Sons of Glasgow built the steamship EUROPE for Ryde & Company of London, specially for the Suez route to

EUROPE
335 x 40 feet
Ryde & Co.
1871

by Green & Co. of Blackwall, London for their own use. Built under Admiralty survey, the VICEROY was a ship of 2,225 tons, 320 × 37 feet with compound engines driving a single screw. She had accommodation for 100 First and 40 Second Class passengers, and a large and well ventilated troop-deck. No expense was spared to alleviate the heat which was so distressing to passengers particularly in the Red Sea. As will be seen from the engraving the engines were placed well to the rear, so that the passengers would not suffer from noise and vibration, their accommodation all being forward of the engines.

The end of 1871 saw two medium-sized vessels completed: the NORTHUMBERLAND, belonging to Money Wigram & Sons of London for traffic to Australia, and the BERTHA, operated by C. M. Norwood & Co. of Hull and belonging to the Red Cross Line, an American company. The NORTHUMBERLAND was built by her owners and, having been launched in September 1871, sailed from the Thames for Melbourne on 28 December the same year. She was 1,898 tons and 270 × 38 feet, with a compound engine driving an auxiliary screw which could be raised out of the water. In addition, the funnel being telescopic could be lowered when under sail. One of a fleet of four similar

India. A comparatively small vessel of 335 × 40 feet, she had accommodation for 120 passengers in addition to cargo. Another medium-sized steamship built for the India service via Suez was the VICEROY, built in 1871

VICEROY
2,225 tons
320 x 37 feet
Green & Co.
1871

BERTHA
2,220 tons
313 × 35 feet
Red Cross Line
1872

vessels had a tonnage of 2,500. The OTHELLO, the first to be completed, was 316 × 36 feet with a two-cylinder compound engine driving a single screw. She had accommodation for 40 First, 20 Second and some Third Class passengers. The saloon which was 50 feet long by 20 feet wide was on the upper deck amidships and was constructed with an overhanging upper deck for the protection of the passengers when in hot climates. Furthermore it also afforded protection from rain, so that the passengers could take exercise whatever the weather. The comfort of passengers was a major consideration, and seven bathrooms were provided, as well as other luxuries which included an ice-house. She left London on 31 March 1872 on her maiden voyage to Calcutta via Suez. The Calcutta service was not very successful and was withdrawn after three years. The OTHELLO was transferred to the Atlantic and made her first voyage from Hull to New York at the end of January 1875. She returned to the India service in 1883, running between Hull and Bombay, until sold at the end of 1895. The COLOMBO was lost at sea in 1877.

In 1870 one of the great names in steam-shipping came into being, the Oceanic Steam Navigation Company, more popularly known as the White Star Line. Starting in 1871 they took delivery of three vessels built for them by Harland & Wolff of Belfast, the OCEANIC, the ATLANTIC and the BALTIC. The following year three more steamships were completed, also built by Harland & Wolff. These were the REPUBLIC, the ADRIATIC and the CELTIC.

The ADRIATIC was 3,888 tons and 452 × 41 feet, with a four-cylinder compound engine driving a single screw 22½ feet in diameter. The ship had accommodation for 150 First Class and 1,000 Steerage passengers.

steamers she made many trips to Australia and back before being sold to Shaw Savill in 1884. Before being sold her engines were removed. On the morning of 10 May 1887 while lying at anchor at Napier, New Zealand, a gale blew up and she was driven onto the rocks and completely wrecked. The figurehead was recovered and for many years adorned a local garden. In 1874 a certain Joseph Sams had sailed in her from London to Melbourne and recorded his journey in a diary which is published by the British Stationery Office, and is referred to in a Chapter One.

The BERTHA was built by Oswald & Co. of Pallion, Sunderland for use on the London to Calcutta route via the Suez Canal. She was 2,220 tons and 313 × 35 feet, with compound engines driving a single screw. She had accommodation for 50 First Class and some Second Class passengers. She could be steered either from the stern or midships and both the steering and the engine-room were under the control of the Master by means of Gisborne's patent telegraph. The BERTHA arrived in the Thames from Sunderland on 15 January 1872, and, taking on cargo and passengers at the Victoria Dock, sailed for Calcutta ten days later.

The firm of Thomas Wilson & Sons of Hull had been in the shipping business for some time operating in the North Sea. Tempted by the opening of the Suez Canal they too decided to enter the India trade, and commissioned two similar steamships: the OTHELLO from Earle's Engineering & Shipbuilding Company of Hull and the COLOMBO from Humphrys of Hull. Both

OTHELLO
2,500 tons
316 × 36 feet
Thomas Wilson & Sons
1872

ADRIATIC
3,888 tons
452 × 41 feet
White Star Line
1872

She sailed from Liverpool on 11 April 1872 on her maiden voyage to New York which she completed in eight days and fourteen hours. The ADRIATIC was the first North Atlantic liner to have general gas-lighting in the Saloon, ladies boudoir, smoking-room, bar, barber's shop, officer's rooms, sleeping rooms and engine room – 300 burners in all. A contemporary description of the ship said that the gas was made from an oil which would not explode, and that a continuous supply could be kept up for any length of time, as the manufacture took place on board ship. The gasometer was in an iron chamber off the engine room. There were three retorts, one of which was sufficient for ordinary purposes, but when the saloon was fully lighted two were required and a third was held in reserve. The ADRIATIC continued in the New York service until November 1897 and was broken up two years later.

All these first six White Star liners had reasonably long service with the company, except the ATLANTIC, which was wrecked near Halifax, Nova Scotia on 1 April 1873 with the loss of 546 lives. The outward bound ATLANTIC (3,707 tons and 420 × 41 feet) had encountered such bad weather that she ran short of coal. Her Captain, therefore, decided to make for Halifax, but she went on the rocks outside the port in appalling weather. The ship was doomed and only about 350 passengers and crew were saved out of a total compliment of 900. Had not the boatswain swum through rough seas carrying a life-line ashore, it is doubtful whether there would have been any survivors.

The loss of life was the worst to date in the North Atlantic. The OCEANIC was chartered in 1875 to the Occidental and Oriental Steam-ship Company to work between San Francisco and Hong Kong until broken up in 1896.

A little after midnight on Wednesday 22 May 1872, the North German Lloyd's steamship BALTIMORE, a vessel of 2,500 tons and 297 × 39 feet, which was on her way from Baltimore to Bremen, having called at Southampton, collided with a small Spanish steamer in the English Channel opposite Hastings and about nine miles from the shore. The commanding officer of the BALTIMORE, finding that the collision had made a large hole in the starboard bow, turned her towards the shore, guided by the lamplights on the Marine Parade at Hastings. The ship took water very quickly and, beginning to sink by the bows, could not have been saved if she had not been beached about 500 yards from the Marine Parade. There were 130 passengers on board and a crew of 80. The cabin passengers were accommodated at the Royal Marine Hotel and the crew were found shelter in the Market Hall by the local secretary of the Shipwrecked Mariners Society. The BALTIMORE was refloated and towed to Southampton for repairs. She had been built in 1868 by Caird & Co. of Greenock and was operated by her owners until she was broken up in 1894.

In 1872 another development in ocean travel came about as a result of the opening of the Suez Canal three years earlier. In order to further shorten the journey to

BALTIMORE
2,500 tons
297 × 39 feet
North German Lloyd
1868

India, it became much quicker to travel by train across France, through the Mont Cenis Tunnel and across Italy to Venice to board the ship there. P & O started this service in July 1872 with the steamship POONAH, a vessel of 2,150 tons which had been built for them by the Thames Ironworks in 1862. She was 335 × 41 feet with compound engines driving a single screw. In 1875 she was lengthened to 414 feet and her weight increased to 3,150 tons. She was sold in 1889.

The CITY OF RICHMOND, a new 1,600 ton Inman Line steamer, built by Tod & McGregor made her maiden voyage from Liverpool to New York on 4 September 1873. The following glowing description, probably taken from a company handout, and engraving appeared in *The Illustrated London News* of 2 May 1874:

'The CITY OF RICHMOND was the last steamer built in the well-known yard of Messrs Tod and McGregor, at Partick, on the Clyde. They constructed for Inman Line alone steamers of the aggregate tonnage of 42,000 tons. The CITY OF RICHMOND is in many respects similar to the CITY OF MONTREAL and other vessels belonging to the company. She is 450 feet in length over all by 43 feet beam

POONAH
2150 tons
335 × 41 feet
P & O
1862

and in depth 36 feet from the spar-deck to keel. Her engines, which are on the compound principle, and the largest size ever made for the merchant service, are 900 horse power nominal, but are capable of working to 5,000 horse power. Like the engines of the CITY OF CHESTER, they are on the high and low pressure principle, with direct-acting cylinders, the larger 120 inches in diameter, and the smaller 76 inches with a stroke of 5 feet. They are supplied with steam by ten boilers, heated by thirty furnaces, the boilers having surface condensers, and all other modern means to ensure economy in the consumption of coal and efficient working of the motive power. The builders have departed from the models of the other boats, by giving two funnels to the CITY OF RICHMOND, so as to afford additional draught to the furnaces. The funnels add to the beauty of the vessel, by aiding to fill up the great space between the main and mizen masts. This new steamer is most strongly built. Every modern appliance which can in any way contribute to her stability and her safety has been employed. Viewed fore and aft, her lines are so beautifully fine that she resembles a very large yacht. It is only by an internal examination that her enormous proportions and her carrying capacity can be seen or understood. She is a full-rigged ship, and carries sufficient canvas to enable her to proceed on her voyage quite independent of steam, should her machinery meet with an accident or break down. But such is the enormous spread of her canvas that, in a gale of wind, her crew, numerous as

they are, would find some difficulty in managing the sails without the steam-winches with which she is provided. These winches are also used for raising the anchors and for lifting and casting overboard the ashes which formed in the stokeholes. When in port, their chief use is for loading and unloading cargo. Communication between the bridge and the engine-room and wheel-house is maintained by Chadburn's telegraph. In the wheel-house is Macfarlane Gray's steam steering gear, by which the vessel may be guided with the greatest ease even in the face of a gale of wind.

'The steamer is built to carry 150 saloon and 1,300 steerage passengers, for the cooking of whose food and for other domestic purposes many hundred gallons of water are daily required. This indispensable article is supplied by means of a condensing apparatus which is capable of furnishing all that is ever likely to be required by passengers and crew. It is comforting to know that provision is made on board for extinguishing that most dreaded of all calamities to sailors – a fire at sea. The steam fire-annihilators are connected with every department of the ship. In addition, there is a powerful steam centrifugal pump capable of raising 2,000 gallons of water per minute, which could be thrown upon a fire. If, by any casualty, a large body of water had entered the engine-rooms and threatened to extinguish the engine fires, the pump could be employed to clear the water off. Hanging in the davits are ten life-boats of great capacity, furnished with the best appliances for safely lowering in case of

CITY OF RICHMOND
4,600 tons
450 x 43 feet
Inman Line
1873

emergency. The internal arrangements of the CITY OF RICHMOND are very convenient. The saloon, as near midships as it can be placed, is a splendid apartment, 44 feet by 42 feet, fitted in a luxurious and tasteful manner. The room is wainscoted in bird's-eye maple, with the outer framework of walnutwood, in the centre of each panel is an elaborate example of inlaid wood. The panels are seperated by Corinthian columns of walnutwood, with gilded capitals. To each window there are crimson curtains, adorned with gold lace. The delicate painting of the ceiling, the richness of the velvet coverings of the lounges, the artistic arrangement of plate glass at each end of the saloon, and the other decorations, are all in perfect taste. They combine to render the saloon as beautiful and as comfortable as any drawing-room could be made at sea. The state-rooms are well ventilated and commodious. They are supplied with hot and cold water, and are fitted with electric communication and Broadfoot's washing-basins. In addition to the rooms already mentioned, are two ladies' boudoirs, one on the upper deck and one immediately adjacent to the saloon. For those who are fond of tobacco there is a capacious smoking-room. For all the saloon passengers an additional promenard-deck has been constructed forward of the funnels. But, in thus providing for the comforts of the saloon passengers, the requirements of those in the steerage have not been overlooked. Their quarters, chiefly on the main deck, are capacious and airy – the most important considerations where the great numbers of persons congregated together by night. In all the arrangements made by the Inman Company, special attention is paid to the comfort of the steerage passengers, as the numbers carried by this line attest.'

The CITY OF RICHMOND continued in the North Atlantic service until she made her last voyage from Liverpool to New York in 1891, the Inman Line having been bought by an American company following the reform of the Inman & International Steamship Company in 1886. The CITY OF RICHMOND was sold in America after this last voyage.

In 1875 the Canadian Shipping Company, which had operated sailing ships for a number of years between Liverpool, Quebec and Montreal, took delivery of the LAKE CHAMPLAIN, their first steamship. The company's house flag incorporated a beaver, and they were generally known as the Beaver Line. In the summer or 'open' season they ran to Quebec and Montreal, but in winter between Liverpool and an American port. The LAKE CHAMPLAIN was built by the London & Glasgow Engineering & Iron Ship-building Company of Govan, who also supplied the engines. She had a gross tonnage of 2,207 and was 321 × 35 feet, with a two-cylinder compound engine driving a single screw. She was classed as 100A at Lloyds, but had been

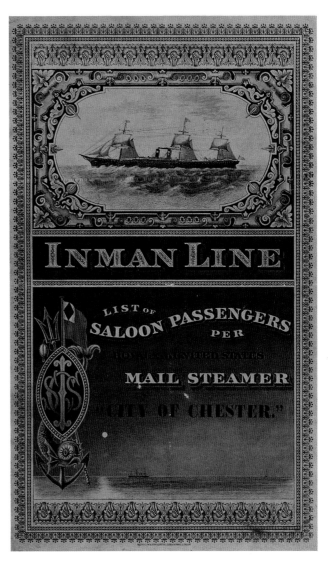

CITY OF CHESTER
passenger list

LAKE CHAMPLAIN
2,207 tons
321 × 35 feet
The Canadian Shipping Co.
1875

built to a specification much in excess of Lloyd's requirements.* She had accommodation for First and Second Class passengers and a Third Class suitable for carrying emigrants. The owners aimed to provide a vessel specially adapted for the Canadian trade, and strong enough to withstand the roughest storms of the North Atlantic. The LAKE CHAMPLAIN was, therefore, specially strengthened where there was the slightest chance of her coming into contact with ice. She left Liverpool on 13 April 1875 for her maiden voyage to Quebec and Montreal.

The previous month the LAKE NEPIGON, a sister ship, had been launched and a third ship the LAKE MEGANTIC was on the stocks, all at the London & Glasgow's yard at Govan. In June 1886 the LAKE CHAMPLAIN went aground off the coast of Antrim, Northern Ireland, but was later salvaged, sold to a British buyer and renamed the LISMORE. During the winter of 1890–91 she was lost without trace.

*Lloyds of London have always been the world's main marine insurers and in the 1860s and 1870s, due to the many losses endured, they required their marine inspectors to pass each ship to ensure it was a viable risk. Previously many ships had not been truly seaworthy. Each ship had to be passed as seaworthy for its intended route. The phrase to designate such a vessel became abbreviated to 'A1 at Lloyds'.

Contemporary advertisement for emigration to the New World

The Inman Steamship Company always had delightfully elegant ships and the CITY OF BERLIN built in 1875 by Caird & Co. of Greenock was no exception. She was a vessel of 5,491 tons and 489 × 44 feet with compound engines driving a single screw. She had accommodation for 202 Cabin and 1,500 Third Class passengers. She sailed from Liverpool on 24 April 1875 on her maiden voyage to New York. With a beam to length ratio of 11:1 she became the 'longest' transatlantic vessel ever built. In September 1875 she made the fastest westbound crossing of the Atlantic and the following

CITY OF BERLIN
5,491 tons
489 × 44 feet
Inman Line
1875

GERMAN
3,149 tons
351 x 39 feet
Union Line
1877

month the fastest eastbound, but only held them for a few months before the White Star Line regained their record. In 1879 she became the first liner with electric light, with six lamps in the saloon, engine-room and boiler-room. In 1887 triple expansion engines were fitted in order to reduce fuel consumption. The CITY OF BERLIN made her last voyage for the Inman Line from Liverpool to New York in March 1893, and was transferred to the American Line with all the other Inman ships. She was renamed simply the BERLIN and made her first transatlantic voyage for her new owners in April 1893. With the exception of two crossings in 1898 she left for her last regular crossing from Southampton on 26 October 1895. She was sold to the United States government in 1898, renamed the MEADE and used as a training ship until broken up in 1921.

The Union Line had a new steamship built for them in 1877 by William Denny of Dumbarton. This was the 3,149 ton GERMAN, a ship of 351 × 39 feet with a two-cylinder compound engine driving a single screw. With a straight stem and only two masts, she carried a minimum of sail. Built for her owners, the Cape Mail service, she made the fastest outward journey to the Cape of 19 days and 8 hours in her first year, and remained on this route until sold in 1896 to the Italian company, Navigazione Generale Italiana, who renamed her the SEMPIONE. Her first voyage for her new owners was in April 1901 from Genoa and Naples to New York. However, she cannot have been too successful on this route, because after two years she was laid up and sold in 1905.

1880–1891

In 1880 John Elder of Glasgow built a new ship for the Castle Line, the KINFAUNS CASTLE, weighing 3,500 tons and being 360 × 43 feet with compound engines driving a single screw. She was a notable ship as she was the first ocean mail steamer to be built of steel. Her accommodation was for 120 First, 100 Second and 160 Third Class passengers, and, in addition, she was designed to be able to carry ten heavy guns and to steam from England to Japan via the Cape of Good Hope without coaling. Thus she could be used either as a cruiser or a troop transport. She made her maiden voyage to Cape Town in January 1880. She could not have been a very successful ship as she was sold in 1883 to the Russian Volunteer Fleet and renamed the MOSKWA. She finished her life as the Russian mine-layer PRUT, and, being chased by the German battle-cruiser GOEBEN off Sevastopol in the Black Sea in October 1914, she was scuttled to avoid capture.

KINFAUNS CASTLE
3,500 tons
360 x 43 feet
Castle Line
1880

TROJAN
3,500 tons
364 x 42 feet
Union Line
1880

Another ship for the South African route was the TROJAN of the Union Line, built by James & George Thomson of Glasgow. With an iron hull she weighed 3,500 tons and was 364 × 42 feet with compound engines driving a single screw. She had accommodation for 116 First, 90 Second and 50 Third Class passengers. The TROJAN made her maiden voyage to Cape Town in June 1880. During the Boer War she served as a hospital ship, and in 1901 was sold to Elder Dempster who renamed her the WASSAU and chartered her to the Beaver Line who used her for four return voyages from Liverpool to Halifax, the first sailing being on 29 January 1901. In January 1902 she was sold to a French owner who renamed her the ISLAM. The following year she was again sold, this time to the Japanese owner Nippon Yusen Kaisha Line, with yet another change of name to TOSA MARU. She was lost without trace during the winter of 1924/25.

When built in 1881 the Cunard Line's SERVIA was their largest ship. She had been built by James & George Thomson. She weighed 7,400 tons and was 530 × 52 feet, with a three-cylinder compound engine driving a single screw. At the time of building she was the largest ship afloat with the exception of the GREAT EASTERN. She was also the first liner to be lit throughout by electric light. She had accommodation for 480 First and 730 Third Class passengers. On 23 August 1881 she left Liverpool on her maiden voyage to New York. While no great record breaker, the SERVIA was one of the outstanding ships on the North Atlantic, a ship in which

CITY OF ROME
8,415 tons
560 × 52 feet
Inman Line
1881

comfort was not sacrificed for speed. After a refit in 1893 her accommodation was changed to 400 First, 200 Second and 500 Third Class passengers, and at the same time she was transferred to the intermediate service to New York after the delivery of the CAMPANIA and the LUCANIA. The SERVIA made her last Atlantic crossing in September 1901 and then did three round trips to South Africa as a troop-ship for the Boer War. At the end of the year she was sold and broken up.

Another famous ship which was completed in 1881 was the Inman Line's CITY OF ROME. Built by the Barrow Shipbuilding Company, she was 8,415 tons and 560 × 52 feet, with a six-cylinder compound engine driving a single screw. She provided accommodation for 520 First, and 810 Third Class passengers. The CITY OF ROME sailed from Liverpool on 13 October 1881 on her maiden voyage to New York. The contract for the CITY OF ROME specified a steel hull, but due to shortages of supplies it was decided to use iron instead. With her clipper bow, three funnels and four masts she was considered the most graceful steamship on the North Atlantic. However, she was a failure as far as performance was concerned. It was said that the main cause was the excessive draught (due to the increased weight caused by using iron instead of steel for the hull) which upset design calculations. Also her tandem compound engines caused trouble.

After five return voyages to New York she was rejected by Inman. A legal case followed which was lost by the Barrow Shipbuilding Company and they had to accept her return. In August 1882 she made one return trip to New York under the flag of the Anchor Line and

SERVIA
7,400 tons
530 × 52 feet
Cunard
1881

was then taken out of service for modification which included a reduction of 300 tons in weight and a simplification of her engines. After her rebuild she had a better performance of $18\frac{1}{4}$ knots and was registered under her builder's name, but sailed under the Anchor Line flag. In 1883 she started working out of Liverpool (as the Clyde was not deep enough at that time) on the New York service, teaming up with various other vessels. Quite a popular ship with her passengers, it is doubtful whether she ever paid her way. In 1890 she was stranded near Fastnet but refloated without damage, and in 1899 she had a minor collision with an iceberg in the North Atlantic, again with little damage done. In 1900 she worked for a few months as a troopship for the Boer War and made her last voyage from Glasgow to New York and back in September 1901, before being sold the following year for breaking up in Germany.

A new shipping company came into being in 1884, Shaw, Savill & Albion, and has survived to this day specialising in the New Zealand trade. Their first ship was the ARAWA. Built by William Denny of Dumbarton, she was a handsome ship weighing 5,050 tons and was 440 × 46 feet with triple expansion engines driving a single screw. She had accommodation for 95 First, 52 Second and 200 Third Class passengers. On her maiden voyage in October and November 1884 she reached Hobart, Tasmania, from Plymouth in 37 days and 15 hours and on her second voyage only took 35 days and 14 hours to Hobart and 38 days and 30 minutes to New Zealand. On the homeward voyage via Cape Horn she took 32 days and 5 hours, a total for a round the world voyage of 70 days and 6 hours steaming, a record that stood for many years. In 1896 she was chartered to Cia TransAtlantica (Italian) and was renamed the COLON, and in 1899 she was sold to Elder Dempster and became a Boer War troop-ship in November. In 1900 she was acquired by the Beaver Line and renamed the LAKE MEGANTIC and on 3 October left Liverpool on her first voyage to Halifax and St. John's (New Brunswick). Three years later when Beaver Line was sold to Canadian Pacific, the LAKE MEGANTIC was not included in the sale and in 1905 she eventually became the property of the Imperial Direct Line who renamed her the PORT HENDERSON. In 1913 she was acquired by an Italian shipowner who named her ANAPO and a year later changed it to PORTO SAID. In 1915 she was sunk by a submarine.

ARAWA
5,050 tons
440 x 46 feet
Shaw, Savill & Albion
1884

EMPRESS OF INDIA
5,900 tons
451 x 51 feet
Canadian Pacific
1891

In 1885 William Denny & Bros of Dumbarton built the TAINUI for the Shaw, Savill Line. She was the sister ship of the ARAWA and these two vessels were among the most beautiful ships of the steam-sail period, probably only exceeded by Inman's the CITY OF ROME. Although they were rigged thy probably did not use sail. The TAINUI was 5,050 tons and 440 × 46 feet, with an elegant clipper bow and triple expansion engines driving a single screw. Her accommodation was for 95 First, 52 Second Class and 200 Emigrant passengers. In 1895 the TAINUI was chartered by the Spanish government to move troops to Cuba under the name of the COVADONGA. In 1899 she was chartered to the Allan Line for their Canadian service, following which Shaw, Savill sold her to the Anchor Line in November 1899. They had her refitted and re-engined and put her to work on their Glasgow to New York service with the name of ASTORIA. She was broken up in 1910.

1891 saw the construction of almost the last steamships which also carried sails. Three ships were built in this year by the Naval Construction & Armaments Company of Barrow-in-Furness for the Canadian Pacific's trans-pacific Service, the first of these being the EMPRESS OF INDIA. All three were sister ships of 5,900 tons and 451 × 51 feet, with triple expansion engines driving twin screws. These three ships, together with the Union Line's SCOT, were the last ocean liners built with a clipper bow and a contemporary description stated that they were 'lightly rigged'. The EMPRESS OF INDIA carried a figurehead which was a bust of Queen Victoria. She had accommodation for 180 First, 32 Second Class and 600 Steerage passengers. In 1907 to meet tighter mail arrangements the EMPRESS OF INDIA and her sisters were modified with enlarged bunkers at the expense of Second Class accommodation and cargo space, as presumably the faster running envisaged would consume more coal. In 1914 the EMPRESS OF INDIA was laid up and later sold to the Maharajah of Gwalior who converted her a hospital ship for Indian troops in the Great War and renamed her LOYALTY. In 1919 she was sold to the Scindia Steam Navigation Company of Bombay for use between Bombay and London, but this was not successful and she was broken up in 1923.

CHAPTER 6

The First Steel Hulls 1879–1900

A new steamer built for the Union Steam Ship Company of New Zealand by William Denny of Dumbarton, the ROTOMAHANA, was launched in June 1879, and would seem to be the first steel-hulled steamer. She was 1,777 tons and 285 × 35 feet, fitted with compound engines. Her maiden voyage to New Zealand via the Cape was completed in a very respectable time with speeds up to 17 knots. An extremely handsome ship with her clipper bow and medium tall single funnel, she was known as the 'greyhound' of the Pacific and according to Dickson Gregory, the well-known writer on Australian shipping, by the less reverent as the 'rotten banana'! Her bow was adorned with the figurehead of a Maori princess. In February 1879 she was described in *The Australian Shipping News* as follows:

'The ROTOMAHANA now being built for USS Co. of New Zealand, is intended to eclipse, if possible, all other steamers in these Colonies in speed, accommodation, and comfort for passengers. A special feature in the new boat will be the "Bridal Chamber" – a large cabin on deck, fitted up for the use of those newly married couples whose purse is long enough, or whose honeymoon is recent enough, to make the additional charge that will be imposed a matter of no consequence.'

The ROTOMAHANA did sterling work between Australia and New Zealand until 1921, when she was laid up and eventually auctioned for scrap in April 1925, realising £1,700. She was finally dismantled in Melbourne in 1927, and at the time it was said she contained 150 tons of lead in her keel, which in those

ROTOMAHANA
1777 tons
285 x 35 feet
Union Steam Ship Co.
1879

S. S. Parisian. (Allan Line.)

PARISIAN
5,350 tons
441 × 46 feet
Allan Line
1881

days was valued at £30 a ton – not bad for the shipbreakers!

In 1881 the PARISIAN was built for the Allan Line by Napier of Clydebank for their service from Liverpool to Canada. She was 5,350 tons and 441 × 46 feet, with double expansion engines driving a single screw. She had accommodation for 150 First, 100 Second Class passengers and 1,000 Steerage. She was notable for being the first steel hulled ship on the North Atlantic service and the first designed with a bilge-keel to minimise rolling. The PARISIAN was modernised while undergoing a refit in 1899 when triple expansion engines were fitted and her appearance altered by the removal of one funnel. In 1902 she was equipped with Marconi wireless telegraphy (radio). In 1912 she was one of the ships which went to the aid of the TITANIC, when she struck an iceberg in the North Atlantic. The PARISIAN was sold to a shipbreaker in January 1914.

The AUSTRAL was built in 1882 by John Elder & Company for the Orient Line. She was 5,500 tons and 456 × 48 feet, with double expansion engines driving a single screw and a steel hull. She was meant for use on the Australian service, but on her second voyage sank on an even keel in Sydney harbour in November 1882, due to water entering her coaling ports. Three months later she was refloated, pumped dry, and was able to return to England under her own steam. She was immediately sent for an extensive refit and had electric lighting installed. Her two funnels were extended by 15 feet and for some reason the extension was of slightly smaller diameter than the lower part, which looked a little odd. On completion of this work she was

chartered to the Inman Line to run on the North Atlantic route with the CITY OF ROME for seven return voyages between Liverpool and New York. She then returned to the Australian service. In 1900 she made one trip to South Africa with troops for the Boer War. She came to the end of her days in 1903 when she was broken up.

The following year, 1883, John Elder built another notable steamer, the OREGON, for the Guion Line. She was 7,400 tons, built of iron (Guion Line could not afford steel!) and 501 × 54 feet, with double expansion engines driving a single screw. No doubt if she had been built of steel she would have been a better ship. She had accommodation for 340 First Class and 1,200 Steerage passengers. The OREGON sailed on her maiden voyage to New York in October 1883. On her third eastward voyage in April 1884 she broke the record to take the Blue Riband from another Guion Line steamer the ALASKA, but her triumph was short-lived; it was her last voyage for Guion, who had not been able to keep up the payments to her builders who repossessed her and sold her to the Cunard Line.

Her first voyage under her new flag was on 7 June 1884. In August 1884, the OREGON won her second Blue Riband of the North Atlantic in both directions for her new owners. In 1885 the British Government, expecting trouble with Russia, chartered the OREGON and fitted her with 10 guns. Her high speed made her an excellent reconnaissance ship, which pleased the Admiralty so much that they decided to continue their policy of chartering suitable vessels in times of trouble. At the end of the year the OREGON was returned to Cunard, but her days were numbered. While approaching New York on 14 March 1886 she was rammed off Fire Island by an unknown ship and holed in two places between the boiler rooms. Because of difficulty with the

OREGON
7,400 tons
501 × 54 feet
Guion Line, later Cunard
1883

PEMBROKE CASTLE
3,936 tons
400 x 42 feet
Castle Line
1883

driving a single screw. She was the first transatlantic record-breaker to be built of steel. On her maiden voyage she crossed from Cobh in southern Ireland to New York in 6 days, 15 hours and 22 minutes giving an average speed of 17.6 knots. On her return voyage she did even better with a time of 6 days, 14 hours and 18 minutes, an average of 17.8 knots. She was in keen competition with the OREGON.

The AMERICA was an extremely handsome ship with her clipper bow, and had a luxurious interior, an outstanding feature being the domed saloon. Her accommodation was for 300 First Class and 700 Steerage passengers. Unfortunately the National Line had no other ship with which to pair her for a regular Atlantic service. The timing of any regular service operated by two ships can only be as fast as the slowest ship and the AMERICA was originally paired with the EGYPT, a much slower vessel. After making a single trooping voyage to India, she was paired with the CITY OF ROME for the 1886 season, but the arrangement was unsatisfactory and could not be justified on financial grounds. The National Line decided to sell the AMERICA to the Italian Navy for a very reasonable price. She was renamed TRINACRIA and was employed as a cruiser-transport, Royal Yacht and Exhibition Ship. She survived until 1925.

In 1885 the Cunard Line took delivery of the second of two sister ships that had been built for them by John Elder of Glasgow. She was the ETRURIA and was 7,700 tons and 502 × 57 feet with compound engines driving a single screw. She had accommodation for 550 First Class passengers and 800 Steerage. The ETRURIA and her sister the UMBRIA were the most powerful single screw ships built at that time and while

water-tight doors she began to fill, and fortunately the North German Lloyd ship FULDA removed the 641 passengers and crew before she went down bow first.

In 1883 the Castle Mail Packet Company acquired a new ship from the Barrow Shipbuilding Company. The PEMBROKE CASTLE was 3,936 tons and 400 × 42 feet with accommodation for 40 First Class, 80 Second Class and 100 Tourist Class passengers. She made her maiden voyage to the Cape in October 1883, and was on the Royal Mail Service to Cape Town until 1893 and again from 1900 to 1902. Between 1893 and 1900 she ran on the Intermediate Service to South Africa. With a service speed of only 12 knots she usually took 21 days from London to Cape Town. On her trials in January 1883 round the north of Scotland, she carried Sir Donald Currie, the Chairman of the operating company and his guests who included Lord Tennyson the Poet Laureate and the Prime Minister, Mr William Gladstone. The cruise was extended to the Norwegian Fjords and Copenhagen where the party was both entertained by and entertained the Danish Royal Family and a party of their royal guests. In 1906 the PEMBROKE CASTLE was sold to the Turkish government and renamed BEZMI ALEM. She was sunk in 1915 by a warship of the Imperial Russian navy.

The AMERICA was built by J. & G. Thomson and delivered to the National Line in 1884. She was 442 × 51 feet and 5,550 tons, with double expansion engines

ETRURIA
7,700 tons
502 x 57 feet
Cunard
1885

performance was good, vibration was excessive, which resulted in continuous propeller shaft trouble. The ETRURIA is recorded as having averaged 20 knots over a six hour trial, but would burn 315 tons of coal a day! Both ships were employed on the North Atlantic. In 1887 and 1888 the ETRURIA gained the Blue Riband in both directions. Both ships were put on reserve sailings in 1907 with the arrival of the LUSITANIA and the MAURETANIA and were laid up the following year. ETRURIA was broken up in 1909.

A second ship to be given the name the ORINOCO was built by Caird & Company of Greenock in 1886 for the Royal Mail Lines. She was 4,550 tons and 410 × 45 feet with triple expansion engines driving a single screw. She had accommodation for 257 First and 26 Second Class passengers. The ORINOCO was the first Royal Mail steamer to have a steel hull and the last to have crossyards on her masts. She sailed on the West Indies service. In November 1906 when entering Cherbourg harbour she collided with the North German Lloyd liner KAISER WILHELM DER GROSSE in very foggy conditions. The German ship was severely damaged, but the ORINOCO with her clipper bow did not suffer too badly. She was taken out of service and broken up in 1909.

The VICTORIA (1887), the BRITANNIA (1887), the OCEANIA (1888) and the ARCADIA (1888) were four sister ships built for the P & O Line. The two built in 1887 were by Caird & Company, and were 6,200 tons and 466 × 52 feet. The latter two were built by Harland & Wolff of Belfast and were 6,200 tons and 468 × 52 feet. All four had triple expansion engines driving a single screw. They were known as the 'Jubilee' class because the first two were delivered in the year of Queen Victoria's Diamond Jubilee and the VICTORIA had her maiden voyage postponed so that she could attend the Jubilee Royal Naval Review. They provided accommodation for 220 First and 160 Second Class passengers. These ships performed well on the Bombay and Australian services. The VICTORIA and the BRITANNIA were used experimentally for troop carrying in 1894 and 1895, which proved very successful and was the beginning of the system, still used today, of chartering passenger liners as troop-ships instead of using government-owned vessels. After this they continued to run on the Bombay and Far East services until withdrawn and broken up in 1909. The second pair lasted a little longer. The OCEANIA while on an outward voyage to Bombay in March 1912 was run into by a German barque off Beachy Head and was a total

s.s. "BRITANNIA."
6,525 Tons.   7,500 h.p.

P AND O

Wishing you all a happy New Year. Tell Uncle F. That I will write to him soon. probably from Aden. — G.C.B.

BRITANNIA
6,525 tons
466 x 52 feet
P & O
1887

loss, although fortunately the £700,000 of gold bullion she was carrying in her strongroom was recovered by divers. The BRITANNIA continued in service until withdrawn and broken up in 1915.

The AUGUSTA VICTORIA was built by Vulkan of Stettin in 1889 for the Hamburg-America Line, and was the first express liner to be built in a German shipyard. She was 7,650 tons and 461 × 56 feet, with twin screws driven by triple expansion engines. It was intended that she should be named the NORMANIA, but following the accession of the Emperor William II to the German throne she was named after his consort. The name was misspelt and remained unaltered until the ship went to Harland & Wolff for major alterations, which included increasing her length to 521 feet, her weight to 8,500 tons, and correcting the spelling of her name to AUGUSTE VICTORIA. After this rebuild she went back to the North Atlantic service. When first built she was the third passenger liner to have twin screws. (The CITY OF PARIS being the first and the TEUTONIC the second). In 1904 she was sold to the Russian Navy and was broken up in 1907.

The TEUTONIC 1889 and the MAJESTIC 1890 were both built by Harland & Wolff for the White Star Line. They were sister ships, each of 9,950 tons and 566 × 58 feet, with triple expansion engines driving twin screws. They had accommodation for 300 First, 175 Second Class and 850 Steerage passengers. They were designed for rapid conversion for Royal Navy use as cruisers, in which capacity the TEUTONIC attended the Royal Naval Reviews of 1889 and the Diamond Jubilee. The MAJESTIC made two troop voyages to South Africa in the Boer War. With the delivery of the OLYMPIC in 1911, the TEUTONIC was transferred to the White Star–Dominion Lines's Canadian service, and two years later was converted to Cabin Class only. The MAJESTIC had been placed on reserve in 1912 because of the delivery of the TITANIC, but, with the loss of this great new ship in April 1912, she returned to the Mail Service in May for a few return trips before being broken up. In September 1914 the British Admiralty requisitioned the TEUTONIC as an armed merchant cruiser for North Atlantic patrol duty, and purchased her outright in 1915. She continued in naval service until 1921 when she was broken up.

The DUNOTTER CASTLE, built by the Fairfield Shipbuilding & Engineering Company for the Castle Line in 1890, was, 5,650 tons and 420 × 50 feet with triple expansion engines driving a single screw. Accommodation was for 160 First Class, 90 Second Class, 100

R.M.S. "Majestic"

MAJESTIC
9,950 tons
566 × 58 feet
White Star Line
1890

White Star-Dominion Canadian Service.

THE LARGEST STEAMERS in the CANADIAN TRADE.

MARCONI'S TELEGRAPHY.

Unsurpassed Accommodation in all Classes.

FIRST CLASS	..	..	From £16 10/-
SECOND CLASS	..	..	,, £9 0/-
THIRD CLASS	..	..	,, £6 0/-

LIVERPOOL to HALIFAX and PORTLAND, Me.
WINTER SERVICE.

From LIVERPOOL (Calling at Halifax)	STEAMER.	From PORTLAND.
1910		1910
Nov. 17...Thurs.	LAURENTIC ...	Dec. 3...Sat.*
,, 24...Thurs.	CANADA	,, 10...Sat.*
Dec. 8...Thurs.	DOMINION ...	,, 24 ..Sat.
		1911
,, 29...Thurs.	CANADA	Jan. 14...Sat.
1911		
Jan. 12...Thurs.	DOMINION ...	,, 28...Sat.
Feb. 2...Thurs.	CANADA	Feb. 18...Sat.
,, 18 ..Sat.	MEGANTIC ...	Mar. 4...Sat.
Mar. 4...Sat.	CANADA	,, 18 ..Sat.
,, 9...Thurs.	DOMINION ...	,, 25...Sat.
,, 18 ..Sat.	MEGANTIC ...	Apl. 1...Sat.
Apl. 1...Sat.	CANADA	,, 15...Sat.
,, 15...Sat.	MEGANTIC ...	,, 29...Sat.

* Calling at Halifax the following day.

Summer sailings to Quebec and Montreal, commencing April 20th.

Apply to—

A later postcard advertisement for the White Star's Canada service, after the invention of telegraphy

DUNOTTER CASTLE
5,650 tons
420 x 50 feet
Castle Line
1890

1915 and used to house workmen at Scapa Flow. In 1915 she was lost in bad weather off Cape Wrath.

In May 1891, the Union Steamship Company took delivery of the SCOT, one of the most handsome ships of her time and one of the last to be built with a clipper bow. She was built by William Denny of Dumbarton. She was 6,850 tons and 502 × 54 feet, with a steel hull which had 14 bulkheads, 10 of which carried up into the upper decks, so that she would not sink if any two compartments were flooded. She had two sets of triple-expansion engines which drove twin screws to give an estimated speed of $18\frac{1}{2}$ knots, a time that was considerably exceeded on her trials. Her clipper bow carried a figurehead of the Scottish patriot and chieftain, Sir William Wallace (1270–1305), and the Royal Arms with a Scottish Lion on her stern. She had accommodation for 208 First Class, 100 Second Class and over 100 Third Class passengers. The Grand Saloon on the upper deck had 190 table seats and was panelled and furnished in sycamore and satinwood. Above this was the Music Room and the Promenade Deck which was 257 feet long. Refrigerating apparatus supplied ice, fresh meat, vegetables and fruit during the voyage. She made a trial trip from the Clyde to Southampton on 31 May 1891 with the Chairman of the company and his guests on

Third Class and 150 'open berth' passengers. In 1894 she ran aground near Eddystone Lighthouse but was refloated. She was laid up in 1904 until 1907 when she was let out on charter. In 1913 she was sold to the Royal Mail Line and, renamed the CARIBBEAN, she was converted for cruising. She was sold to the Admiralty in

SCOT
6,850 tons
502 x 54 feet
Union Steamship Co.
1891

OPHIR
6,800 tons
465 x 53 feet
Orient Line
1891

Poster advertising
the Orient-Royal Mail's
service to Australia

board. She sailed from Southampton on her maiden voyage to the Cape on 24 July 1891.

The OPHIR was built by Robert Napier of Glasgow for the Orient Line in 1891. She was 6,800 tons and 465 × 53 feet, with triple expansion engines driving twin screws. A fine-looking ship, she had been built for speed, and was the first twin-screw steamer on the Australian run. She was the second twin-screw vessel to go through the Suez Canal, being preceded by the Bibby Line's CHESHIRE. As may be imagined with a name like the OPHIR, her accommodation was luxurious and she could carry 220 First and 150 Second Class passengers as well as 520 emigrants. She left Plymouth on 7 November 1891 on her maiden voyage to Australia. The OPHIR had been designed to comply with certain Royal Naval requirements, namely that she should have sufficient coal in her bunkers for 130 days steaming at 10 knots and the machinery should be placed between the two sets of boilers. In the event, coal consumption proved very heavy at a daily rate of 125 tons. This famous Orient liner was extremely popular with passengers, but very expensive to operate, and, as a result, she was usually laid up during the slack season. The Admiralty chartered the OPHIR from November 1900 to the end of 1901 to take the Duke and Duchess of York (later King George V and Queen Mary) to Australia to open the first Commonwealth Parliament. She was crewed by Royal Navy personnel and was painted white overall. In 1915 the Admiralty bought her for conversion into an auxiliary cruiser. The OPHIR finished her life as a hospital ship and was finally broken up in 1922.

1893 saw the commissioning of two new Cunarders, both built by the Fairfield Shipbuilding & Engineering Company of Govan, the CAMPANIA and the LUCANIA. Competition had been hotting up in the Atlantic trade and Cunard had decided they must have some faster ships. These two sister ships were 12,950 tons and 598 × 65 feet, with triple expansion engines driving twin screws. They had accommodation for 450 First, 280 Second Class and 1,000 Steerage passengers. The CAMPANIA left Liverpool on 22 April 1893 for New York, and the LUCANIA left on her maiden voyage on 2 October from Liverpool. Between them these two ships held the Blue Riband of the North Atlantic for Cunard from 1893 to 1897. In 1903 the LUCANIA became the first ship to make radio contact with both sides of the Atlantic at the same time. On 14 August 1909, she was destroyed by fire while at the dockside in Liverpool. With the delivery of the

LUCANIA
12,950 tons
598 x 65 feet
Cunard
1893

CAMPANIA
12,950 tons
598 × 65 feet
Cunard
1893

AQUITANIA in 1914, the CAMPANIA was put on reserve and made her last North Atlantic sailing in October 1914. She was then sold to the Admiralty and converted into an aircraft carrier, working with the Royal Navy. Six days before the signing of the Armistice for the end of the First World War, she sank when in collision with a British battleship in the Firth of Forth.

The CALEDONIA was built by Laird for P & O in 1894. She was 7,550 tons and 486 × 54 feet, with two funnels, four masts, triple expansion engines and a single screw. Her accommodation provided for 316 First and 175 Second Class passengers. She was built for the Bombay trade and painted white with yellow funnels. Her speed on trials was $19\frac{1}{2}$ knots, and her fastest trip to Bombay via Suez was $12\frac{1}{2}$ days after leaving Marseilles. In 1908 she completed the voyage from London to Calcutta in 24 days 21 hours (Marseilles to Colombo in $13\frac{1}{2}$ days). The CALEDONIA continued on the London-Calcutta service until she struck a mine near Marseilles late in 1915. The passengers and most of the crew were safely taken off and a skeleton crew got her into port. After repairs she was requisitioned by the British Ministry of War Transport as a troop-ship. When released from war service she was rebuilt and refitted in 1920.

When the NORMAN was built by Harland & Wolff in 1894, she was the largest vessel of the Union Line. She was 7,550 tons and 491 × 53 feet, powered by triple expansion engines driving twin screws, which were designed to give a service speed of 15 knots. While not as fast as the SCOT built three years earlier, her accommodation was better. On her maiden voyage to the Cape from Plymouth, the NORMAN made the journey in 14 days and 9 hours (SCOT's time was 15 days and 3 hours). Her accommodation was for 187 First, 108 Second and 125 Third Class passengers. In 1896 she ran aground at Port Shepstone, south of Durban on the Natal Coast, but was refloated. In 1910 she was placed on reserve until August 1914, when together with the DUNVEGAN CASTLE she brought

R.M.S. CALÉDONIA
Péninsular Oriental Co - In storm weather

CALEDONIA
7,550 tons
486 x 54 feet
P & O
1894

S.S.S⸀LOUIS

ST LOUIS
11,629 tons
554 x 63 feet
American Line
1895

South African troops to Britain. Thereafter she returned to the South African Mail Service until May 1918 when she again became a troop ship. The NORMAN was derequisitioned in 1919 and chartered by P & O for one return voyage to Australia, after which she returned to the South African Mail service. In 1923, the NORMAN was transferred to the Union Castle round Africa service until 1926 when she was broken up.

When they were built in 1895 by William Cramp of Philadelphia, the two sister ships of the American Line, the ST LOUIS and the ST PAUL were the largest ships owned by a non-European shipping company and the third and fourth largest ships in the world. They were both 11,629 tons and 554 × 63 feet, with quadruple expansion engines driving twin screws giving an estimated speed of 19 knots. They had accommodation for 320 First, 220 Second Class passengers and 800 Steerage. The ST PAUL sailed from New York on 9 October 1895 on her maiden voyage to Southampton, but after one return trip went back to her makers for modification because her speed was unsatisfactory. In 1898 she was fitted up as an auxiliary cruiser for the Spanish-American war. In 1899 the ST PAUL had Signor Marconi as a passenger on a voyage from New York to Southampton. He had receiving equipment with him and made contact with a station in the Isle of Wight and Cobh, thereby establishing a 'first' in the history of North Atlantic radio communications. In 1907 during a major overhaul she had new boilers fitted; a year later she was in collision at Southampton with the British cruiser HMS GLADIATOR which sank with the loss of 27 lives. Following the outbreak of the First World War, the ST PAUL used Liverpool as her English port. In 1918 she was taken over by the US Navy for fitting out as an armed transport and was

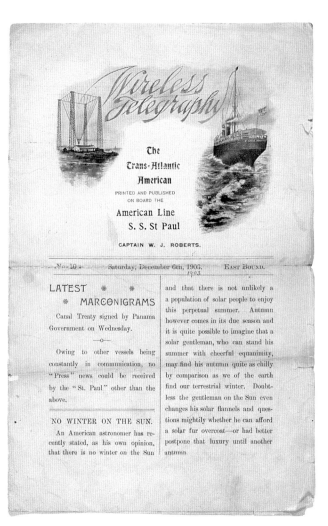

renamed KNOXVILLE. However, before the job was completed she capsized and sank. By March 1920, having been refloated, repaired and handed back to her owners with her old name of ST PAUL, she started sailing again on the North Atlantic using various European ports. In July 1923 she was laid up and broken up later in the same year.

In 1903, the ST LOUIS suffered boiler damage while at Southampton and had to sail to her home port at very reduced speed, before going to Philadelphia for repairs. In 1917 she was taken over by the US Navy and used as an armed transport renamed LOUISVILLE. In 1920 she was returned to her owner and regained her original name, but during her refit she caught fire and sank. She was eventually raised and in 1922 sold to the Anderson Overseas Corporation of New York who planned to restore her. Alas, this proved impractical and two years later she was sold to an Italian Company to be broken up in Genoa.

CANADA
8,800 tons
500 × 58 feet
Dominion Line
1896

The Dominion Line accepted delivery of the CANADA from Harland & Wolff in 1896. She was 8,800 tons and 500 × 58 feet, with triple expansion engines driving twin screws. Accommodation was provided for 200 First, 20 Second Class and 800 Steerage passengers. At that time she was considered to be the finest ship sailing between Great Britain and the St Lawrence. After two Canadian trips she started serving Boston, Massachusetts. Between 1899 and 1902 she was used as a troop-ship for the Boer War, after which she returned to her North Atlantic duties. In 1910 she had a refit and became a Cabin Class ship. The CANADA again became a troop-ship in the First World War bringing troops

PHILADELPHIA
(formerly CITY OF PARIS)
10,499 tons
560 × 63 feet
Inman Line
1889

across the Atlantic. She survived until 1926 when she was broken up.

In 1888 and 1889 the Inman Line had taken delivery of the first two steamships of over 10,000 tons to be built since Brunel's GREAT EASTERN, which was 18,915 tons and had made her maiden voyage 28 years earlier. In contrast, P & O did not have a vessel over 10,000 tons until 1903. These two new Inman ships, the CITY OF NEW YORK and the CITY OF PARIS were built by J. & G. Thomson on Clydebank. They were 10,499 tons and 560 × 63 feet, with triple expansion engines driving twin screws. They had accommodation for 540 First, 200 Second Class passengers and 1,000 Steerage. The CITY OF PARIS started her maiden voyage on 3 April 1889 from Liverpool to New York, and the following month took the Blue Riband of the North Atlantic in both directions. In 1890 the CITY OF PARIS travelling at speed broke her starboard propeller shaft, causing the engines to race and break down. The vibration caused leaks in the hull and the water put the other engine out of action, necessitating a tow to Queenstown.

The Inman Line, although registered in Britain, had been owned by an American company, the International Navigation Company, who also owned the American Line. In 1893 both the CITY OF NEW YORK and the CITY OF PARIS were transferred to the American Line and Inman ceased to trade. At the time of the transfer their names were changed to the NEW YORK and the PARIS, and they both started sailing from New York to Southampton. In 1899 the PARIS ran aground off the

CITY OF NEW YORK
10,499 tons
560 × 63 feet
Inman Line
1888

S. S. "PHILADELPHIA"

S. S. "New York"

Cornish coast and, after salvage and temporary repairs, she was sent to Harland & Wolff for refitting and the installation of quadruple expansion engines. One funnel was removed and when she went back into service in August 1901 she bore the name the PHILADELPHIA. She continued on the Southampton to New York route until the outbreak of the First World War, when Liverpool became her English port. From 1917 to 1919 she became an armed transport in the US Navy and was named the HARRISBURG. In March 1920 she returned to the North Atlantic service under her old name PHILADELPHIA. Two years later she was sold to the New York–Naples Steamship Company of New York and sailed for Naples in July 1922. On the voyage a mutiny broke out and an attempt was made to sink the ship. On arrival in Naples she was laid up and never used again. PHILADELPHIA was broken up the following year.

1896 saw the completion of a famous German class of liners, named the Barbarossa Class after the second ship to be completed, which was also the first German vessel of over 10,000 tons. Altogether there were eleven ships in the class: FREDERICH DER GROSS (1896), BARBAROSSA (1897), KONIGINBLUISE (1897), BREMEN (1897), KONIG ALBERT (1899), HAMBURG (1900), GROSSER KURFUST (1900), PRINZESS IRENE (1900), KIAUTSHON (1900), MOLTKE (1902) and BLUCHER (1902). All were owned by North German Lloyd of Bremen. Seven were about 10,500 tons while four were over 10,500 tons: GROSSER KURFUST (13,180), the KIAUTSHON (10,900), the MOLTKE (12,335) and BLUCHER (12,335). These ships were built by various German yards – Vulkan of Stettin, Blohm & Voss of Hamburg, and Schichau of Danzig. It is not possible to recount the interesting histories of all these fine vessels and one will have to suffice – the BREMEN, a famous enough name in years to come. Built by Schichau of Danzig, she was completed in 1897, and was 550 × 60 feet and 10,552 tons, with quadruple expansion engines driving twin screws giving a desired service speed of $14\frac{1}{2}$ knots. Accommodation was for 230 First Class, 250 Second Class and 1,850 Steerage passengers, with a crew of 250. Her maiden voyage from Bremerhaven to New York commenced on 5 June 1897 and from then on she was used on both North Atlantic and Australian services. On 30 June 1900 she was involved in a serious fire that broke out at the North German Lloyd pier at New York in piles of cotton bales. It rapidly spread from the warehouse to the ships moored alongside. The SAALE, a 5,000 tonner

MOLTKE
12,335 tons
North German Lloyd
1902

THE UNION CASTLE LINE INTERMEDIATE STEAMER "GASCON" (6288 tons)

GASCON
6,288 tons
430 × 52 feet
Union Steamship Co.
1897

built in 1886 was the most seriously damaged and was sold to an American company who refitted her as a cargo steamer. The MAIN, the second ship of this name, which had been built in 1899, was repaired as was KAISER WILHELM DU GROSSE, a 14,000 tonner and the largest vessel in the fleet. The BREMEN and the MAIN both ran aground and had to be towed away from the wharf by tugs. In all 300 lives were lost, 12 being from the crew of the BREMEN. After temporary repairs the BREMEN sailed back to Germany and was sent to Vulkan at Stettin for repairs and a refit, during the course of which she gained 25 feet in length and almost 1,000 tons in weight. In 1905 while on a voyage from New York to Bremen she suffered a broken propeller shaft and had to be towed into Halifax (Nova Scotia). In 1908 she took 1,000 refugees from the island of Sicily to Naples when the volcano Etna had a serious eruption. In 1919 the BREMEN passed to the British government as part of war reparations and was operated on their behalf by the P & O company on services to Australia until sold to the Greek Byron Steam Navigation Company in 1921 who renamed her CONSTANTINOPLE and used her between Paris and New York. In 1924 she was renamed KING ALEX-

ANDER and continued in Byron's service until sold to an Italian ship breaker in 1929.

In the last three years before the amalgamation of the Union Steamship Company of Southampton and the Castle Line in 1900, the Union Company had three ships from Harland & Wolff – the GASCON (6,288 tons) and the BRITON (10,248 tons) in 1897 and the SAXON (12,970 tons) in 1900. The GASCON was 430 × 52 feet and had triple expansion engines driving twin screws. She had accommodation for 78 First Class, 118 Second Class and 180 Third Class passengers. Between 1897 and 1910 she operated on the Intermediate Service to South Africa and between 1910 and 1914 on the East African Service and to Durban. The GASCON was a hospital ship for most of the First World War, returning to the Intermediate Service in 1920 until 1926 when she transferred to the Round-Africa Service until sold in 1928 to Scottish shipbreakers.

Meanwhile between 1896 and 1899, the Castle Mail Packet Company took delivery of two ships from the Fairfield Shipbuilding and Engineering Company – the DUNVEGAN CASTLE and the KINFAUNS CASTLE. The DUNVEGAN CASTLE was delivered in 1896 and was 5,958 tons and 450 × 50 feet with triple expansion

S.S. DUNVEGAN CASTLE leaving TABLE BAY.

Union-Castle Line.

CASTLE LINE
Royal Mail Service.

WEEKLY SAILINGS

For the GOLD FIELDS of SOUTH AFRICA.

LONDON, SOUTHAMPTON, MADEIRA, GRAND CANARY, CAPE COLONY, NATAL,
DELAGOA BAY, BEIRA, MADAGASCAR, AND MAURITIUS.

THE ROYAL MAIL STEAMERS OF THE CASTLE MAIL PACKETS COMPANY, LIMITED,

Leave London every alternate Friday, and sail from Southampton on the following day, with Mails, Passengers,
and Cargo, for Cape Colony and Natal, calling at Madeira.
Intermediate Steamers are despatched every 14 days from London and Southampton, for Cape Colony,
Natal, Delagoa Bay, &c., via Grand Canary, thus forming, with the Mail Steamers, a weekly service to
South Africa.
Passengers and Cargo are taken every fortnight for Delagoa Bay, every four weeks for Madagascar and
Mauritius, and at stated intervals for St. Helena and Beira.
Through bookings from the Continent.
Return Tickets issued for ALL PORTS. Handbook of information for Passengers gratis on application.
LOADING BERTH—East India Dock Basin, Blackwall, London. *Free Railway Tickets from London to Southampton.*
Experienced Surgeon and Stewardesses on every Steamer. Superior Accommodation. Excellent Cuisine.

DONALD CURRIE & Co.,

LONDON—1, 2, 3 & 4, Fenchurch Street, E.C.; MANCHESTER—15, Cross Street;
LIVERPOOL—Castle Street; GLASGOW—40, St. Enoch Square.

Advertisement for the
Castle Line

(Top)
DUNVEGAN CASTLE
5,958 tons
450 × 50 feet
Castle Line
1896

171 Second Class and 148 Third Class passengers. Apart from service during the First World War, she was used on the Royal Mail Service to South Africa until being placed on the reserve list in 1925 and sold for scrap in 1927.

Immediately after the amalgamation, the Union-

KINFAUNS CASTLE
9,664 tons
515 × 59 feet
Castle Line
1899

DONALD CURRIE & Co.

A CASTLE LINER

Built in 1899 at Fairfield Works, Glasgow.
Tonnage, 9664; Horse Power, 12,000;
Speed, 18¾ knots; Length, 515 ft.;
Breadth, 59 ft.; Depth, 40 ft.
South African service.

W. & A. K. JOHNSTON LTD. EDINR — COPYRIGHT.

engines driving a single screw. Her accommodation was for 287 First Class, 96 Second Class and 130 Third Class passengers. Apart from Royal Mail service to South and East Africa, in 1914 and 1918 she was a troop-ship while in 1915 and 1916 she was a hospital ship. In 1919 she was used briefly by the French government before being placed in reserve from 1921 to 1923 and used only for occasional voyages. In December 1923 she was sold to a German firm of shipbreakers. The KINFAUNS CASTLE, delivered in 1899 was 9,664 tons and 515 × 59 feet with quadruple expansion engines driving twin screws. Her accommodation was for 266 First Class,

ARMADALE CASTLE
12,973 tons
590 × 64 feet
Union Castle Line
1903

KENILWORTH CASTLE
12,973 tons
590 × 65 feet
Union Castle Line
1903

Castle Mail Steamship Company ordered a further three ships, the WALMAN CASTLE from Harland & Wolff (completed 1902), the ARMADALE CASTLE from Fairfield (completed 1903) and the KENILWORTH CASTLE from Harland & Wolff (completed 1903).

The ARMADALE CASTLE was 12,973 tons and 590 × 64 feet, with quadruple expansion engines driving three screws, giving an average service speed of 17 knots. Accommodation was provided for 350 First Class, 200 Second Class and 270 Third Class passengers with a crew of 260. She made her maiden voyage in 1903 leaving Southampton on 5 December for Cape Took. At the commencement of the First World War she was almost immediately taken over by the Government as an auxiliary cruiser and was also used as a troop transport. In 1918 she was released from war service and after a refit returned to the South African service until she was laid up in 1935 and broken up in 1936.

Between 1898 and the end of 1902, the White Star Line took delivery of nine new steamers, all of about 12,000 tons and all built by Harland & Wolff. Except for the CYMRIC, the others were for the Australian and New Zealand services. They were the AFRIC 1899 (11,816 tons), the MEDIC 1899 (11,985 tons), the PERSIC 1899 (11,973 tons), the the RUNIC 1900 (12,482 tons), the SUEVIC 1901 (12,531 tons), the ATHENIC 1902 (12,234 tons), the CORINTHIC 1902 (12,231 tons) and the IONIC 1902 (12,232 tons).

The CYMRIC at 599 × 64 feet was the largest, while the last two, the CORINTHIC and the IONIC were the smallest at 516 × 63 feet. All had quadruple expansion engines driving twin screws. Of these nine ships, two, the CYMRIC and the AFRIC were sunk by German submarines in 1916 and 1917. Three were sold to whaling companies – the RUNIC, the SUEVIC and the ATHENIC. Of these the RUNIC, the SUEVIC, together with the MEDIC were sunk by German action in the Second World War, while the PERSIC had been broken up in 1927, the CORINTHIC in 1932 and the IONIC in 1937. The ATHENIC had the longest life, for, despite being captured by the Germans and sunk at Kirkeness in 1944, she was refloated in 1945, repaired and returned to whaling until broken up in 1962.

The North German Lloyd company of Bremen had five large passenger liners built over a 10-year period. The first, KAISER WILHELM DER GROSSE by Vulkan of Stettin in 1897 at 14,349 tons and 655 feet x 66 feet was the world's largest ship when completed. The other ships were KAISER FRIEDRICH 1898 (12,481 tons and 600 × 64 feet) built by Schichau of Danzig; and three ships by Vulkan – KRONPRINZ WILHELM 1901 (14,908 tons and 664 × 63 feet), KAISER WILHELM II 1903 (19,361 tons and 707 × 72 feet) and KRONPRINZESSIN CECILIE 1907 (19,306 tons and 707 × 72 feet.

KAISER WILHELM DER GROSSE was for some time the pride of the German mercantile fleet. She had triple expansion engines driving twin screws to give an estimated service speed of 22 knots. She had accommodation for 558 First Class, 338 Second Class and 1,074 Steerage passengers with a crew of 488, and had an unusual appearance with her four funnels being in

CYMRIC
12,500 tons
599 × 64 feet
White Star Line
1899

RUNIC
12,482 tons
565 × 63 feet
White Star Line
1900

two groups of two. Her maiden voyage from Bremerhaven to New York commenced on 19 September 1897 and on a return trip in November of the same year she made a west to east crossing at an average speed of 22.35 knots, thereby capturing the Blue Riband of the Atlantic for Germany for the first time. In February 1900 she was one of the first vessels to be fitted with a radio, albeit of very limited range. On 30 June 1900 she narrowly escaped destruction in the North German Lloyd wharf fire in New York. By 1913 she had become outdated as far as providing a rapid Atlantic service was concerned and was refitted to accommodate Third Class and Steerage only. On the

outbreak of the First World War she was taken over by the German Navy as an auxiliary cruiser to act as a commercial raider. In spite of her early success in the first few days of the war, she was greatly handicapped by her heavy coal consumption of about 520 tons every 24 hours. On 27 August 1914 while coaling off Rio de Oro (Spanish West Africa) she was found by the British cruiser HIGH FLYER and was so seriously damaged that she was scuttled by her crew – thus ending the life of Germany's first Blue Riband holder.

The KRONPRINZ WILHELM was completed a few years after KAISER WILHELM DER GROSSE and was a little larger, being 14,908 tons and 664 × 66 feet, with

SUEVIC
12,531 tons
565 × 63 feet
White Star Line
1901

PERSIC
11,973 tons
570 × 63 feet
White Star Line
1899

KAISER WILHELM II
19,361 tons
707 x 72 feet
North German Lloyd
1903

KAISER WILHELM
DER GROSSE
14,349 tons
655 x 63 feet
North German Lloyd
1897

Bremerhaven (inset)

quadruple expansion engines driving twin screws. She had accommodation for 367 First Class, 340 Second Class and 1,054 Steerage passengers. She sailed on her maiden voyage from Bremerhaven to New York on 17 September 1901. On the outbreak of the First World War she was in New York and, sailing for home the day before hostilities commenced, she met up with a German naval cruiser, who armed her as a raider and enabled her two days later to sink over 60,000 tons of allied shipping. In April 1915 sailing into Newport News (America was still neutral) with supplies exhausted and in generally bad condition, she was

interned. Two years later after America had entered the war, she was taken over by the US Navy Transport and named VON STEUBEN. She was laid-up in 1919 and eventually scrapped in 1923.

Two years after KRONZPRINZ WILHELM went into service, a larger North German Lloyd liner, the KAISER WILHELM II, joined the fleet in 1903. Built by Vulkan, she was 19,361 tons and 707 x 72 feet with Vulkan's own quadruple expansion engines. Her accommodation was for 775 First Class, 343 Second Class and 770 Steerage pasengers with a crew of 600. She made her maiden voyage from Bremerhaven to

KRONPRINZ WILHELM
14,908 tons
664 x 66 feet
North German Lloyd
1901

KRONPRINZESSIN
CECILE
19,360 tons
707 x 72 feet
North Gerrman Lloyd
1907

New York in April 1903. In June 1906 she took the Atlantic Blue Riband record with an average speed of 23.58 knots between Sandy Hook and the Eddystone Lighthouse. In 1914 she was interned in New York until 1917 when she was seized by the US government and used as a naval transport under the name AGEMEMNON. In 1919 she was taken over by the US Shipping Board, but no one wanted to use her. In 1929 she was renamed the MONTICELLO, but remained unused. Eventually she was broken up in 1940, after she had been offered to the British government and rejected yet again.

The last ship in the North German Lloyd 'Express' fleet was the KRONPRINZESSIN CECILIE. Once again built by Vulkan, she sailed on her maiden voyage from Bremerhaven to New York on 6 August 1907. She was 19,360 tons and 707 × 72 feet, with four sets of quadruple expansion engines driving twin screws (two engines to each propeller shaft). She had accommodation for 742 First Class, 326 Second Class and 740 Steerage passengers. At the outbreak of the First World War she was in mid-Atlantic on a homeward voyage with a considerable amount of gold bullion on board, so she turned back to America and was interned until

taken over by the US Navy in 1917. At that time she was renamed the MOUNT VERNON and used as a US transport. In September 1918 she was torpedoed about 200 miles off the French coast, but made port, and eventually returned to America and was laid up. Efforts were made to sell her without success and she was finally cut-up in 1940.

The Atlantic Transport Line was taken over by the Atlantic Transport Company of West Virginia in 1898 and the new company placed an order with Harland & Wolff for two ships of 13,400 tons, which were both delivered in 1900 – the MINNEAPOLIS and the MINNEHAHA. The MINNEAPOLIS made her maiden voyage from London to New York in May 1900 and the MINNEHAHA in August 1900. Both ships had accommodation for 250 First Class passengers. They were an unfortunate pair of vessels. The MINNEAPOLIS became a military transport in 1915 and was sunk the following year by torpedo with the loss of 12 lives. The MINNEHAHA, running aground off the Scilly Isles in 1910, was refloated and returned to service after major repairs, but eventually had a similar fate to her sister ship when she was torpedoed off Ireland in 1917 with the loss of over 40 lives.

MINNEHAHA
13,400 tons
616 × 63 feet
Atlantic Transport Co.
1900

OCEANIC 17274 TONS
LENGTH 705 FT 6 INS.

OCEANIC
17,272 tons
685 × 68 feet
White Star Line
1899

The Empress Dock, Southampton

Empress Dock
Southampton

White Star Line poster

The OCEANIC built for the White Star Line in 1899 by Harland & Wolff, was the largest ship in the world from the time of her delivery until 1901 when the same company built the CELTIC, followed by the CEDRIC and the BALTIC (all for the White Star). The OCEANIC was 17,272 tons and 685 × 68 feet, with triple expansion engines driving twin screws giving an average service speed of 19 knots. There was accommodation for 410 First Class, 300 Second Class and 1,000 Steerage. She commenced her maiden voyage from Liverpool to New York on 6 September 1899. Although not as heavy, she was the first ship to exceed the length of the GREAT EASTERN. She was the last White Star liner designed primarily for a fast Atlantic crossing and in this respect she was a failure because of excessive vibration from the engines. However, the standard of accommodation was most luxurious, and the company from then on decided to settle for comfort rather than speed in all future ships. In 1907 she started using Southampton as her home port although still registered at Liverpool. In August 1914 she was taken over by the British Admiralty as an auxiliary cruiser, but within four weeks she was stranded on the Shetlands and, efforts to refloat having failed, she was declared a total loss. However, the hull had such strength that it weathered the ravages of the sea for ten years until broken up as she lay in 1924.

On 4 July 1900 the Hamburg-America Line's the DEUTSCHLAND sailed from Hamburg via Plymouth to New York on her maiden voyage. Built by Vulkan of Stettin, at 16,500 tons and 684 × 67 feet she was the

DEUTSCHLAND
16,500 tons
684 x 67 feet
Hamburg-America Line
1900

Hamburg
Schnelldampfer „Deutschland" 1900

largest German ship afloat. She had quadruple expansion engines driving twin screws and accommodation for 450 First, 300 Second and 300 Third Class passengers, with optional accommodation for 1,000 Steerage. The DEUTSCHLAND won the Blue Riband of the North Atlantic for a western crossing on her maiden voyage with a time of 5 days, 15 hours and 46 minutes, and the record for an eastern passage on her return trip with a time of 5 days 14 hours and 6 minutes. While the DEUTSCHLAND was a very fast and prestigious ship, she was not a very comfortable one to sail in as the vibration from her engines when travelling at speed was excessive. In 1902 attempts were made to cure this fault, but they were not successful. She remained in service on the North Atlantic until October 1910, when she returned to the shipyard at Stettin for conversion to

a cruise liner, and her two six-cylinder engines were reduced to two four-cylinders with a reduction of power output and vibration.

Her first voyage after rebuilding was in September 1911 when she sailed under the name of VICTORIA LOUISE. In August 1914 she was fitted out as an auxiliary cruiser, but was never used. In 1919 she was not taken over as part of reparations because of her poor condition, and so remained as the only large passenger steamer under the German flag. In 1920 she again went to Stettin for overhaul and emerged in October 1921 with two instead of four funnels and a new name, the HANSA. She made her first voyage from Hamburg to New York in October 1921 and continued to sail on the North Atlantic until October 1924 when she was laid up and sold for scrap.

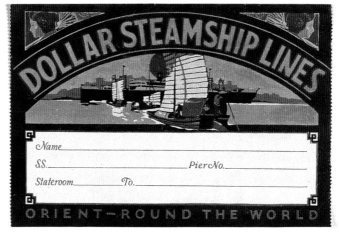

A collection of luggage labels

CHAPTER 7

Edwardian Splendour 1900–1909

In 1900 the Cunard Steamship Company took delivery of two similar vessels, the INVERNIA built by Swan Hunter of Newcastle-on-Tyne, weighing 13,799 tons, and the SAXONIA built by John Brown of Clydebank, weighing 14,281 tons. Apart from the difference in weight other details were almost identical. The INVERNIA was slightly longer at 600 × 64 feet 9 inches to the SAXONIA's 600 × 62 feet 2 inches. Quadruple expansion engines driving twin screws gave a service speed of 15 knots. Accommodation was provided for 164 First Class, 200 Second Class and 1,600 Steerage passengers. When built these were the largest ships in the Cunard fleet. Because some of Cunard's ships were occupied transporting troops for the Boer War, the IVERNIA started life with a maiden voyage between Liverpool and New York on 14 April 1900. She made

three trips on this route before starting regular voyages to Boston. The SAXONIA's maiden voyage was to Boston on 22 May 1900. During 1911 and 1912 the two ships started sailing from Trieste, the IVERNIA to New York and the SAXONIA to Boston. The IVERNIA was torpedoed and sunk on 1 January 1917 near Cape Matapan with the loss of 36 lives. In 1912 the SAXONIA had been altered to Second Class and Steerage, and in 1914 she started service as a troop-ship. Towards the end of 1914 she was used for a short period to accommodate German prisoners of war while moored on the Thames before resuming troop transport on March 1915. In January 1919 she returned to the North Atlantic service between Liverpool and New York and the following year had a refit at Tilbury in which her accommodation was altered to 471 Cabin and 978

SAXONIA
14,281 tons
600 × 62 feet
Cunard
1900

The Cunard Steam Ship Company Limited
21 to 24 State Street
New York, October 27, 1919.

CABIN:
PASSENGER DEPARTMENT.

KINDLY QUOTE
C
IN YOUR REPLY.

"SAXONIA" will not sail before Nov. 1.

    The labor conditions prevailing in this port at the present time indicate that we will probably not be able to dispatch this steamer before the above date. Confirmation of actual sailing date will be immediately advised.

    Should the additional delay make any change in your plans for sailing, immediate advice will be appreciated.

    Very truly yours,

    The Cunard Steam Ship Company Limited

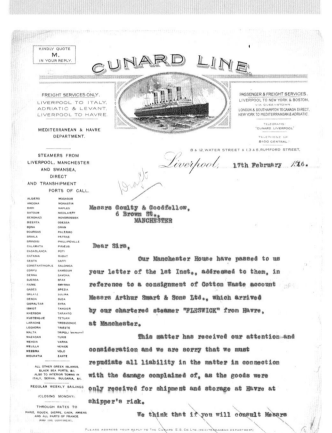

Ephemera from the
Cunard Line

Third Class passengers. In her last years of service she ran on the New York route out of London. In 1925 she was sold for breaking up in Holland.

In 1900, the Red Star Line (the fleet name of the American-owned International Mercantile Marine Company) took delivery of the first of four steamers for their Antwerp–New York service. They were the VADERLAND, the ZEELAND, the KROONLAND and the FINLAND. The first two were about 12,000 tons and the last two 17,760 tons. The VADERLAND and the ZEELAND were built by John Brown on Clydebank, while the KROONLAND and the FINLAND were by Cramp of Philadelphia (USA). The first of the group, VADERLAND, sailed on her maiden voyage on 8 December 1900 from Antwerp to New York. In 1914 she was transferred to the White Star Dominion Line and sailed from New York to Liverpool. She was renamed SOUTHLAND in 1915 and transferred to the Liverpool–Montreal service for a short while before being taken over as a troop-ship. On 4 June 1917 she was sunk off Tony Island off the coast of Donegal, Northern Ireland, by a German submarine. This was the second time she had been torpedoed, the first time

being in September 1915 in the Aegean Sea when she had managed to reach safety.

In 1915 the ZEELAND was renamed the NORTH-LAND and was used as a troop transport. In 1920 she returned to the Red Star Line and was converted to oil-firing. In 1927 she was sold to the Atlantic Transport Line and renamed the MINNESOTA before being sold for scrap in 1929. The KROONLAND and the FINLAND had identical careers: in 1916 they were used by the American Line for Atlantic service. In 1918 they were taken over by the US navy as armed transports before being returned to Red Star in 1920. In 1923 they were sold twice remaining with the Panama Pacific Line until sold for scrap in 1927.

In 1901, the first of what became known as the White Star Line's 'Big Four' was delivered from Harland & Wolff. The CELTIC was 20,094 tons and 700 × 75 feet, with quadruple expansion engines driving twin screws to give a service speed of 16 knots. She had accommodation for 347 First Class, 160 Second Class and 2,350 Steerage passengers and sailed on her maiden voyage from Liverpool to New York on 26 July 1901. At that time she was the largest ship in the world and

ATLANTIC TRANSPORT LINE

S.S. MINNESOTA. 11,904 TONS.

ZEELAND
(later MINNESOTA)
11,905 tons
580 × 60 feet
Red Star Line
1900

CEDRIC
White Star Line
1902

remained so until 1903 when the third of the class the BALTIC claimed that distinction with a weight of 23,884 tons and 726 × 75 feet 6 inches. The CELTIC was taken over in 1914 as an auxiliary cruiser and commenced troop carrying in 1916. In March 1917 she was hit by a torpedo while in the Irish Sea but survived and was repaired in Belfast. Very soon after the Armistice in November 1918, the CELTIC was back in North Atlantic service between Liverpool and New York. In 1920 she had a refit and passage accommodation was altered to 347 First Class, 160 Second Class and 2,350 Steerage. On 10 December 1928 she ran aground off Roches Point at the entrance of Cobh and, efforts to refloat her having failed, she was sold to a Danish company for scrap or breaking up. The other three making up the 'Big Four' were the CEDRIC (1902), the BALTIC (1904) and the ADRIATIC (1907).

By the early 1900s good services to the Antipodes became more urgent and the P & O line embarked on the building of four larger sister steamers, to be followed by three more. These were known as the 'M' class. The first, the MARMORA, was completed at the end of 1903 and the second, MACEDONIA, early in 1904. Both were built by Harland & Wolff.

The P & O's MARMORA was the first P & O liner over 10,000 tons, being 10,509 tons and 530 feet × 60 feet, with two funnels and two masts. Quadruple expansion engines driving twin screws gave an

Twin-Screw Steamer "Baltic."

AU REVOIR.

ONWARD she ploughs through the
mighty expanse,
Disregarding all moods of the
weather;
Onward she sails to the land of
fair chance !
Bringing friends that were parted together.
Some she takes out to new homes in
the West;
Some few to fortune and fame;
Some to go under, broken down and
distressed,
To return to the home-land again.
Yet the wish of the "Baltic" goes out
with you all,
Wherever your footsteps may roam;
Good luck to the great ! Good luck to
the small !
And good luck to the loved ones at home.

Postcard from the
BALTIC

estimated average speed of 17 knots. Passenger accommodation was for 377 First Class and 187 Second Class with a crew of 370. In 1914 she was requisitioned by the British government and used by the Royal Navy as an auxiliary cruiser, being purchased by the Admiralty in 1916. On 23 July 1918 she was sunk by a German submarine off the south coast of Ireland.

Two more were built in 1908, one by Barclay, Curle & Co. of Glasgow (the MOREA) and the other by Caird of Greenock (the MALWA), and yet another in 1909 also by Caird (the MANTUA). Two years later a further two 'M' class ships were built, one by Harland & Wolff (the MALOJA), the other by Caird (the MEDINA). Three of the seven ships were sunk during the First World War – the MARMORA, the MALOJA and the MEDINA – while the other four survived. The MACEDONIA was taken over as an auxiliary cruiser and troop transport in 1914. The MOREA was a hospital ship in 1915, a troop-ship in 1916 and an auxiliary cruiser in 1917. The MALWA became a troop-ship in 1917. The MANTUA was used for cruising in 1913 before being taken over as an auxiliary cruiser in 1914. All four returned to P & O after the war in 1919 or 1920 and were sold for scrap in the early 1930s.

The MEDINA, the last of the class, was 12,350 tons and 625 × 63 feet with quadruple expansion engines driving twin screws to give a service speed of 18 knots. She had accommodation for 460 First Class, 220 Second Class passengers and carried a crew of 400. Although completed in October 1911 she did not make her first

MOREA
10,890 tons
562 × 61 feet
P & O
1908

MACEDONIA
10,500 tons
530 × 60 feet
P & O
1904

service voyage, which was from London to Sydney, until 28 June 1912, because on 11 November 1911 she sailed from Portsmouth to Bombay as the Royal Yacht carrying King George V and Queen Mary to the Delhi Durbar. For this purpose an extra mast was fitted just forward of the front funnel to bear the Royal Standard when the sovereign was on board. In 1917, the MEDINA, which remained in company service, was torpedoed and sunk off Strait Point on 28 April with the loss of six lives.

In 1903, Harland & Wolff started building two liners for the British Wilson & Furness–Leyland Line, but the contract was cancelled before completion and they were laid up in Belfast until bought by the Hamburg–America Line of Hamburg. The ships were finally completed in 1907 as the PRESIDENT LINCOLN and PRESIDENT GRANT. They were almost identical, being 18,100 tons and 600 × 68 feet (various authorities differ on the exact dimensions). They had quadruple expansion engines driving twin screws to give a service speed of 14½ knots. Accommodation was provided for 324 First Class, 152 Second Class and 1,004 Third Class passengers. Both were completed and made their maiden voyages in 1907 from Hamburg to New York. In 1914 they were both interned in New York and in 1917 seized by the US Navy as transports. The PRESIDENT LINCOLN was sunk by enemy action in the North Atlantic on 31 May 1918 with the loss of 26 lives. The PRESIDENT GRANT survived under American ownership, being renamed the REPUBLIC, until sold for breaking up in 1951.

PRESIDENT GRANT
18,100 tons
600 × 68 feet
Hamburg-America line
1907

In 1905 the Allan Line of Glasgow took delivery of two liners, the VICTORIAN built by Workman, Clark & Co. of Belfast and the VIRGINIAN by Alexander Stephen & Sons of Glasgow. They were almost identical in weight and size and both were fitted with direct action turbines, being the first ships with this type of engine on the North Atlantic. They were also the first liners in the world to have triple screws giving a service speed of 18 knots. They were 10,700 tons and 520 × 60 feet. Their accommodation was slightly different with the VICTORIAN carrying 346 First Class, 344 Second Class and 1,000 Third Class passengers. Both vessels acted as auxiliary cruisers in the First World War and ownership was transferred to the Canadian Pacific when this company purchased the Allan Line. Both ships were returned to CP in 1920. The VICTORIAN was used occasionally on the Canadian service, while the VIRGINIAN was sold and, amidst several changes of ownership and name (1920 DROTTNINGHOLM, 1948 BRASIL and 1951 HOMELAND), she was used as an International Red Cross ship from 1940–45, before being finally sold for scrap in 1955.

In 1906 the French Compagnie Générale Transatlantique (CGT) took delivery of the largest ship at that time, LA PROVENCE built by Penhoët of St. Nazaire. She was 13,753 tons 627 × 65 feet, with triple expansion engines driving twin screws, designed to give a service speed of 21 knots. She had accommodation for 422 First Class, 132 Second Class and 808 Steerage passengers. She commenced her maiden voyage from Le Havre to New York on 21 April 1906. She continued in

VICTORIAN
10,700 tons
520 × 60 feet
Allan Lines
1905

"La Provence"

C¹ᴱ G¹ᴱ **TRANSATLANTIQUE**
(FRENCH LINE)

LA PROVENCE
13,753 tons
627 × 65 feet
CGT
1906

CANADIAN PACIFIC LINE

S.S. EMPRESS OF BRITAIN

EMPRESS OF BRITAIN
14,190 tons
570 × 65 feet
Canadian Pacific
1906

this service until 1914 when she was taken over by the French Navy as an auxiliary cruiser and renamed LA PROVENCE II. Together with two other CGT ships, LA LORRAINE and LA SAVOIE, she helped cover the landing of French troops at the Dardanelles in the spring of 1915. Later she transported troops from France to Salonica and while so doing was sunk by a German submarine in the Aegean Sea in February 1916; of the 1,700 on board only 870 were saved.

1906 saw the completion for the Canadian Pacific Line of two new liners which were to be their fleet leaders. They were the last British North Atlantic liners to be powered by quadruple expansion engines (all later ones were turbine). The EMPRESS OF BRITAIN and the EMPRESS OF IRELAND were both built by Fairfield Shipbuilding & Engineering Co. of Govan, Glasgow and delivered in 1906. They were of similar dimensions, 14,190 tons and 570 × 65 feet with twin screw. Accommodation was for 310 First Class, 500 Second Class, 500 Third Class and 270 Steerage. The EMPRESS OF BRITAIN set off on her maiden voyage from Liverpool to Quebec on 5 May 1906 and her sister seven weeks later. The EMPRESS OF BRITAIN became an auxiliary cruiser in August 1914 and a troop transporter a year later. In 1919 she was returned to her owners and was refitted and converted to oil-firing by Fairfield. In 1924 she had a further refit and was renamed the MONTROYAL. In 1927 she ran between Antwerp and Canada, but was laid up in 1929 and sold for scrap the following year. The EMPRESS OF IRELAND had only a short life; on 29 May 1914 she was rammed in the St

Lawrence river in thick fog by a Norwegian collier STORSTAD and she sank in a few minutes. The accident occurred just after midnight and loss of life was very heavy, 840 of her 1,050 passengers and 171 out of her crew of 400. The subsequent enquiry placed the blame entirely on the Norwegian vessel, for what was one of the worst disasters of the North Atlantic sea route.

ARAGON
9,450 tons
513 × 60 feet
Royal Mail Line
1905

ALMANZORA
16,034 tons
589 × 67 feet
Royal Mail Lines
1915

The Royal Mail Line's 'A' class vessels were all built by Harland & Wolff, except the ARAGUAYA (1906) which was built by Workman, Clark & Co. of Belfast. Altogether there were nine ships in the class, the other seven being the ARAGON (1905), the AMAZON (1906), the AVON (1907), the ASTURIAS (1908), the ARLANZA (1912), the ANDES (1913) the ALCANTARA (1914) and the ALMANZORA (1915). Whilst classed as a group, they varied considerably over the period in which they were built.

The first of the class, the ARAGON was delivered in 1905 and sailed between Southampton and La Plata. She was 9,450 tons and 513 × 60 feet, with quadruple expansion engines driving twin screws, being the first Royal Mail steamer to have twin screws. She had accommodation for 305 First Class, 66 Second Class and 632 Steerage passengers. She was used for trooping in the First World War and was sunk by a German submarine off Alexandria on 30 December 1917 with 610 lives lost. The AMAZON was 10,050 tons and 530 × 60 feet, with quadruple expansion engines driving twin screws. She was the only 'A' class ship left in her owner's service during the First World War and continued to sail to La Plata, but was sunk by a German submarine on 15 February 1918 off the north coast of Ireland. The ARAGUAYA was 10,537 tons and 532 × 61 feet. In 1917 she was used as a hospital ship, returning to the Royal Mail in 1920. In 1930 she was sold to Jugoslavensk-Lloyd and renamed KRALJICA MARIJA. In 1940 she was sold to the French government and, renamed the SAVOIE, was used on the South American service. In 1942 she was sunk off Casablanca during the North African landings. The AVON, 11,073 tons and

535 × 62 feet, ran on the La Plata service until taken over for war service in 1914. She survived the war and refitted for cruising until laid up and sold for scrap in 1929.

The ASTURIAS was 12,000 tons and 535 × 62 feet, with quadruple expansion engines driving twin screws. She had accommodation for 300 First Class, 140 Second Class and 1,200 Third Class passengers. She made her maiden voyage on the Australian service, London to Brisbane, on 24 January 1908 and then went on the South American run until she was taken over as a hospital ship in 1914 and torpedoed by a German submarine on 20 March 1917 off Start Point with the loss of 44 lives. She was left to the insurers and subsequently bought by the British Admiralty to be eventually towed into Plymouth and used as a store ship. At the end of the war she was bought back by the Royal Mail line and towed to Belfast for repair and refit. When the work was completed in 1923 she was used as a cruise liner under the name the ARCADIAN, until being laid up in 1930 and sold for scrap three years later.

ARLANZA, built in 1912 and 15,050 tons in weight, had a change of engine design from her elder sisters, namely triple expansion engines exhausting to a low pressure turbine. Apart from acting as an auxiliary cruiser from 1915 to 1919, the ARLANZA remained on the South American service until sold for scrap in 1938. The last and largest of the class, the ALMANZORA at 16,034 tons and 589 × 67 feet was not completed by Harland & Wolff until 1915 and was straight away used as an auxiliary cruiser. In 1919 she was released from Naval Service, refitted for passenger service and made her maiden commercial voyage to La Plata in January

1920. In 1939 she again returned to war service as a troop-ship until 1947 when she was laid up. The following year she was sold for scrap.

In 1907 the Cunard Line took delivery of two large ships which were to become household names. First to be delivered in August was the LUSITANIA built by John Brown of Clydebank. At 31,550 tons, and 787 feet × 88 feet she was the largest ship in the world for three months until the slightly larger MAURETANIA was delivered in November. She was powered by turbines driving four screws and comprised accommodation for 563 First Class, 464 Second Class and 1,138 Third Class passengers with a crew of 802. On 7 September 1907 she started her maiden voyage from Liverpool to New York, gaining the Blue Riband at an average speed of 23.99 knots on her second westerly voyage. The LUSITANIA and her sister ship, the MAURETANIA, were not used by the Navy as auxiliary cruisers as it was

The Cunard 'Big Three'
MAURETANIA, BERENGARIA
and AQUITANIA
1920s

MAURETANIA
31,938 tons
790 × 88 feet
Blue Riband holder for
20 years
Cunard
1907

CHIYO MARU(right)
13,450 tons
575 × 62 feet
Toyo Kisen KK
1908

MAURETANIA
at Cherbourg

decided they were too large, and they were, therefore, left on the North Atlantic service. On 1 May 1918 the LUSITANIA was sunk by a torpedo fired by a German submarine off the Old Head of Kintale in Southern Ireland. Loss of life was very heavy – 791 passengers (124 American) and 404 crew out of a total complement of 1,956 perished. This event did much to prepare the way for America to enter the war.

The MAURETANIA was built by Swan Hunter and Wigham Richardson of Newcastle-on-Tyne and was delivered on 7 March 1907. At 31,938 tons and 790 × 88 feet she was just a little bigger than her sister ship and was therefore the largest ship in the world until the advent of the OLYMPIC in 1911. She was also the fastest, gaining the Atlantic Blue Riband from the LUSITANIA after a short struggle and holding it for twenty years. She was powered by turbines driving quadruple screws and had accommodation for 560 First Class, 475 Second Class and 1,300 Third Class passengers. The MAURETANIA did limited service in 1915 and 1916 after which she was laid up until March 1918 when she was used to ferry troops across the English Channel. In June 1919 she resumed the North Atlantic sailings from Southampton to New York. In 1921 she had a refit and was converted to oil firing. From 1930 onwards she was mainly used for cruising and in 1935 was sold for breaking up.

In 1908 Japan entered the large steamship field (over 10,000 tons) with two liners completed in that year, the TENYO MARU and the CHIYO MARU both built by Mitsubishi of Nagasaki for Toyo Kisen KK of

Yokohama. They were 13,450 tons and 575 × 62 feet, powered by turbines driving triple screws. There was accommodation for 275 First Class, 54 Second Class and 800 Third Class passengers. Both made their maiden voyages from Hong Kong to San Francisco. The CHIYO MARU ran aground on an island a little south of Hong Kong and was a total wreck. The TENYO MARU was taken over by Nippon Yusen KK in 1926, was laid up in 1930 and broken up three years later. In 1911 a similar ship the SHINYO MARU had been built at the same yard to a comparable specification. She ran on the same Pacific run and was also taken over in 1926 by Nippon Yusen KK and run until laid up in 1932 and broken up in 1936.

Nippon Yusen
baggage label

LUSITANIA
31,550 tons
787 × 88 feet
Cunard
1907

MAURETANIA and LUSITANIA
interiors

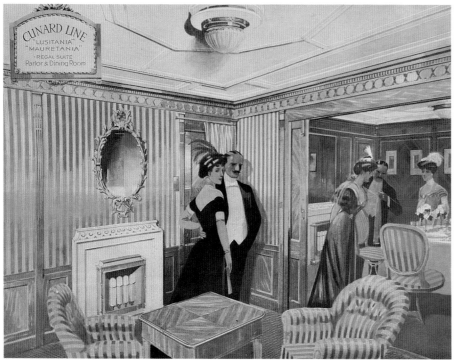

116. LE HAVRE
Le Transatlantique " France "
The Transatlantic " France "

Très grand transatlantique français, attaché spécialement au service postal rapide entre Le Havre et New-York. Ses dimensions sont de 220 mètres de long et 23 de large et jauge net 21 000 tonnes. Il est actionné par 4 hélices qui lui donnent une vitesse de 23 nœuds et demi à l'heure.
Ses 4 cheminées qui ont 34 mètres de hauteur et 5m30 de diamètre, reçoivent les fumées de 120 foyers. Il transporte dans ses diverses classes 2.000 passagers et occupe un personnel de 600 hommes. Il est muni de la télégraphie sans fil et franchit ses 6 000 kilomètres en moins de 6 jours.

FRANCE
23,666 tons
713 × 75.5 feet
CGT The French Line
1912

In 1912 Compagnie Générale Transatlantique took delivery of the liner the FRANCE which at 23,666 tons was nearly twice the size of any of their other ships, and was the pride of the fleet. Built by Penhoët of St Nazaire she was 713 × 75 feet 6 inches powered by turbines driving quadruple screws to give an expected service speed of 23 knots. She had accommodation for 534 First Class, 442 Second Class, 250 Third Class and 800 Steerage passengers with a crew of 500. Her maiden voyage from Le Havre to New York on 20 April 1912 was completed in 6 days exactly and she was the third fastest ocean liner in the world, led only by the LUSITANIA and the MAURETANIA. Unfortunately she

OTRANTO
12,124 tons
554 × 64 feet
Orient Line
1909

had to run a service in conjunction with three slower ships and her power was kept in reserve to ensure regularity of time-keeping in varying weather conditions. In 1914 she was taken over by the French government as an auxiliary cruiser and renamed FRANCE IV. In 1916 she was converted to a hospital ship and in 1917 was used to transport United States troops to Europe. In 1919 she returned to CGT and, reverting to the name of the FRANCE, was used to repatriate American troops sailing from Brest to New York. In August 1919 she returned to her old Atlantic service, Le Havre–New York. In 1923 as part of a refit she was converted to oil-firing. She was laid up in 1932 and broken up three years later.

In 1909 the Orient Line took delivery of five of a series of six ships for their Australian service. The first five were of similar size varying from 12,036 tons to 12,133 tons. They were the ORSOVA (12,036 tons, 553 × 63 feet, by John Brown), the OTWAY (12,077 tons, 552 × 63 feet, by Fairfield), the OSTERLEY (12,129 tons, 553 × 63 feet, by London & Glasgow Shipbuilding Co.), the OTRANTO (12,124 tons, 554 feet × 64, by Workman Clark & Co.), and the ORVIETO (12,133 tons, 554 × 64 feet, by Workman, Clark & Co.). They had quadruple expansion engines driving twin screws. The ORAMA, delivered two years later, was 12,927 tons and 569 × 64 feet. She was built by John Brown and had triple expansion engines plus a low pressure turbine and triple screws. All the ships saw war service between 1914 and 1918; two were lost by enemy action and a third, the OTRANTO, in an accident. The OTRANTO commenced her maiden voyage from

ORVIETO
12,133 tons
554 × 64 feet
Orient Line
1909

(Scotland) and ran aground with the loss of the ship and 431 lives.

In 1909 Lamport & Holt of Liverpool took delivery of the VASARI, the first of four similar vessels for their New York to La Plata service. Built by Raylton Dixon of Middlesbrough she was completed in April 1909 and straight away went into service from New York to La Plata. She was 10,117 tons and 516 × 53 feet, with quadruple expansion engines driving a single screw. Accommodation was for 250 First Class, 130 Second Class and 200 Third Class passengers. In 1928 she was sold, her passenger accommodation removed and she was renamed ARCTIC QUEEN. In 1935 she was sold to the Soviet Union and renamed the PISCHEVAYA. This old ship soldiered on until 1979, when she was broken up in the Far East.

In 1911–12 three more ships were built for Lamport & Holt by Workman & Clark of Belfast – the VANDYCK (10,328 tons), the VAUBAN (10,660 tons) and the VESTRIS (10,494 tons). Bigger than the VASARI, they were 511 × 60.5 feet with quadruple expansion engines driving twin screws. They provided accommodation for 280 First Class, 130 Second Class and 200 Third Class passengers.

The VANDYCK sailed on 8 September 1911 on her maiden voyage from New York to La Plata. In October 1914 she was sunk in the South Atlantic by the German cruiser KARLSRUHE after the passengers and crew had been taken off. The VAUBAN was delivered in April 1912 and chartered by the Royal Mail Line for their Southampton to La Plata service under the temporary name of ALCALA. She was returned to Lamport & Holt at the end of 1913. After the war she was chartered by both the Royal Mail Line and Cunard and returned to Lamport & Holt's New York to La Plata service in 1922. She was laid up in 1930 and broken up two years later. The VESTRIS was completed in September 1912 and was on the New York to La Plata service until 1919 when she was chartered by both Royal Mail and Cunard, returning to Lamport & Holt in 1922. In November 1928, soon after leaving New York for La Plata she ran into a storm which shifted some of the cargo and bunker coal. Developing a severe list she sank shortly afterwards with the loss of 112 of the 325 passengers who were on board.

Poster advertising the Lamport & Holt line

London to Brisbane on 1 October 1909. In 1914 she was taken over by the Royal Navy as an auxiliary cruiser. Just before the end of the war on 6 October 1918 while acting as a convoy escort and troop carrier on a voyage from New York to Britain, she collided with the P & O liner KASHMIR off the Isle of Islay

CHAPTER 8

Peril on the High Seas 1910–1920

The year 1910 saw delivery of two almost identical ships to the Union Castle Line, the BALMORAL CASTLE built by Fairfield of Glasgow and the EDINBURGH CASTLE by Harland & Wolff. Both ships were a little over 13,300 tons and 590 × 64 feet, with quadruple expansion engines driving twin screws to give a service speed of 17 knots. Accommodation was provided for 320 First Class, 220 Second Class and 250–270 Third Class. Shortly after her maiden voyage to Cape Town and back she was taken over as the Royal Yacht to take members of the British Royal Family to Cape Town to open the Union of South African Parliament. In 1917 she acted as a troop transport and in 1919 returned to her normal South African service. In 1914 the EDINBURGH CASTLE was taken over as an

armed merchant cruiser, returning to the South African run in 1919. Laid up in 1939 at Southampton she was then moved to Freetown as a depot ship, having been taken over by the Admiralty, who bought her from the company the next year. In 1945 she was towed out to sea and sunk by naval target practice.

The Cunard Line's FRANCONIA and LACONIA were very handsome sister ships built by Swan Hunter & Wigham Richardson of Newcastle-on-Tyne, and delivered in 1911. Both were 18,100 tons and 625 × 71 feet, with quadruple expansion engines driving twin screws giving an estimated service speed of 17 knots. With accommodation for 300 First Class, 350 Second Class and 2,200 Third Class passengers, the FRANCONIA made her maiden voyage from Liverpool

BALMORAL CASTLE
13,361 tons
590 x 64 feet
Union Castle Line
1910

Impromptu dance on the
Union Castle Line

to New York on 23 January 1911 and the LACONIA made hers on the same route on 20 January 1912. Both ships then went on to the Liverpool–Boston service. In 1915 the FRANCONIA was taken over as a troop transport and on 4 October 1916 she was torpedoed in the Mediterranean by a German submarine with the loss of 12 lives. The LACONIA was taken over as an auxiliary cruiser in 1914, but was returned to her owners and re-commenced North Atlantic crossings on 9 September 1916. Whilst still in commercial service she was torpedoed and sunk 160 miles north west of Fastnet also with the loss of 12 lives.

In 1911 and 1912 the White Star Line took delivery of two liners which in turn were to hold the title of the largest ship in the world. First was the OLYMPIC completed in May 1911 and then the very slightly larger TITANIC delivered in April the following year. The OLYMPIC, built by Harland & Wolff, as were all White Star ships at this time, was 45,324 tons and 882 × 92 feet 6 inches, with triple expansion engines exhausting into a low pressure turbine driving triple screws to give an estimated service speed of 21 knots. Accommodation was provided for 1,054 First Class, 510 Second Class and 1,020 Third Class passengers. On 14 June 1911 she sailed from Southampton for New York on her maiden

voyage. On 20 September 1911, while leaving Southampton, she collided with the British cruiser HMS HAWKE and both ships were severely damaged. The OLYMPIC had to return to Belfast for repairs and while there the TITANIC disaster occurred. As a result, modifications were made to the OLYMPIC's water-tight bulkheads and extra lifeboats were added. In September 1915, she was requisitioned as a troop transport. In May 1918 she was attacked by a German submarine, but avoided the torpedoes. In 1919 she was returned to White Star and went to Belfast for overhaul and refit and, after conversion to oil firing, she returned to the North Atlantic service. In 1934 she became part of the Cunard–White Star fleet and was eventually laid up in 1935 and sold for scrap.

The TITANIC, also built by Harland & Wolff and completed ten months after OLYMPIC, was just over 1,000 tons heavier at 46,392 tons, and one foot longer than her predecessor as 'largest ship in the world'. Her passenger accommodation was also slightly different, providing for 905 First Class, 564 Second Class and 1,134 Third Class passengers with 900 crew. Her tragic life is well known. She commenced her maiden voyage on 2 April 1912 from Southampton bound for New York. On 14 April she was in collision with an iceberg

TITANIC
46,392 tons
883 × 92.5 feet
White Star
1912

OLYMPIC
45,324 tons
882 × 92.5 feet
White Star Line
1911

and subsequently sank with the loss of 1,503 lives. Many accounts and films of this disaster have been made.

Following the disaster, White Star planned an even larger liner to be called the BRITANNIC. She was 48,158 tons and 850 × 94 feet, with triple expansion engines and low pressure turbines driving triple screws. Launched in February 1914 at the Belfast yard of Har-

land & Wolff, she was not completed before the outbreak of the First World War. Accordingly she was taken over by the British Admiralty and, having been completed as a hospital ship, was commissioned on 12 December 1915. Almost a year later on 21 November 1916 she ran into a minefield in the Aegean Sea. She sank within an hour with a loss of 21 lives out of the 1,134 on board.

BRITANNIC
48,158 tons
850 × 94 feet
White Star
1914

In 1911 Denny's of Dumbarton built an 11,270 ton steamer called the REMEURA for the New Zealand Line. At 502 × 62 feet with triple expansion engines driving twin screws, she had accommodation for 60 First Class, 90 Second Class and 380 Third Class passengers. In September 1911 she made her maiden voyage from London to Wellington, New Zealand. In 1920 she was converted to oil-firing and had a refit in 1933. In

REMUERA
11,270 tons
502 × 62 feet
New Zealand Line
1911

S.S. "OXFORDSHIRE."

OXFORDSHIRE
8,600 tons
475 × 55 feet
Bibby Line
1912

August 1940 while on a return voyage from New Zealand she was sunk by enemy action off the north coast of Scotland.

The Bibby Line was one of the main transport contractors to the British government in both peace and war. None of the vessels were very large and the OXFORDSHIRE was typical. Built by Harland & Wolff in 1912, she was 8,600 tons and 475 × 55 feet with triple expansion engines driving twin screws. She was an army Red Cross ship during the First World War and served in a similar capacity for the Royal Navy in the Second World War. Between the wars she was used for troop transport and carried a limited number of fare-paying passengers. From 1945 to 1951 she continued in this capacity until sold to the Pan Islamic Steamship Company of Karachi and renamed SATINA-E-ARAB.

In 1912–13 the Royal Mail Line took delivery of five ships of 11,500 tons and 590 × 64 feet – the DESEADO, the DEMERARA, the DESNA, the DARRO and the DRINA. All were built by Harland & Wolff and became known as the 'D' class. They had quadruple expansion engines driving twin screws, giving a service speed of $13\frac{1}{2}$ knots, and were used on the Liverpool–La Plata service. Accommodation was provided for 95 First Class, 40 Second Class and 860 Third Class passengers. The DESEADO sailed for La Plata on her maiden voyage on 27 June 1912 and the ships were the largest on this service until sold for scrap in 1934. The others had been scrapped a year earlier, except for the DRINA which was a casualty of war in 1917 off the Pembrokeshire coast.

DESEADO
11,500 tons
590 x 64 feet
Royal Mail Line
1912

modation. She was sunk by enemy action in the Indian Ocean in June 1944.

In 1913 the Canadian Pacific Company took delivery of two ships from Fairfield of Glasgow for service in the Pacific. Both ships were very similar except for a slight variation in their weight, namely the EMPRESS OF RUSSIA was 16,810 tons and the EMPRESS OF ASIA 16,909 tons. Both were 592 × 68 feet with turbines driving quadruple screws giving a service speed of 20 knots. Accommodation was for 284 First Class, 100 Second Class and 808 Third Class with a crew of 475. Both ships made a maiden voyage from Liverpool to Hong Kong and then entered service between Vancouver and Yokohama. They saw service in the First World War as auxiliary cruisers and troop transports, returning to the Canadian Pacific Line in 1919 after undergoing an overhaul. The Second World War saw them again used as troop transports, but although EMPRESS OF RUSSIA survived the war she was destroyed by fire in 1945 while being repaired and refitted at Barrow-in-Furness. The EMPRESS OF ASIA suffered air attack from the Japanese off Singapore on 5 February 1942, caught fire and sank. For many years these two fine ships had been the fastest liners on the Pacific Ocean.

In 1913 Harland & Wolff completed a 15,620 ton steamer for the Royal Mail Line, named ANDES, she

The NELLOR was one of four small P & O steamers built in 1913, which were mainly used for cargo but carried some fare-paying passengers. She was built by Caird of Greenock and was 7,000 tons and 450 × 52 feet with quadruple expansion engines driving twin screws. She was used on the London to Calcutta service until 1930 when she was transferred to the Eastern Australian Steamship Company for service between Australia and Japan with additional passenger accom-

NELLOR
7,000 tons
450 x 52 feet
P & O
1913

ATLANTIS
(formerly ANDES)
15,620 tons
589 × 67 feet
Royal Mail Lines

ROYAL MAIL
"ATLANTIS"
ABSTRACT OF LOG

Ship's log

was 589 × 67 feet with triple expansion engines exhausting to a low pressure turbine driving triple screws. Accommodation was provided for 380 First Class, 250 Second Class and 700 Third Class passengers. She sailed from Liverpool to Chile on her maiden voyage in September 1913. In 1915 she was taken over as an armed merchant cruiser and in 1916 was involved in an action with a German auxiliary cruiser GRIEF in the North Sea in which her sister ship ALCANTARA was sunk. After the war in 1939 she resumed sailing to La Plata. In 1930 she was fitted out as a cruise liner and converted to oil firing, painted white and renamed the ATLANTIS. In 1919 she was sold to the British government and fitted out as a hospital ship. In 1948 the ATLANTIS was converted for use as an emigrant ship sailing to Australia and New Zealand. In 1952 she was broken up.

The White Star liner CERAMIC, built by Harland & Wolff and delivered in 1913 for service between Liverpool and Sydney, was the last ship built for White Star's Australian service. She was 18,500 tons and 655 × 69 feet, with triple expansion engines and low pressure turbines driving triple screws. A one-class ship, she

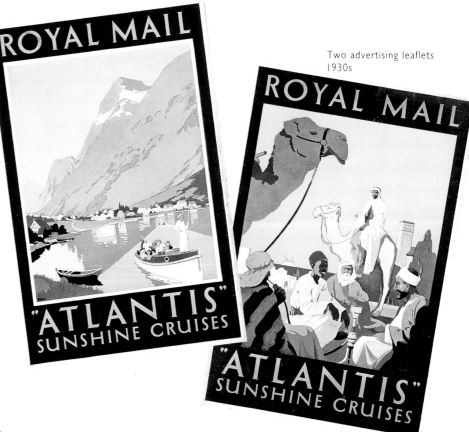

Two advertising leaflets
1930s

The Blue Funnel Line steamship ULYSSES was built by Workman, Clark & Company of Belfast in 1913. She was 14,499 tons and 580 × 68 feet with triple expansion engines driving twin screws. She had accommodation for 350 First Class passengers and sailed from Liverpool on her maiden voyage to Australia in October 1913. In 1915 she was employed as a troop ship and in 1920 returned to her Australian service. In April 1942 she was sunk by a German torpedo off the coast of Florida.

In 1913 the German Hamburg–America Line of Hamburg took delivery of what was then the largest ship in the world. The IMPERATOR, built by Vulkan of Hamburg, was 52,117 tons and 909 × 98 feet, with turbines driving quadruple screws giving an estimated service speed of 23 knots. She had accommodation for 908 First Class, 972 Second Class, 942 Third Class and 1,772 Steerage passengers. On June 10 1913 she commenced her maiden voyage from Cuxhaven to New York. From August 1914 she was laid up at Hamburg for the duration of the First World War. She left Hamburg for the last time on 27 April 1919 as part of the reparations package and was briefly used by the United States Navy as a transport until being laid up in New York in August. In February 1920 she was handed on to Great Britain and, under charter to the Cunard Line, was used on the New York service. In February 1921 she was sold to Cunard, renamed the BERENGARIA and sent to Armstrong Whitworth of Newcastle-on-Tyne for overhaul and refit which included conversion to oil firing. When this

BERENGARIA
(formerly IMPERATOR)
52,117 tons
909 × 98 feet
Hamburg-America Line
1913

ULYSESS
14,499 tons
580 × 68 feet
Blue Funnel Line
1913

originally had accommodation for over 800 emigrants. She was used as a troop transport in the First World War. She was acquired by Shaw, Savill & Albion in 1934 and sailed between Liverpool and Brisbane. In 1940 she was again a troop transport for a short while, before being sunk by a German submarine on 6 December 1942 whilst on a civilian voyage to Australia. There was only one survivor.

work was completed in May 1922 she returned to the North Atlantic service. In March 1938 she was badly damaged by fire while in New York and returned to Southampton with only the crew on board, before being sold for scrap in November.

The Hamburg–America Line took delivery of the second of three large vessels with which they hoped to conquer the Atlantic trade in 1914. The VATERLAND, built by Blohm & Voss of Hamburg, was completed in April 1914 and with a weight of 54,282 tons took over the title of the world's largest ship from the IMPERATOR, a title she retained until 1922 when the BISMARK was completed and handed over to the British. The VATERLAND was 948 × 100 feet with turbines driving quadruple screws designed to give a service speed of $23\frac{1}{2}$ knots. Accommodation was provided for 752 First Class, 535 Second Class, 850 Third Class and 1,772 Steerage passengers with a crew of 1,234. Her maiden voyage on 14 May 1914 was from Cuxhaven to New York. In August 1914 she was interned in New York, and in April 1917, having been taken over by the United States Navy and renamed LEVIATHAN, she was used as a transport. In 1919 she was laid up in New York until February 1922 when she

went to the Newport News Shipbuilding & Dry Dock Company. In 1923 her weight was reclassified as 59,956 tons thus making her the world's largest ship for the second time (in 1922 on completion of the BISMARK-/MAJESTIC she had lost this title by about 2,000 tons). Her first voyage for United States Liners commenced on 4 July 1923 from New York to Southampton, and she remained in this service until laid up in 1932. In 1931, because the dock dues assessed on tonnage were so severe, her weight was reassessed at 48,950 tons, leaving the MAJESTIC as the largest yet again. She made four Atlantic crossings in 1934 and was then laid up in New York until sold for scrap and towed to Rosyth, Scotland in 1938.

The third German giant was the BISMARCK. Built by Blohm & Voss of Hamburg, she was 56,550 tons and 956 × 100 feet, with turbines driving quadruple screws to give her an estimated service speed of $23\frac{1}{2}$ knots. Accommodation was planned for 750 First Class, 545 Second Class, 850 Third Class and a crew of 1,000. She was incomplete at the outbreak of the First World War and remained in the docks at Hamburg. In 1919 she was handed over to the British Government who sold her in 1921 to the White Star Line. When completed

MAJESTIC
(formerly Bismarck)
56,550 tons
956 x 100 feet
White Star Line
1922

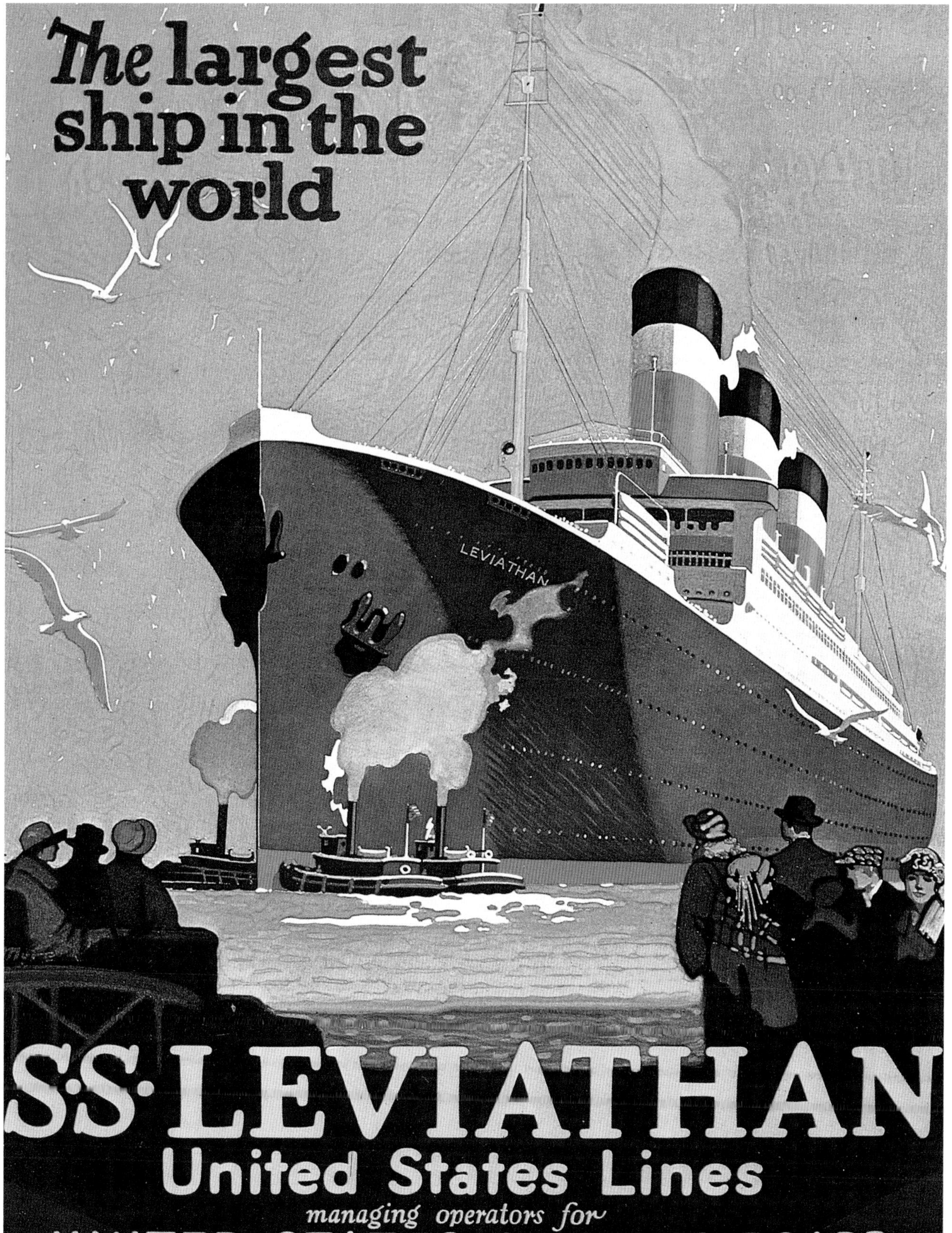
The largest ship in the world
LEVIATHAN
S·S·LEVIATHAN
United States Lines
managing operators for
UNITED STATES SHIPPING BOARD

LEVIATHAN
(formerly VATERLAND)
54,282 tons
948 x 100 feet
Hamburg-America Line
1914

she was the largest ship in the world. In March 1922 she was sailed round to Liverpool for trials, after which she was renamed the MAJESTIC and left on her maiden voyage from Southampton to New York on 10 May 1922. In 1936 she was sold for breaking up, but re-sold by the breakers to the British Admiralty to be fitted out as a training ship. She was stationed at Rosyth in Scotland and given the name CALEDONIA. In 1939 it was planned to refit her as a transport, but within a few weeks she was burned out completely and sank and was sold for scrap the following year.

Between 1913 and 1914 Cunard had four 'A' class steamships laid down, three at Scott's of Greenock and one at Swan Hunter on the Tyne. The first to be complete was the ANDANIA at Scott's. She was 13,400 tons and 540 × 64 feet with quadruple expansion engines driving twin screws to give a service speed of $14\frac{1}{2}$ knots. She had accommodation for 520 Second Class and 1,620 Third Class passengers. She sailed from Liverpool on her maiden voyage to Montreal in July 1913. In 1914 she was taken over as a troop-ship. In January 1918, the ANDANIA was sunk by a German

AQUITANIA
45,647 tons
901 × 97 feet
Cunard
1914

torpedo. Two other 'A' class ships were sunk by enemy action, and the fourth the ALBANIA was not completed until 1920, continuing in service until 1930 when she was sold to an Italian company who renamed her the

ANDANIA
13,400 tons
540 × 64 feet
Cunard
1913

AQUITANIA
in camouflage for troop-
ship duty, 1915

Celluloid pocket
calendar, 1917

but in November 1939 she was again put to work as a troop-ship. At the end of the war in Europe she helped repatriate American troops and made some voyages carrying emigrants to Canada. In March 1948 she returned to Cunard and, after a minor overhaul, started sailing in May between Southampton and Halifax, being subsidized by the Canadian Government. The AQUITANIA continued in this service until the end of

1920s poster of
AQUITANIA

CALIFORNIA. In 1941 she was sunk by a British torpedo in the Mediterranean.

The AQUITANIA was on the North Atlantic run for longer than most large ocean-going liners. Delivered to the Cunard Line in May 1914 by her builders John Brown of Clydebank, she was 45,647 tons and 901 × 97 feet, with turbines driving quadruple screws to give a service speed of 23 knots. She had accommodation for 618 First Class, 614 Second Class, 1,998 Third Class and a crew of 972. She was considered the most handsome of the North Atlantic 'giants'. Her maiden voyage from Liverpool to New York commenced on 30 May 1914. She only completed three round voyages before the outbreak of the First World War. She was taken over as an American cruiser but after only a month it was decided that she was too large a vessel for these duties, and the spring of 1915 saw her being used first as a troop transport and later as a hospital ship in the Dardanelles, remaining there until the end of 1916. In 1917 she was laid up until taken over in March as a troop ship to take American troops to Europe, with 1919 seeing her taking troops in the opposite direction. In 1920 she was overhauled and converted to oil firing. She resumed regular North Atlantic services from Southampton to New York in August 1920.

With the advent of the QUEEN MARY in 1936, she had to run a fortnightly service with the new 'Queen' and to meet this schedule, redesigned propellers were fitted allowing her to make service crossings at an average speed of 24 knots. When the Second World War started she was nearing the end of her useful life,

Wireless news sheet, 1927

Cunard menu, 1919

German propaganda

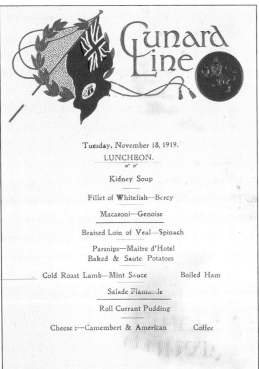

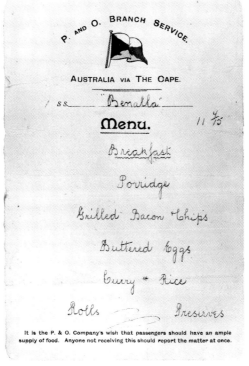

P & O breakfast menu

1949 when she was sold for scrap – a sad end to the long life of a great ship.

Two ships were added to the Hamburg–South America Line in 1914. The CAP TRAFALGAR was first, built by Vulkan of Hamburg and delivered in March 1914. In the same month she commenced her maiden voyage from Hamburg to La Plata. She was 18,805 tons and 613 × 72 feet, with triple expansion plus low pressure turbines driving triple screws to give an estimated speed of 17 knots. Accommodation was provided for 400 First Class, 274 Second Class and 912 Third Class with a crew of 436. At the beginning of August 1914 she was in port at Buenos Aires and was ordered to remain there pending instructions. Three weeks later she had a rendezvous with a German Naval vessel who provided her with armaments and thereafter she acted as an auxilliary cruiser. In mid-September she was located and sunk by the British auxilliary cruiser CARMANIA (Cunard) which was also damaged.

The CAP POLONIO was built for the Hamburg–South America Line by Blohm & Voss in 1914, but was not completed before the outbreak of the First World War. She was taken over in an incomplete state by the

German Government and fitted out as an auxilliary cruiser, entering naval service in 1915 as the VINETA. She was 20,576 tons and 662 × 72.5 feet, with triple expansion engines and low pressure turbines driving triple screws. On trial she failed to achieve her designed speed of 17 knots and after six days she was taken out

CAP POLONIO
20,576 tons
662 x 72 feet
Hamburg-South
America Line
1915

CAP TRAFALGAR
18,805 tons
613 x 72 feet
Hamburg-South
America Line
1914

CARMANIA sinking the
CAP TRAFALGAR in 1914

LLANSTEPHAN CASTLE
11,293 tons
519 × 63 feet
Union Castle Line
1914

KASHMIR
9,000 tons
480 × 58 feet
P & O
1915

of service and handed back to her owners. Her original name was reinstated, but although completed in 1916 to accommodate 356 First Class, 250 Second Class and 949 Third Class passengers, she remained unused. In 1919 she was handed on to the British Government and chartered to Union Castle for one voyage to Cape Town and back, before being taken over by P & O for one voyage to Bombay and back. However there had been further trouble with her engines and, her performance being judged unacceptable, she was laid up. In 1921 the Hamburg–South America Line bought her back for overhaul and conversion to oil firing. In February 1921 she sailed from Hamburg to La Plata, her troubles apparently cured. In 1931 she was laid up and did not sail again, being sold for scrap in 1935.

Two new ships were completed in 1914 for the Union Castle Line, the LLANSTEPHAN CASTLE and the LLANDOVERY CASTLE. These were virtually sister ships. The LLANSTEPHAN CASTLE was built by Fairfield of Glasgow and the LLANDOVERY CASTLE by Barclay & Curle of Glasgow. The first was 11,293 tons and 519 × 63 feet, while the latter was 11,423 tons and 517 × 63 feet. Both had quadruple expansion engines driving twin screws to provide an estimated service speed of 14 knots. Each had accommodation for 213 First Class, 116 Second Class and 100 Third Class passengers. The LLANSTEPHAN CASTLE ran on the London–East African service until the outbreak of the First World War and from then on sailed mostly to South Africa. In 1920 she returned to the East African service. In the Second World War she was used by the

Ministry of War Transport. At the conclusion of the war she sailed again for Union Castle on the London–round Africa–London service until sold for scrap in 1952. The LLANDOVERY CASTLE also started on the East Africa Service in 1914 but on the outbreak of the First World War was transferred to West African ports. In 1917 she was commissioned as a hospital ship and was sunk by a German submarine while on this service about 100 miles west of Iceland with the loss of 234 lives.

Between 1914 and 1915, P & O ordered five ships for their Yokahama service, three from Cammell Laird of Birkenhead and two from Caird & Co. of Greenock. They were all 9,000 tons and 480 × 58 feet with quadruple expansion engines driving twin screws. They had accommodation for 79 First Class and 68 Second Class passengers. The KASHMIR was completed in 1915 by Caird. She was immediately taken over for war service and did not start on P & O's Far Eastern duties until after the end of the First World War. She was broken up in 1932.

At the outbreak of the First World War, Canadian Pacific had two ships on the stocks at the yards of Barclay, Curle & Company. They were sister ships of 13,469 tons and 250 × 64 feet with quadruple expansion engines driving twin screws. Both ships were completed in 1915 – the METAGAMA in March and the MISSANABIE in October. They worked on the Canadian service out of Liverpool during the war. In September 1918 the MISSANABIE was torpedoed off Cork with the loss of 45 lives, while the METAGAMA survived and

METAGAMA
13,469 tons
250 × 64 feet
Canadian Pacific
1915

HOMERIC
34,351 tons
774 × 82 feet
North German Lloyd
taken over by
White Star Line
1919

continued sailing to Canada until laid up in 1930 and sold to shipbreakers in 1934.

In 1913 Schichau of Danzig launched a new liner for North German Lloyd which was only partly completed at the outbreak of the First World War and was left in an incomplete state for the whole of the war. In 1919 she was handed over to the British government before being sold on a year later to the White Star Line who renamed her HOMERIC and supervised her completion. HOMERIC was 34,351 tons and 774 × 82 feet , with triple expansion engines driving twin screws to give a service speed of 18 knots. She had accommodation for 529 First Class, 487 Second Class and 1,850 Third Class passengers. When completed she was the largest twin-screw liner in the world, and as such, was steady rather than swift and did not fit readily into the sailing schedule with the OLYMPIC and MAJESTIC. She sailed from Southampton on 15 February 1922 on her maiden voyage to New York. A year later she was sent to Harland & Wolff for a refit and conversion to oil firing, thereby improving her speed to 19½ knots. The HOMERIC crossed the Atlantic on a service voyage for the last time in January 1932, after this being used only for cruising. She was laid up in 1935 and sold for scrap the following year.

In 1913 the German yard of Vulkan at Stettin launched what was to be a 21,000 ton vessel named the ADMIRAL VON TIRPITZ. Before she was completed the name was shortened to the TIRPITZ, but in August 1914 all work on her was halted because of the outbreak of war. She was not completed until the end of

November 1920 and straightaway was handed over to Great Britain and managed by P & O as a troop ship. When completed she was 21,498 tons and 615 × 75 feet, with her twin screws driven by geared turbines. Her accommodation was for 370 First Class, 190 Second Class, 415 Third Class passengers and 1,000 Steerage.

In 1921 she was sold to Canadian Pacific and renamed the EMPRESS OF CHINA but never sailed under this name as she immediately went for a refit in Hamburg and at John Brown of Clydebank. She eventually sailed on 16 June 1922 as the EMPRESS OF AUSTRALIA to Vancouver for service in the Pacific between Canada and Japan. In September 1923 she was just about to sail from Tokyo when the great earthquake took place.

EMPRESS OF AUSTRALIA
(formerly TIRPITZ)
21,498 tons
615 × 75 feet
P & O (then CP)
1920

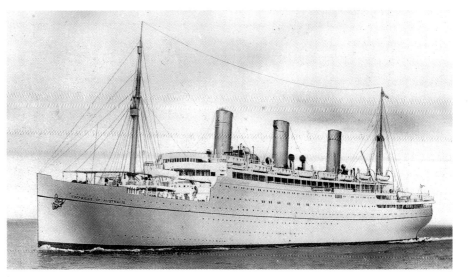

Fortunately she was not seriously damaged and was able to rescue many people from this terrible disaster. In 1926 she was re-engined with Parsons turbines by Fairfield of Glasgow. When completed her speed had been increased to 19 knots and her passenger accommodation altered to 400 First, 150 Second and 630 Third Class passengers. After sailing to Canada, she was used for cruising. In 1933 her passenger accommodation was again altered and she continued cruising until requisitioned for troop transport in 1939. After the war she was retained by the British Government and continued as a troop-ship until sold for scrap in 1952.

In 1913 the Compagnie Générale Transatlantique placed an order with Penhoët of St. Nazaire for what was to be by far their largest ship, to be named the PARIS. On the outbreak of the First World War building was halted and she was left on the stocks until 1916 when she was launched in an incomplete state to free the berth and be towed to a place of safety. She was finally completed in 1921 and on 15 June sailed on her maiden voyage from Le Havre to New York. When complete she was 34,569 tons and 764 × 85 feet, with quadruple screws driven by Parsons turbines with a designed service speed of 21 knots. Accommodation was provided for 563 First Class, 460 Second, 1,000 Third Class passengers and a crew of 648. In 1929 she was severely damaged by fire. In April 1939 she again caught fire this time at Le Havre and, keeling over onto her side, sank at her berth. Due to the war, salvage could not be completed and the wreck was eventually cut up in 1947.

Another ship which was commenced in 1913 and launched the following year was the North German Lloyd ZEPPELIN built by Bremer Vulkan. Work continued on her until she was completed in 1915 but she was then laid up for the duration of the war. In 1919 she was handed over to the British Government and managed for the Controller of Shipping by the White Star Line. She was 14,167 tons and 570 × 67 feet, with her twin screws being driven by quadruple expansion engines to give an estimated service speed of $15\frac{1}{2}$ knots. Her accommodation was for 319 First, 156 Second, 342 Third Class passengers and 1,348 Steerage. In 1920 she was sold to the Orient Steam Navigation Company and renamed ORMUZ. The accommodation was not suited to Orient's needs and so a refit followed to give 293 First and 882 Third Class passenger places. She made her first voyage to Australia in November 1921 and remained in this service until sold in 1927 to North German Lloyd. She was renamed DRESDEN and made her first voyage from Bremerhaven to New York in August. She was later transferred to cruising, until on 20 June 1934 she was wrecked while on a cruise off the coast of Norway.

Completed in October 1914 the P & O ship KAISER-I-HIND commenced her maiden voyage to Bombay almost immediately. Built by Caird of Greenock she was 11,430 tons and 540 × 61 feet, with quadruple expansion engines driving twin screws to give an estimated service speed of 17 knots. On her first trip between London and Bombay, she set a record time of 17 days and 21 hours. Passenger accommoda-

KAISER-I-HIND
11,430 tons
540 × 61 feet
P & O
1914

NARKUNDA
15,825 tons
605 × 67 feet
P & O
1920

P. & O. R.M.S. KAISAR-I-HIND, 11,500 TONS GROSS.
India Mail and Passenger Service.

P. & O. INDIA-CHINA-AUSTRALIA MAIL AND PASSENGER SERVICES.
S.S. "NARKUNDA" { 16,000 TONS. { 20,000 H.P.

LANCASHIRE
9,450 tons
482 x 51 feet
Bibby Line
1917

tion was for 315 First and 223 Second Class passengers. In 1916 she started working from London to Sydney until requisitioned for troop transport. In 1919 she returned to the London–Bombay service. For a short while in 1921 she was chartered by the Cunard Line to operate trips between Southampton and New York under the temporary name of EMPEROR OF INDIA. As soon as she returned to P & O she resumed her old name. She was eventually broken up at Blyth in 1938.

In 1914 a new ship for the Bibby Line was launched by Harland & Wolff named the LANCASHIRE. When war broke out that same year building was halted and was not completed until 1917. She was 9,450 tons and 482 × 51 feet, with quadruple expansion engines driving twin screws. As soon as she was completed she went to do service in the Indian Ocean and was based at Rangoon. In 1930 she was refitted as a troop-ship and operated under a government contract. In 1944 she was one of a quartet of Bibby ships that took part in the Normandy landings, together with the CHESHIRE, the WORCESTERSHIRE and the DEVONSHIRE, the latter being a motor vessel. The LANCASHIRE continued in government service until she was broken up in 1956.

Two more P & O liners, the NARKUNDA and the NALDERA, some 4,500 tons bigger than the KAISER-I-HIND at 16,000 tons, were built in this difficult period of the First World War. Although started in 1914 it was 1920 before they were completed. The NALDERA, 16,118 tons and 606 × 70 feet, was built by Harland & Wolff and had a fairly uneventful life working between England and the Far East and Australia until scrapped in 1938. The NARKUNDA, built by Caird of Greenock, was 15,825 tons and 605 × 67 feet. She was converted to oil firing in 1938 and two years later became a troop-ship. In November 1942 she was sunk in enemy action off North Africa.

CHAPTER 9

Reconstruction 1921–1930

In 1921 the Union Castle Line took delivery of a 19,000 ton vessel built by Harland & Wolff, named the ARUNDEL CASTLE. She was 631 × 72 feet and had geared turbines driving twin screws to give a designed speed of 17 knots. Passenger accommodation was for 234 First Class, 362 Second Class and 274 Third with 300 Steerage. Her maiden voyage to Cape Town started on 22 April 1921. She remained in this service until re-engined and refitted by Harland & Wolff in 1937. Externally her four funnels were replaced by two and a new bow was fitted bringing her length to 661 feet. Her speed was increased to 20 knots, and her passenger accommodation altered. In 1939 she was requisitioned for troop transport. After the war she returned to Union Castle and in 1949 had a general overhaul and refit in Belfast, returning to the Cape service in 1950.

She sailed from Southampton for the Cape for the last time in December 1958 and then proceeded to Hong Kong for breaking up. Her sister ship the WINDSOR CASTLE was sunk by enemy action in 1943.

In 1921–22 two sister ships, the CAMERONIA and the TYRRHENIA were built by Beardmore of Glasgow for the Anchor Line, although the TYRRHENIA was transferred to Cunard before completion. They were both 16,250 tons and 578 × 70 feet, with geared turbines driving twin screws to give a service speed of $16\frac{1}{2}$ knots. The TYRRHENIA was completed in 1922 and made her maiden voyage on 13 June from Glasgow to Montreal, transferring the following year to the Hamburg–New York service. In 1924 her passenger accommodation was altered and she was renamed the LANCASTRIA. From 1932 onwards she was mostly used for cruising. In 1940 she was taken over as a troop transport, and on 16 June, having taken on board an

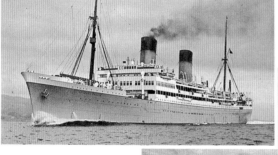

ARUNDEL CASTLE
19,000 tons
631 x 72 feet
Union Castle Line
1921

WINDSOR CASTLE
18,967 tons
631 x 72 feet
Union Castle Line
1921

LANCASTRIA
passenger list

LANCASTRIA
(formerly TYRRHENIA)
16,250 tons
578 x 70 feet
Cunard
1921–22

estimated 5,500 British troops being evacuated from France via St. Nazaire, she was anchored off the port awaiting other ships to make up a convoy for England. The following morning she was attacked by German bombers and, suffering a number of direct hits, sank within 20 minutes with the rescue of only 2,500. The loss of 3,000 lives in one ship was one of the heaviest in marine history, and may have been even higher if accounts from unofficial sources, stating there were 9,000 on board, are true.

The Glasgow-based Anchor Line who had sold TYRRHENIA/LANCASTRIA to Cunard before accepting delivery had three other similar vessels, the CAMERONIA (1921), the TUSCANIA (1932), and the CALIFORNIA (1923). Of the three, the TUSCANIA had the longest life. Built by Fairfield of Glasgow and delivered in September 1922, she was 16,990 tons and 580 x 70 feet, with geared turbines driving twin screws which gave a service speed of $16\frac{1}{2}$ knots. Passenger accommodation was for 240 First Class, 377 Second and 1,818 Third Class with a crew of 346. She sailed from Glasgow on 16 September on her maiden voyage to New York. In 1926 she commenced sailing between London and New York under charter to the Cunard Line. In October 1930 she was laid up for 10 months

prior to working as a cruise liner with some service voyages from Liverpool to India until April 1939, when she was sold to the Greek Line and renamed the NEA HELLAS. After a refit her passenger accommodation was altered to 179 First Class, 404 Cabin and 1,399 Tourist Class. In May she sailed on her first voyage from Piraeus to New York. In 1941 she was requisitioned by

TUSCANIA
16,990 tons
580 x 70 feet
Anchor Line
1922

NEW YORK
(formerly TUSCANIA)
16,990 tons
580 x 70 feet
Greek Line
1954

SCYTHIA
19,730 tons
601 x 74 feet
Cunard
1921

the British Government as a war transport and managed by her old owners the Anchor Line. At the beginning of 1949 she was returned to Greek Line who put her back on their New York service. In 1954–5 she underwent a refit and in March under the name NEW YORK started working between Bremerhaven and New York until 1959, when she returned to the Piraeus service for a couple of months before being laid up and finally sold for scrap in 1961.

In 1921 Cunard received delivery of a class of five ships of between 19,600 to 20,277 tons from four different yards: the SCYTHIA by Vickers of Barrow (19,730 tons); the SAMARIA by Cammell Laird & Co. of Birkenhead (19,602 tons); the LACONIA by Swan Hunter & Wigham Richardson of Newcastle-on-Tyne (19,680 tons); the FRANCONIA by John Brown of Clydebank (20,158 tons), and the CARINTHIA by Vickers (20,277 tons). All five ships had similar passenger accommodation and geared turbines driving twin screws giving a service speed of 16 knots. All were in service on the North Atlantic until requisitioned by the British Ministry of War Transport in 1939. All survived the war, except for the LACONIA which was sunk by a German submarine in September 1942 in the South Atlantic with 2,732 people on board, including 1,800 Italian prisoners of war on a voyage from Egypt to Britain. The LACONIA sinking showed the German U-boat commanders at their best. The sinking was carried out by U156, who then summoned two other U-boats in the area to help collect the lifeboats and to take on board a large number of survivors. The authorities at

Dakar were then informed and a French cruiser was sent for the survivors who were taken to Casablanca. In all, 1,111 people were saved, but the losses among the Italian prisoners was very heavy.

Canadian Pacific took delivery of their second largest liner, the EMPRESS OF CANADA in May 1922. (Their largest liner being the EMPRESS OF SCOTLAND, 25,000 tons, the ex-Hamburg–America Lines KAISERIN AUGUSTE VICTORIA built by Vulkan of Stettin in 1906 and transferred to CPR in January 1922). Built by Fairfield of Glasgow, she was 21,517 tons and 650 × 77 feet with geared turbines driving twin screws which gave a service speed of 18 knots. Her maiden voyage was from Falmouth to Hong Kong and

KAISERIN AUGUSTE
VICTORIA (later
EMPRESS OF SCOTLAND)
Canadian Pacific
25,000 tons
1922

she was then employed on the Vancouver to Yokohama route. In 1928 she returned to Fairfield for new engines and the following year was back on the Pacific service. In 1939 she was requisitioned as a troop transport. She was sunk in the South Atlantic in March 1943 while on a voyage from Egypt to Britain via the Cape by an Italian submarine.

Between 1921 and 1926, Cunard Line had six new ships built to replace those lost during the war. Ranging between 13,900 and 14,000 tons they comprised: the ANTONIA (1922) built by Vickers of Barrow; the AUSONIA (1921) built by Armstrong Whitworth of Newcastle-on-Tyne; the ANDANIA (1923) by Hawthorn Leslie of Newcastle-on-Tyne; the ASCANIA

(1925) by Armstrong Whitworth; the AURANIA built by Swan Hunter & Wigham Richardson of Newcastle-on-Tyne and the ALAUNIA (1925) built by John Brown of Clydebank. All six spent most of their commercial life on the British–Canadian service until requisitioned for war duties in 1939. The ANTONIA, the AUSONIA, the AURANIA and the ALAUNIA were sold to the British Admiralty in 1942 and fitted out as repair ships. the ASCANIA was returned to Cunard in 1947 and resumed her sailings to Canada until broken up in 1957, while the ANDANIA had been sunk by enemy action south of Iceland in June 1940.

In 1921–2 the Commonwealth Government Line of Australia took delivery of five sister ships known as the

CARINTHIA
20,277 tons
601 x 74 feet
Cunard
1921

ANDANIA (above)
13,950 tons
520 x 65 feet
Cunard
1923

ASCANIA (below)
14,013 tons
520 x 65 feet
Cunard
1925

'Bay' Class: the MORETON BAY (1921), the HOBSON'S BAY (1922) and the JERVIS BAY (1922) by Vickers of Barrow; the LARGS BAY (1921) and the ESPERANCE BAY (1922) by Beardmore of Glasgow. All were 13,800 tons and 550 × 68 feet (with a slight variation of about two feet). All had geared turbines driving twin screws and provided accommodation for 12 First and over 700 Third Class passengers. Originally all five ships sailed between London and Brisbane. In 1928 they were sold to the White Star Line and in 1933 were taken over by the Aberdeen & Commonwealth Line. All five ships were taken over by the British Ministry of War Transport, of which all but the JERVIS BAY survived and returned to civilian service until broken up in the mid-1950s. The JERVIS BAY, while serving as an armed merchant cruiser on November 5 1940, was the sole escort to a convoy of 37 ships to Halifax (HX84) when they were attacked by

JERVIS BAY
13,800 tons
550 × 68 feet
Commonwealth Govt
Line of Australia
1922

the German pocket battleship, ADMIRAL SCHEER. The convoy scattered and the JERVIS BAY turned to attack. Although no match for the German 11-inch guns, her brave action enabled most of the convoy to escape before she was sunk. After dark a Swedish merchantman returned to pick up 65 survivors.

In 1921 Lamport & Holt took delivery of a new ship from Workman Clark of Belfast, the 13,230 ton VANDYCK, which was 559 × 64 feet with twin screws driven by geared turbines. She had accommodation for 300 First Class, 150 Second Class and 230 Third Class passengers. She was for use on the company's South American service. In 1939 she was taken over as a troopship and sunk by enemy action off the Norwegian coast in June 1940. Her sister ship, VOLTAIRE was completed two years later at the same yard and went into service in November 1923. For a time in the early 1930s she was laid up before being used as a cruise ship. In 1939 she was taken over as an armed merchant cruiser and was sunk by enemy action in April 1941.

Lamport & Holt
matchbox cover

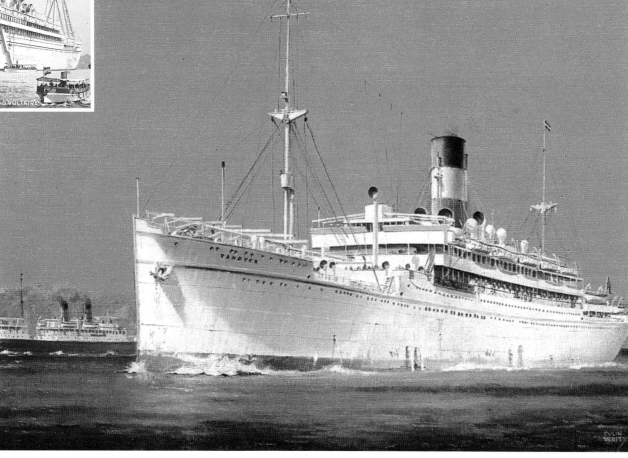

VOLTAIRE
13,230 tons
559 × 64 feet
Lamport & Holt
1923

VANDYCK
13,230 tons
559 × 64 feet
Lamport & Holt
1921

TAMAROA
(formerly SOPHOCLES)
12,350 tons
519 × 63 feet
Aberdeen Line
1922

In 1922, the Aberdeen Line received two sister ships from Harland & Wolff, the SOPHOCLES and the DIOGENES. Both were 12,350 tons and 519 × 63 feet, with geared turbines driving twin screws with accommodation for 131 First and 422 Third Class passengers. Both ships worked on the London–Brisbane service until 1926 when they were chartered to Shaw, Savill & Albion and at the same time converted to oil firing. The SOPHOCLES was renamed the TAMAROA and the DIOGENES, the MATAROA before they started sailing between London and Wellington (New Zealand). Six years later they were purchased by Shaw, Savill &

Albion. Both vessels served in the Second World War as troop transports until 1948 when they returned to the New Zealand service before being broken up in 1957.

The White Star Line took delivery of a new liner from Harland & Wolff in 1923 which was named the DORIC. She was 16,484 tons and 601 × 67.5 feet, with twin screws driven by geared turbines. Her accommodation was for 600 Cabin Class and 1,700 Third Class passengers. She commenced her maiden voyage from Liverpool to Montreal on 8 June 1923. In 1933 she was transferred to cruising and the following year was taken over by the amalgamated company Cunard-White Star. On 5 September 1935 she was involved in a collision in fog off Cape Finistère and managed to reach safety, but was subsequently sold for scrap.

In 1914 North German Lloyd of Bremen had had a new ship laid down at AG Weser. She was 18,900 tons and 615 × 71 feet with quadruple expansion engines driving twin screws to give a service speed of 17 knots. She had accommodation for 229 First Class, 523 Second Class and 630 Third Class passengers. Building was suspended during the First World War and was not completed until 1923 when she was handed over to the Royal Mail Line as war reparations and named the OHIO. She made her maiden voyage to New York in April 1923. In 1927 she was sold to the White Star Line, who renamed her the ALBERTIC and used her on the Montreal service until she was laid up in 1933 and sold for scrap the following year.

DORIC
16,484 tons
601 × 67.5 feet
White Star Line
1923

White Star line
matchbox cover

OTRANTO
20,032 tons
660 × 75 feet
Orient Line
1926

ORONTES
19,970 tons
660 × 75 feet
Orient Line
1929

The Blue Funnel Line had a new ship from Cammell Laird in 1923, the turbine steamer SARPEDEN. She was 11,320 tons and 520 × 62 feet with accommodation for 155 First Class passengers. In May 1923 she made her maiden voyage from Liverpool to Singapore and beyond. In 1946 she was transferred to the Australian service until sold to breakers in 1953.

The Orient Line had five 20,000 ton ships built for them between 1924 and 1929: the ORAMA (19,777 tons) in 1924, the OTRANTO (20,032 tons) in 1926 and the ORFORD (19,941 tons) in 1928 by Vickers of Barrow, the ORONSAY (20,001 tons) by John Brown of Clydebank 1925, the ORONTES (19,970 tons) by Vickers-Armstrong of Barrow in 1929. All

SARPEDEN
11,320 tons
520 × 62 feet
Blue Funnel Line
1923

STATENDAM
29,511 tons
697 x 81 feet
Holland-America Line
1929

Class passengers. In December 1939 she was laid up in Rotterdam. Five months later during fighting in the Rotterdam area, she was hit by German bombs, caught fire and was completely burned out.

In the 1920s, the P & O Line began building new ships for their London–Bombay and London–Sydney services, with seven ships being completed in 1925: the RAZMAK, the RAWALPINDI and the RAJPUTANA by Harland & Wolff; the RANPURA and the RANCHI by Hawthorn, Leslie; the CATHAY and the COMORIN by Barclay, Curle & Co. and the CHITRAL by Alexander Stephen & Co. An eighth and much larger vessel was the VICEROY OF INDIA built by Alexander Stephen & Co. in 1929. The first seven were all in a range of 15,000 to 16,000 tons and were powered by quadruple expansion engines driving twin screws. All seven were involved in the war in various capacities, but only three survived. The RAWALPINDI, while serving as an armed merchant cruiser, was sunk in November 1939 in the North Atlantic by the 'pocket battleships' GNEISNAU and SCHARNHORST with a loss of 270 lives. The RAJPUTANA was sunk by German submarines in April 1941, while the CATHAY was bombed and sunk in November 1942 while landing allied troops in North Africa with a loss of only one life. The COROMIN was lost by fire in 1941 in mid-Atlantic with no loss of life. The VICEROY OF

RAWALPINDI
Christmas menu
1936

were approximately 660 × 75 feet with twin screws driven by geared turbines. Their main work was on the London to Brisbane service until requisitioned for war duties as troop transports and only the OTRANTO and the ORONTES survived. The ORAMA was sunk on 8 June 1940 by the German cruiser ADMIRAL HIPPER while evacuating troops from Norway. At the time she was sunk there were no troops on board and the crew of 280 were rescued by the Germans.

The ORONSAY was sunk on 9 October 1942 by an Italian submarine off the west coast of Africa with the loss of five lives. The ORFORD was attacked by German aircraft off Marseilles on 1 June 1940 and was beached and totally wrecked. The other two both returned to the London–Sydney service after the war until broken up, the OTRANTO in June 1957 and the ORONTES in March 1962.

Although started in 1921, the STATENDAM built by Harland & Wolff for the Holland-America Line of Rotterdam, was not launched until September 1924. This was due to a slump in the North Atlantic trade in 1922–23 caused by restrictions on immigration to the United States. Even after launching in 1924 all further work was halted. In April 1927 the uncompleted ship was towed to Rotterdam for completion by Wilton's Shipway & Engineering Company, but she was not ready to sail to New York on her maiden voyage until April 1929 – eight years after being laid down. The STATENDAM was 29,511 tons and 697 × 81 feet, with twin screws driven by geared turbines designed to give a service speed of 19 knots. She had accommodation for 510 First Class, 344 Second, 374 Third and 426 Tourist

RAWALPINDI
being sunk by German
battleships, 1939
(Courtesy P & O)

COMORIN
15,116 tons
545 x 70 feet
P & O
1925

INDIA was 19,548 tons and 612 ×76 feet, with turbo-electric power, an unusual feature. Turbo generators gave power for British Thomson-Houston electric motors which drove twin screws. In February 1929 she made her maiden voyage from London to Bombay. In November 1942 she was sunk by a German submarine off North Africa after landing Allied troops. Only four lives were lost. The VICEROY OF INDIA was the first large turbo-electric passenger ship in the world.

Two very handsome three-funnel liners were built for the Anchor Line in 1925. The TRANSYLVANIA by Fairfield of Glasgow was 16,923 tons and 552 feet x 70 feet, while the CALEDONIA, built by Alexander Stephen of Glasgow, was 17,043 tons with the same overall measurements. Both had twin screws driven by

geared turbines. They had their maiden voyages from Glasgow to New York within three weeks of each other on 12 September and 3 October 1925 respectively. In 1939, both ships were taken over as armed merchant cruisers and at this time the CALEDONIA was renamed the SCOTSTOUN. Both ships were sunk in 1940 by German submarines – the SCOTSTOUN on 13 June and the TRANSYLVANIA on 10 August.

Two comparatively small passenger liners were built in 1926–27 for the Union Castle Line, the LLAN-DOVERY CASTLE by Barclay Curle & Co. of Glasgow at 10,609 tons and $487 \times 61\frac{1}{2}$ feet and the LLANDAFF CASTLE by Workman, Clark & Co. of Belfast at 10,786 tons and $490 \times 61\frac{1}{2}$ feet. Both had twin screws which were driven by quadruple expansion engines and both

P. & O. S.S. VICEROY OF INDIA, 19,700 TONS GROSS.
India Mail and Passenger Service.

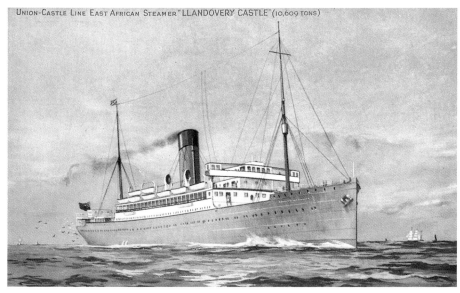

UNION-CASTLE LINE EAST AFRICAN STEAMER "LLANDOVERY CASTLE" (10,609 TONS)

VICEROY OF INDIA
19,648 tons
612 × 76 feet
1929

LLANDOVERY CASTLE
10,609 tons
487 × 61.5 feet
Union Castle Line
1926–7

worked on the London–round Africa service. The LLANDOVERY CASTLE started her maiden voyage on 25 September 1925 and the LLANDAFF CASTLE on 6 January 1927. During the war the LLANDOVERY CASTLE did service as a hospital ship and was returned to her owners in September 1946. After a refit, she went back on the round Africa service in May the following year. In 1953 she was sold for breaking up. The LLANDAFF CASTLE was employed on war service as a troop transport and did not survive, being sunk off the south-east coast of Africa by a German submarine on 30 November 1942.

At the time of her building in 1927, the ILE DE FRANCE was the largest ship in the CGT fleet. Built by Penhoët at St. Nazaire she was 43,153 tons and 792 ×

$91\frac{3}{4}$ feet, with geared turbines driving quadruple screws to give a service speed of $23\frac{1}{2}$ knots. She started her maiden voyage from Le Havre to New York on 22 June 1927. In September 1939 she was laid up in New York, but early in 1940 she was used to move French troops to Indo-China. At the time of the French capitulation she was in Singapore and was taken over by the British and used as an allied troop-ship with French crew under the management of Cunard–White Star. After the war she was handed back to her owners and in 1947 had a complete overhaul and refit, which included the removal of one funnel. She returned to the Le Havre–New York service on 21 July 1949. At the end of 1958 she was sold to a Japanese company to be broken up.

TRANSYLVANIA
16,923 tons
552 × 70 feet
Anchor Line
1925

ILE DE FRANCE
43,153 tons
792 × 91.75 feet
CGT
1927

QUEEN FREDERICA
(formerly MALOLO)
17,232 tons
582 x 83 feet
Matson Navigation Co.
1927

change of name to the ATLANTIC, she began sailings between Genoa and New York. In 1952 she began sailing from Southampton to Canada. In 1954 she underwent a further refit and was again renamed, this time the QUEEN FREDERICA. In 1955 she was put to work between New York and Piraeus (Athens). In 1965 she was sold to Dimitri Chandris of Piraeus and sailed between Southampton and Australia with cruising fitted in when feasible. In 1971 she was laid up in the river Dart in England and in 1973 started Mediterranean cruising.

In 1927, the Matson Navigation Co. of San Francisco took delivery of the largest vessel in the US maritime fleet, the MALOLO built by W. Cramp & Sons of Philadelphia. She was 17,232 tons and 582 feet x 83 feet, with twin screws driven by geared turbines to give a service speed of 21 knots. An accident while on trials in May 1927 caused her delivery to be delayed and she sailed from San Francisco to Honolulu on her maiden voyage on 16 November 1927. Ten years later she had a refit and was renamed the MATSONIA. In February 1942 she was taken over by the US Navy Transport and was released in April 1946. After overhaul she went back to the Honolulu service until 1948 when she was sold to Home Lines of Panama and, after a refit and a

At the time of her building in 1927, the Hamburg-South America Line's CAP ARCONA was the largest ship in the German mercantile fleet. Built by Blohm & Voss of Hamburg she was 27,560 tons and 676 × 84 feet, with twin screws driven by geared turbines giving a service speed of 20 knots. She had accommodation for 575 First Class, 275 Second and 465 Third Class passengers with a crew of 630. She left Hamburg on her maiden voyage to La Plata on 19 November 1927 and remained on this route most of her life. At the outbreak of war she was in German waters and in 1940 was converted into an accommodation (barracks) ship for the German Navy at Gotenhafen. In 1945, when Germany was being over-run from the East by the Russians, she was used to move civilians from that area and in three voyages she moved 26,000 people. In April she had 5,000 people on board from a concentration camp, and at the beginning of May was attacked by British aircraft, capsizing with the loss of all on board.

The LAURENTIC was the last steamer built for the White Star Line. Completed in November 1927 at the

CAP ARCONA
27,560 tons
676 x 84 feet
Hamburg-South
American Line
1927

LAURENTIC
18,724 tons
600 x 75 feet
White Star Line
1927

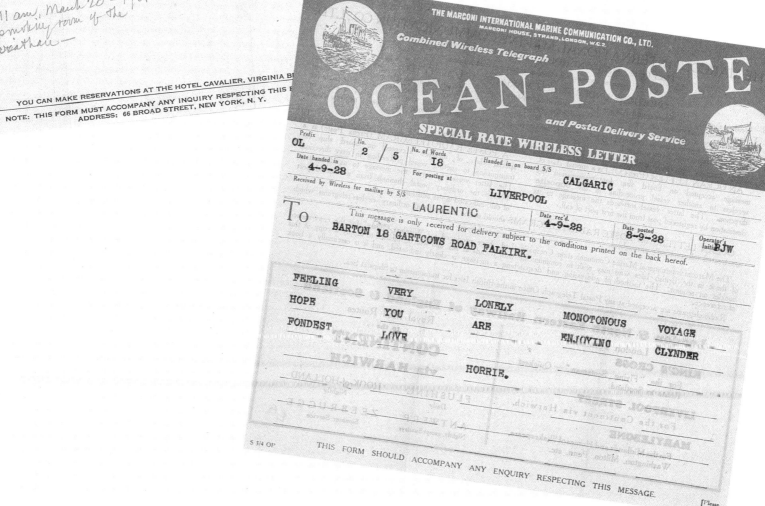

Two telegrams from
the 1920s

ARGENTINA
(formerly PENNSYLVANIA)
20,526 tons
613 × 80 feet

EMPRESS OF FRANCE
(formerly DUCHESS
OF BEDFORD)
20,123 tons
601 × 75 feet
CPR
1928

yard of Harland & Wolff, she was 18,724 tons and 600 × 75 feet, with triple screws driven by triple expansion engines plus a low pressure turbine to give a service speed of 16 knots. She had accommodation for 594 Cabin, 460 Tourist and 500 Third Class passengers. She sailed on her maiden voyage from Liverpool to New York on 12 November 1927. The following year she moved to the Liverpool to Montreal service. In 1934 she was taken over as part of the Cunard–White Star fleet. In August 1935 she was involved in a collision in the Irish Sea and was laid up at Birkenhead for repairs. In 1936 she made one voyage to Palestine as a troopship and was then laid up first at Southampton and then at Falmouth. In August 1939 she was taken over by the Royal Navy as an armed merchant cruiser and must have been the largest ocean-going coal-fired ship operated by the Royal Navy. In November 1940 she was sunk by a German submarine off the Irish coast. An unfortunate end for a not too successful ship.

It fell to the USA to build the next big turbo-electric steamer, the American liner PENNSYLVANIA which came from the yard of Newport News Ship Building & Dry Dock Company and was 20,526 tons and 613 × 80 feet. The turbo-electric equipment was made by the General Electric Company and drove twin screws to give a service speed of $18\frac{1}{2}$ knots. Completed in July 1929 she served on the San Francisco to New York service via Panama. In 1937 she was sold to the US Maritime Commission and rebuilt as a one-class vessel (500 passengers) for the South American service. At the same time she had her aft funnel removed, and a year later under her new name the ARGENTINA, she started

sailing between New York and Buenos Aires under the flag of the American Republic Line, although she was managed by Moore & McCormack. In 1942 she was taken over by the US War Shipping Administration. Five years later she was released and again operated on the South American service for Moore & McCormack until 1963 when she was sold for breaking up.

1928 and 1929 saw the delivery to Canadian Pacific of the first of four 20,000 ton sister ships: the DUCHESS OF ATHOLL (20,119 tons) built by Beardmore of Glasgow in 1928, the DUCHESS OF BEDFORD (20,123 tons) 1928, the DUCHESS OF RICHMOND (20,022 tons) 1928 and the DUCHESS OF YORK (20,021 tons) 1929. The latter three were all by John Brown of Clydebank 1929. They were all 601 × 75 feet, except the DUCHESS OF RICHMOND which apparently lost 12 inches in her length and was only 600 feet. All had twin screws driven by geared turbines to give a service speed of 18 knots. The first two sailed between Liverpool and Montreal and the second pair between Liverpool and St. Johns. In 1939 all four were seconded to troop transport duties. The DUCHESS OF ATHOLL was sunk by German submarines on 10 October 1942 near Ascension Island, and the DUCHESS OF YORK was attacked by German bombers west of the Portuguese coast while on a voyage from Glasgow to Freetown. In the latter incident all but 11 of the troops and crew were taken off by three naval vessels and the burning wreck was abandoned. The other two ships returned to their owners after the war. The DUCHESS OF BEDFORD had an overhaul and refit in 1947 at Fairfield of Glasgow, being renamed the EMPRESS OF INDIA

EMPRESS OF CANADA
(formerly DUCHESS OF
RICHMOND)
20,022 tons
600 × 75 feet
CPR
1928

BREMEN
51,656 tons
938 × 102 feet
North German Lloyd
1929

51,656 tons and 938 × 102 feet with quadruple screws driven by geared turbines. Her accommodation was for 800 First, 500 Second, 300 Tourist and 600 Third Class passengers with a crew of 990. Her maiden voyage on 16 July 1929 was from Bremerhaven to New York and she made an average speed of 27.83 knots from Cherbourg to Ambrose Light thereby gaining her the Blue Riband. On the return journey between Ambrose and Eddystone she did even better, averaging 27.92 knots, but she only held the record until March 1930 when the title was wrested from her by the EUROPA. The EUROPA held the Riband until June 1933 when the BREMEN regained it after alterations, but only for two months whereupon the record was again broken by the Italian liner the REX. At the outbreak of war in 1939, the BREMEN managed to return to Germany via Murmansk, but it was mid-December before she eventually ran the gauntlet and arrived back in Bremerhaven. In 1940 it had been proposed to refit her for the invasion of England but this never happened. In March 1941 she was completely wrecked by fire as the result of arson.

The EUROPA, which was slightly different to BREMEN was built for North German Lloyd by Blohm & Voss of Hamburg and was 49,746 tons and 941 × 102 feet. Her machinery was similar to that of BREMEN, but her accommodation was different, with 687 First, 524 Second, 306 Tourist and 507 Third Class passengers and a crew of 970. She should have been ready at the same time as BREMEN (they had been launched only two days apart), but a fire while fitting out delayed her until March 1930, when on her maiden voyage she took

and then seven months later having yet another change to EMPRESS OF FRANCE. The refit completed, she went into service in September 1948 on the Liverpool–Montreal route until she was withdrawn from service in 1960 and sold for scrap. The DUCHESS OF RICHMOND also went for a refit to Fairfield in 1946, reappearing in July 1947 with a new name the EMPRESS OF CANADA and immediately going back on the Liverpool to Montreal service. In January 1953 she was destroyed by a fire at Liverpool and sank at the dockside. She was raised 18 months later and sold for scrap.

North German Lloyd entered the Blue Riband of the Atlantic race in 1929 with the BREMEN which was built by Deschimag, AG 'Weser' of Bremen. She was

EUROPA
49,746 tons
941 × 102 feet
North German Lloyd
1930

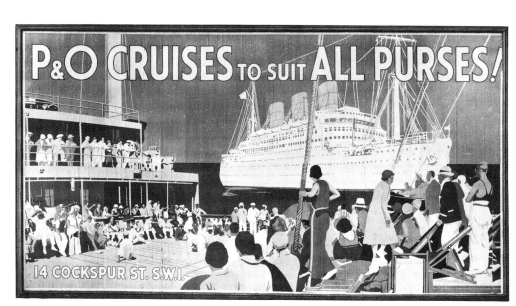

1930s ephemera
(clockwise, from top
left)

Canadian Pacific brochure

Farewell dinner menu

Cunard sailing list

Blue Funnel Line leaflet

P & O poster

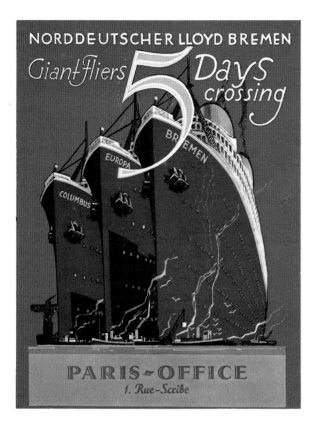

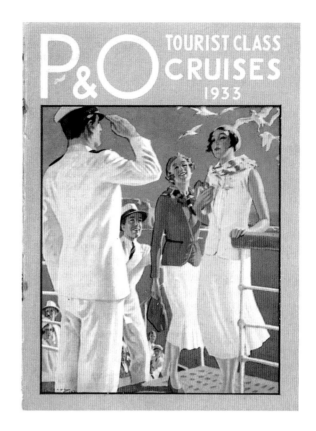

1920s and 1930s ephemera (clockwise from top left)

Two North German Lloyd leaflets

P & O leaflet, 1933

Three price lists

the Blue Riband from her sister. At the outbreak of war she was at Bremerhaven, and it was also planned that she should be used for the invasion of England. In 1945 she was seized by the USA and used as a Navy transport on the North Atlantic, and in June 1946 she was handed over to France's CGT and renamed LIBERTÉ. Six months later while at Le Havre she broke away from her moorings in a storm, was damaged and sank. It was 1950 before repairs and reconstruction work was complete and she made her first voyage from Le Havre to New York on 17 August, continuing on this service until December 1961 when she was sold for scrap.

The EMPRESS OF JAPAN was built for the Canadian Pacific Line in 1930 by the Fairfield Shipbuilding & Engineering Company of Govan. She was a vessel of 26,313 tons and 644 × 84 feet with geared turbines driving twin screws. She had accommodation for 399 First, 164 Second and 100 Third Class passengers with extra space for 510 Asiatic Steerage. At the time of building she was the largest Canadian Pacific liner, and as her name implied she was destined for the Pacific service out of Vancouver. After a maiden crossing from Liverpool to Canada and back she went out to the Far East and Vancouver via Suez. She soon became the fastest ship on the Pacific and in April 1931 did the voyage from Yokohama to Victoria, British Columbia, in a little under eight days at an average of 22.27 knots. In 1939 the EMPRESS OF JAPAN was requisitioned for trooping and in 1942 was renamed the EMPRESS OF SCOTLAND because of the entry of Japan into the war. She was not released from troop transport duties until 1948 when she had a complete refit at Glasgow and Liverpool. On her return to the company she was assigned to the North Atlantic service and made her first crossing in May 1950. She continued in this service, with some winter cruising until January 1958, when she was sold to the Hamburg–Atlantic Line and after a refit worked the North Atlantic in summer and did cruising in winter, under the new name of the HANSEATIC and with only two funnels. In September 1966 she was badly damaged by fire while at New York. As a result she had to be towed back to Hamburg and after inspection was sold for breaking up. So ended the life of a fine ship that had been the undoubted Queen of the Pacific.

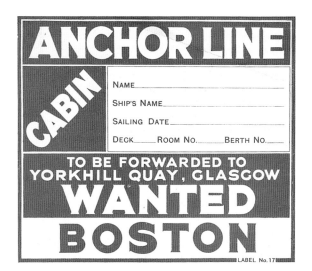

Seven luggage labels,
1930s

ANCHOR LINE

CABIN

NAME_____
SHIP'S NAME_____
SAILING DATE_____
DECK_____ROOM NO._____BERTH NO._____

TO BE FORWARDED TO
YORKHILL QUAY, GLASGOW
WANTED
BOSTON

LABEL No.17

ANCHOR-DONALDSON LINE
TOURIST ✦ CLASS

TO BE FORWARDED TO:—
SOUTH PIER, PRINCES DOCK, GLASGOW

NAME_____
S.S._____ SAILING_____
LANDING AT_____
Thence RAIL to_____

NOT WANTED

ANCHOR LINE

3RD CLASS

NAME_____
SHIP'S NAME_____
SAILING DATE_____

TO BE FORWARDED TO
YORKHILL QUAY, GLASGOW
HOLD
NEW YORK

LABEL No.6

Bestimmung:
Destination: **NEW YORK**

N.D.L.

Norddeutscher Lloyd
Name des Passagiers:
Passengers name:

1

Bett
Berth N°._____
Abfahrt von
From
Für Gepäckraum. Hold

Dampfer:
S.S.

BREMEN

CABIN

2nd CLASS.   CABIN No.

NAME _____
R.M.S. _____
LOADING AT _____

ENGLAND

UNION-CASTLE LINE.
— LONDON. —

CABIN **P&O 1** CABIN

BERTH N°
S.S.
To
NAME

FIRST CABIN   SECOND CABIN
AROUND THE WORLD
THE CUNARD S.S. CO. LTD.
$498 $380
21-24 State Street, New York

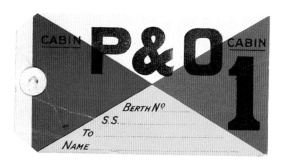

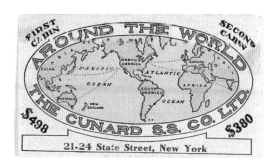

CHAPTER 10

Luxury Giants 1931–1941

The EMPRESS OF BRITAIN – a proud name for a proud ship. Built by John Brown of Clydebank for the Canadian Pacific Line, she was expressly designed for North Atlantic service and cruising. She was 42,350 tons and 760 × 97 feet with geared turbines driving quadruple screws. She had accommodation for 465 First, 260 Tourist and 470 Third Class passengers. She sailed from Southampton on 27 May 1931 on her maiden voyage to Quebec. Apart from the recently built BREMEN and EUROPA, she was the fastest large liner afloat, and it was the hope of her owners to attract mid-United States traffic by providing a quicker door-to-door service than ships sailing from New York. In the winter months the EMPRESS OF BRITAIN was used for cruising and she was designed to be able to negotiate the Panama Canal for this purpose. She was also built so she could cruise on only two screws, thus saving on fuel and reducing possible vibration. In November 1938 she was taken over for troop transport. Almost a year later on 26 October 1940, while on a return trip from Canada, she was attacked by a German bomber about 70 miles west of the Scottish Western Isles and set on fire. Those on board took to the boats and were picked up while the EMPRESS OF BRITAIN was taken in tow

by a destroyer, but she was sunk two days later by a German submarine's torpedoes. 49 lives were lost.

Four years after completing ILE DE FRANCE, Penhoët of St. Nazaire built another large liner L'ATLANTIQUE this time for Cie Sudatlantique of Bordeaux. She was 42,500 tons and 744 × 92 feet, with geared turbines driving quadruple screws. Accommodation was for 414 First, 158 Second and 584 Third Class passengers. She left Bordeaux on 29 September 1931 for her maiden voyage to Buenos Aires. On 4 January 1933 while on a voyage without passengers between Bordeaux and Le Havre, a fire broke out in the small hours when nearing the Channel Isles. About four hours later the crew had to abandon ship and take to the boats. The blazing liner drifted in the English Channel for two days before being taken by tugs to Cherbourg. Three years later the hulk was sold to ship-breakers.

The Booth Line, a comparatively small British shipping company, specialised in servicing the Amazon ports as far as 1,000 miles up stream. For this reason they did not have any very large ships. The HILARY was built for them by Cammell Laird of Birkenhead. She was 7,400 tons and 424 × 56 feet, with triple expansion engines and low pressure turbines driving a

EMPRESS OF BRITAIN
42,350 tons
760 × 97 feet
CPR
1931

L'ATLANTIQUE
42,500 tons
744 × 92 feet
Cie Sudatlantique
1931

EMPRESS
OF
BRITAIN

CANADIAN PACIFIC

EMPRESS OF BRITAIN
brochure

Round the world cruises
became popular in the
1930s

ROYAL MAIL
LINE
TO
SOUTH AMERICA

PLEASURE CRUISES
TO
MEDITERRANEAN,
NORWAY, NORTH CAPE,
BALTIC, WEST INDIES,
ROUND BRITAIN, Etc.
according to season.

For full particulars apply—
THE ROYAL MAIL STEAM PACKET COMPANY,
America House, Cockspur Street, S.W.1.
Royal Mail House, E.C.3.
SOUTHAMPTON, LIVERPOOL, MANCHESTER, BIRMINGHAM, GLASGOW,
CARDIFF, ETC.

RIO DE JANEIRO, Capital of Brazil, the world's loveliest and most spectacular harbour.

Royal Mail Lines to
South America

HILARY
7,400 tons
424 × 56 feet
Booth Line
1931

NEW AUSTRALIA
(formerly MONARCH OF
BERMUDA)
22,250 tons
579 × 76 feet
Shaw, Savill & Albion
1949

single screw. Accommodation was for 80 First and 214 Third Class passengers. She ran a regular service from Liverpool to Manaus. In January 1941 she was requisitioned for war service until July 1942. On 16 October 1942 she was hit by a torpedo while in a convoy in the Atlantic, but it failed to explode. After the war she returned to the South American trade until she was broken up in 1959.

In 1931, Vickers-Armstrong of Newcastle-on-Tyne built the The MONARCH OF BERMUDA for the Furness Withy Company which was registered in Hamilton, Bermuda. She was 22,250 tons and 579 × 76 feet, with a turbo-electric power unit driving quadruple screws. Accommodation was for 830 First Class passengers only. MONARCH OF BERMUDA and her sister ship the QUEEN OF BERMUDA were known as the 'Millionaires' Ships'. In November 1931, the MONARCH made her maiden voyage from New York to Hamilton. An average voyage took a little less than 40 hours and the two ships often did two return journeys of a week each. In 1939 she was taken over for troop transport and survived, but in March 1947 while undergoing an overhaul and refit, she was almost completely destroyed by fire. The Ministry of Transport bought the wreck and had it completely rebuilt at Southampton after which her appearance was considerably altered with only one funnel. When completed at the end of 1949 she was re-named the NEW AUSTRALIA and used for carrying emigrants to Australia under the management of Shaw, Savill & Albion. She left Southampton on 15 August 1950 on her first voyage to Australia, and she continued

in this work until 1957. In January 1958 the Ministry sold her to the Greek Line, and after a refit at Hamburg she was renamed ARKADIA. In May 1958 she started sailing between Bremerhaven and Montreal. After a further refit in 1961, she was finally broken up in December 1966.

The Matson Navigation Company of Los Angeles had three new sister ships built by the Bethlehem Ship Building Corporation of Quincy in 1932 and 1933. They were all 18,000 tons and 632 × 79 feet, with geared turbines driving twin screws. The first was the MARIPOSA which had accommodation for 475 First and 229 Cabin Class passengers, while the accommodation of her sister ships was slightly different. MARIPOSA sailed from San Francisco on 2 February 1932 on her maiden voyage to Honolulu and Sydney and worked on the Pacific until taken over as a transport by the US Navy. At the end of the war she was laid up in 1946 until 1953 when she was sold to Home Lines of Panama. After an engine overhaul she sailed to Trieste for the refitting of her passenger accommodation and was renamed the HOMERIC. In January 1955 she made her first voyage after overhaul from Venice to New York. In the next eight years she stayed on the North Atlantic using various European and North American ports. In the latter part of 1963 she commenced cruising which she was still doing in 1973 when a serious fire at sea caused considerable damage, but was dealt with by the crew with no loss of life. The HOMERIC was taken to Genoa for repairs but, as the damage was more serious than anticipated and repairs

HOMERIC
(formerly MARIPOSA)
18,000 tons
632 × 79 feet
Matson Navigation Co.
1932

CARTHAGE
14,300 tons
540 × 71 feet
P & O
1932

REX
51,050 tons
880 × 67 feet
Flotta Riunite Line
1932

would have proved uneconomical, in January 1974 she was broken up.

The P & O steamer CARTHAGE was built by Alexander Stephen & Co. of Glasgow. She was 14,300 tons and 540 × 71 feet with geared turbines driving twin screws. She had accommodation for 175 First and 196 Second Class passengers. She made her maiden voyage from London to Hong Kong over the turn of the years 1931-32 and continued in this service until 1940 when she was taken over by the Royal Navy as an armed merchant cruiser. In 1943 she became a troop-ship. In 1947-48 she had a 'post-war' overhaul and refit, and was altered externally as she had one of her two funnels removed and her hull was painted white. In 1948 she returned to the London–Hong Kong service until 1961 when she was sold to ship breakers.

The pride of the Italian mercantile fleet, the REX was built by Ansaldo, Sestri Ponente for Italia, Flotta Riunite of Genoa. She was 51,050 tons and 880 × 67 feet with Parsons geared turbines driving quadruple screws. She had accommodation for 601 First, 378 Second and 410 Tourist Class passengers. On 27 September 1932 she sailed from Genoa on her maiden voyage to New York. In August 1933 she took the Blue Riband of the Atlantic for an east–west crossing with an average speed of 28.92 knots which she held until 1935. During the Second World War she was laid up near Trieste. On 8 September 1944 she was attacked by British aircraft and sunk in shallow water. At the end of the war scrapping operations started but were not completed until 1958.

1933 and 1934 were lean years as far as ship building was concerned due to the seriousness of the world depression and building was halted on the QUEEN MARY and slowed down on the NORMANDIE. No new ships of note were put into service in this period. However, one major liner, the ASTURIAS, owned by the Royal Mail Line and built by Harland & Wolff with diesel engines in 1926, was converted to steam-driven geared turbine engines. After refit she was 22,050 tons and 666 × 78 feet with accommodation for 330 First Class, 220 Second Class and 768 Third Class passengers.

ASTURIAS
22,050 tons
660 × 78 feet
Royal Mail Line
1926

NORMANDIE
79,300 tons
1,030 × 118 feet
CGT
1935

emigrants from Southampton to Sydney. In 1953 she reverted to being used a a troop-ship until being broken up in 1957.

The NORMANDIE took to the high seas in May 1935. Built by Penhoët of St. Nazaire for CGT of Le Havre, she was the largest ship in the world at 79,300 tons and 1,030 × 118 feet with a turbo-electric power unit driving quadruple screws. She had accommodation for 848 First, 670 Tourist and 454 Third Class passengers. She left Le Havre on 29 May 1935 on her maiden voyage to New York. On her first voyage she broke REX's Blue Riband record with an average speed of 29.98 knots on the outward leg and 30.31 knots on her return, thereby becoming the undisputed queen of the North Atlantic – but not for long. On 28 August 1939 she was laid up in New York because of the threat of war. With the collapse of France she was seized in December 1941 by the US Maritime Commission and after 12 days she was handed over to the US Navy and renamed the LAFAYETTE. Work started immediately to convert her to a navy transport, but on 9 February 1942 while this work was being carried out a fire started which spread rapidly. The New York fire brigade pumped so much water into her upper decks that she became top heavy and, heeling over on her side, she sank at the pier side. In 1942 she was righted and plans were made to convert her to an aircraft carrier, but these were not carried out. In October 1946 she was sold for scrap.

The conversion was finished in September 1934 and she was employed on the Royal Mail's South American service. On the outbreak of the Second World War she was taken over by the Royal Navy as an armed merchant cruiser and her forward funnel was removed. In July 1943 she was torpedoed in the South Atlantic but not sunk and was towed to Freetown. Having been considered a total loss by the Royal Mail Line she was bought by the British Admiralty in 1945 and taken to Belfast where she was repaired and fitted out for trooping. She started in this service in 1947 and was operated on behalf of the Ministry of Transport by her original owners. In 1949 the ASTURIAS was employed to take

The Orient Line took delivery in 1935 of the ORION built by Vickers-Armstrong of Barrow-in-Furness. She was 23,350 tons and 665 feet x 82 feet, with geared turbines driving twin screws. Accommoda-

Luggage label

Page 163
NORMANDIE poster

Lloyd Triestino
VICTORIA poster

White Star brochure
cover

M·V "BRITANNIC" DINING SALOON

Designed in the Louis XIV style, this room has dignity and character. The colour scheme is old ivory, relieved with ormolu, and tinted panelling. The walls are finished to represent French Masonry of the period. The furniture is in Walnut.

WHITE STAR LINE

M·V "BRITANNIC"

M·V "BRITANNIC" STATE ROOMS

The State rooms are furnished and appointed in excellent taste, and special electric light fittings concealed in shades which give a soft warm glow are installed. The various colour schemes, curtains and floor coverings are all in keeping with the idea of restfulness and comfort.

WHITE STAR LINE

M·V "BRITANNIC"

Interior from the
White Star liner BRITANNIC

M·V "BRITANNIC"
SWIMMING
BATH

The large well-lit swimming bath, fitted with every convenience, will enable passengers to enjoy a form of recreation at present available on but few liners. The system of flood and reflected lighting, which eliminates shadows, adds to the charm of this apartment.

WHITE STAR LINE

M·V " BRITANNIC "

M·V "BRITANNIC"
CHILDREN'S
PLAYROOM

Many a child will here discover the playroom of his dreams. The walls are adorned with illustrations of stories dear to the young mind; and all manner of toys, to suit children of various ages, are available.

WHITE STAR LINE

M·V " BRITANNIC "

ORION
23,350 tons
665 × 82 feet
Orient Line
1935

QUEEN MARY
80,750 tons
975 × 118 feet
Cunard White Star
1936

Cunard matchbox

tion was for 486 First and 653 Tourist Class passengers. After a Mediterranean cruise in August she left London on 29 September 1935 on her maiden voyage to Brisbane. In September 1939 she was taken over for troop transport. After the war she was reconditioned at Barrow and on 25 February 1947 was the first de-requisitioned Orient Line ship to return to commercial work with a voyage from London to Sydney. She was regularly employed until May 1963 when she went to Hamburg to act as a hotel for the International Gardening Exhibition. The following month she went to the ship-breakers yard.

Although laid down in December 1930 it was April 1936 before the Cunard QUEEN MARY was completed. The delay was due to the economic world climate, and construction of what was then known as '534' – the number of the order given to her by her builders John Brown of Clydebank – was completely halted between the end of 1932 and April 1934 when the British government came to their aid by advancing a £3,000,000 loan to complete '534' on condition that Cunard Line and White Star amalgamated. '534' was launched in September 1934 and much speculation was ended when she was named QUEEN MARY. During her trials she averaged 32.84 knots. When completed she was 80,750 tons and 975 × 118 feet with Parsons geared turbines driving quadruple screws. Accommodation was for 776 Cabin, 784 Tourist and 579 Third Class passengers. The QUEEN MARY left Southampton on 27 May 1936 on her maiden voyage to New York.

After a short running-in period (six return trips)

she made an attempt on NORMANDIE's Blue Riband time and did the westward crossing in 4 days and 27 minutes and the eastward voyage in 3 days, 23 hours and 57 minutes. In the following year the NORMANDIE beat both these times, before in August the QUEEN MARY made her fastest outward time of 3 days, 21 hours and 48 minutes and a home time of 3 days, 20 hours and 42 minutes, a record which stood until July 1952. In fact such a contest was rather 'splitting hairs', as there was not much to choose between these two magnificent ships as far as speed was concerned. However, the NORMANDIE had the edge over the QUEEN MARY in the luxury of her appointments and passenger comfort.

In September 1939 the QUEEN MARY was laid up in New York until March 1940 when she went to Sydney to be fitted out as a troop-ship, to carry Australians and New Zealanders to Egypt. At the end of the war she was released and went to John Brown of Clydebank for an overhaul and the refitting of her passenger accommodation before returning to the Southampton to New York service until July 1947. In 1958 she had Denny Brown stabilisers fitted. In August 1967 the QUEEN MARY was sold to the City of Long Beach, California as a floating hotel and conference centre, sailing from Southampton for the last time on 31 October 1967.

The Union Steam Ship Company of New Zealand took delivery of a new vessel in 1936, the AWATEA built by Vickers-Armstrong of Barrow-in-Furness. She was 13,500 tons and 545 × 74 feet with geared turbines

Cunard 1930s ephemera
(clockwise, from top left)

Post card showing
QUEEN MARY interior

Front cover of a
QUEEN MARY brochure

Envelope from the
QUEEN MARY

Programme of events

T.S.S. "AWATEA"

T.S.S. "CITY OF BENARES"

AWATEA
13,500
545 × 74 feet
Union Steamship
Company
1936

CITY OF BENARES
11,100 tons
509 × 63 feet
Ellerman Line
1936

driving twin screws. Accommodation was provided for 377 First, 151 Tourist and 38 Third Class passengers. The AWATEA left Birkenhead for her delivery voyage to Wellington in early August and sailed from Sydney on 15 September on her maiden voyage to Auckland. For a short while from 1940 until 1941 she ran through from Sydney and Auckland to Vancouver, taking over from the company's AURANGE which had been requisitioned for war service. In September 1941 the AWATEA herself was taken over as a troop-ship. On 10 March 1942 she was attacked by German bombers while in Bougle Bay, Algeria and sank.

The Ellerman Line which ran services to India took delivery of their largest ship in 1936. She was the CITY OF BENARES and, built by Barclay, Curle & Co. of Glasgow, was 11,100 tons and 509 × 63 feet with geared turbines driving a single screw. She had accommodation for 219 passengers all in one class. The CITY OF BENARES left Liverpool on 24 October 1936 on her maiden voyage to Bombay. On 17 September 1940 while on a voyage from England to Halifax with 406 people on board, including 90 children being evacuated to Canada, she was torpedoed by a German submarine. Loss of life was heavy and only seven children survived, with altogether 248 lives lost. It was this disaster that ended the British government policy of evacuating children overseas.

Shipbuilding in 1937 had been limited and the first ship of note to be commissioned in 1938 was the NIEUW AMSTERDAM built by Rotterdasche DD MK for the Holland–America Line. She was 36,300 tons and 759 feet × 88 feet with Parsons geared turbines and twin screws. Her accommodation was for 556 First, 455 Tourist and 209 Third Class passengers. She left Rot-

terdam on 10 May 1938 on her maiden voyage to New York. In September 1939 she was laid up at New York due to the outbreak of war. In 1940 she started cruising from New York, but following the German invasion of Holland she was made available to the British Government and in September she was refitted as a troop-ship at Halifax with accommodation for 8,000 troops and placed under Cunard management. In April 1946 she returned to Amsterdam for overhaul and refit and at the end of October 1947 she made her first post-war voyage from Rotterdam to New York. From 1971 onwards she was used for cruises only and in 1974 was sold for scrap.

The CANTON was the last liner built for P & O before the Second World War. She was built by Alexander Stephen of Glasgow and was 15,800 tons and

Luggage label

Holland-America Line 1ˢᵗ

NIEUW AMSTERDAM
36,300 tons
759 × 88 feet
Holland America Line
1937

CANTON
15,800 tons
563 × 73 feet
P & O
1938

563 × 73 feet, with geared turbines driving twin screws. She had accommodation for 260 First and 220 Second Class passengers. On 7 October 1938 she left Southampton on her maiden voyage to Hong Kong. In November 1939 she was taken over as an armed merchant cruiser and operated mostly in the Indian Ocean. In 1944 she was converted into a troop-ship in Cape Town where she had gone with a damaged propeller shaft, which could only be patched up there. She left Cape Town at the end of February 1945 for Britain with RAF personnel on board (including the author). She steamed unescorted to Gibraltar and five days later proceeded to Greenock in convoy. In 1947 she was refitted as a passenger liner and October of that year saw her first post-war voyage from Southampton to Hong

Kong. In August 1962 she was broken up in Hong Kong.

A second MAURETANIA was completed in 1939 for the Cunard Line by Cammell Laird of Birkenhead. She was 35,750 tons and 772 × 90 feet with Parsons geared turbines driving twin screws. Accommodation was for 440 Cabin, 450 Tourist and 470 Third Class passengers. On 17 June 1939 she sailed from Liverpool on her maiden voyage to New York, although from August onwards she sailed from Southampton. In December 1939 she was laid up at New York, and in the following March was transferred to Sydney to be converted to a troop-ship. In September 1946 she was released from war service and went to her builders for overhaul. In April 1947 she made her first post-war voyage from Liverpool to New York and from June

MAURETANIA (II)
35,750 tons
772 × 90 feet
Cunard
1939

ANDES
25,700 tons
669 x 83 feet
Royal Mail Line
1939

onwards she sailed from Southampton. In December 1962 the MAURETANIA was painted bright green and mainly used for cruising. In November 1965 she was broken up.

The last Royal Mail steamer to be built before the Second World War was the ANDES by Harland & Wolff. She was 25,700 tons and 669 feet x 83 feet, with geared turbines driving twin screws. Accommodation was to have been for 403 First and 204 Second Class passengers. It had been planned that she would have her maiden voyage on 24 September 1939 and would be the largest and fastest liner on the South American route. In the event, this voyage was cancelled because of the outbreak of war and she was requisitioned as a troop-ship, making her first voyage in December to Canada to bring the initial batch of Canadians to Great Britain. In May 1945 the ANDES took the exiled Norwegian Government back to Oslo following the liberation of their country from German occupation. Before being finally released from troop transport duties she made the fastest ever 'round-the-world' voyage from Liverpool via Panama, Wellington, Karachi, Suez and back to Great Britain in 72 days. She was released from government service in 1947 and went straight to her builders in Belfast to have her passenger accommodation reinstated, before finally

making her first voyage from Southampton to La Plata on 22 January 1948. At the end of 1959, work was started to refit her as a cruise liner to take 480 passengers, all in one class. She started her new cruising career on 10 June 1960. In May 1971 she was sent to the breakers yard.

The last large French liner to be completed just before the Second World War was the PASTEUR built by Penhoët of St. Nazaire for Cie Sudatlantique of Bordeaux. She was 29,250 tons and 697 × 88 feet, with Parsons geared turbines driving quadruple screws. Her accommodation was for 287 First, 126 Second and 338 Third Class passengers. She was to have sailed from Bordeaux on 10 September 1939 on her maiden voyage to Buenos Aires, but it was cancelled because of the outbreak of war. On 2 June 1940 she made her first voyage which was from Brest to Halifax and carried with her the French gold reserves. In August she started her career as a troop-ship under the management of Cunard White Star. On 11 April 1946 she was returned to the French Government and continued as a troop transport under the management of her owners. In July 1956 she was laid up at Brest and awarded the 'Croix de Guerre' for her war services, before being promptly sold to the Germans. In September 1958 she was sold to North German Lloyd and in January 1958 rebuilding

BREMEN
(formerly PASTEUR)
29,250 tons
697 x 88 feet
Cie Sudatlantique

started at Bremen. When completed in 1959 she looked very different and on 9 July 1959 made her first voyage as the BREMEN for her new owners from Bremerhaven to New York. In 1971 she was sold to International Cruises SA, Dimitri Chandris of Piraeus, and in January 1972 she was delivered to her new owners who named her the REGINA MAGNA and used her for cruising. In October 1974 she was laid up. In 1977 she was taken over as an accommodation ship at Jeddah for workers from the Philippines and renamed SAUDIPHIL I. In

1980 she was lost at sea while being towed for breaking up in the Far East.

Probably the most famous and certainly the largest ship in the world was the QUEEN ELIZABETH built for Cunard White Star by John Brown of Clydebank in 1940. She was 83,650 tons and 1,029 × 118 feet, with Parsons geared turbines driving quadruple screws. Her accommodation was for 823 First, 662 Cabin and 789 Tourist Class passengers. On 2 March 1940 the nearly completed QUEEN ELIZABETH slipped out of the

QUEEN ELIZABETH
83,650 tons
1,029 × 118 feet
Cunard
1940

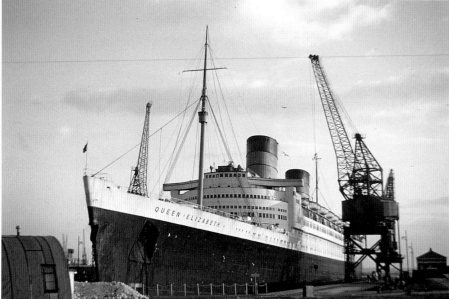

QUEEN ELIZABETH
at Southampton and on
the open seas (right)

QUEEN ELIZABETH
at Southampton Docks

AMERICA
26,450 tons
723 x 93 feet
United States Line
1940

AMERICA after
her refit as the
AUSTRALIS
1965

Clyde ostensibly to go to Southampton, but in fact she arrived in New York on 7 March to join the MAURETANIA and the QUEEN MARY. She subsequently also sailed to Sydney to be fitted out as a troop-ship. In March 1946 the QUEEN ELIZABETH was the first Cunarder to be released from government service and, after refitting as a passenger ship, she sailed from Southampton on 16 October 1946 on her maiden voyage to New York. She plied the Atlantic until 1968 when she was sold to the Elizabeth Corporation at Everglades where it was planned to use her as a convention centre and tourist attraction. The following year she officially changed owners to another Everglades company, Queen Limited, and the QUEEN ELIZABETH became plain ELIZABETH. In 1970 Queen Limited went bankrupt and ELIZABETH was sold by auction to a Chinese ship owner from Hong Kong. The ship was moved to Hong Kong in February 1971 and her registered owner was Seawise Foundation Limited who renamed her the SEAWISE UNIVERSITY with the intention that she should be a floating university and educational cruise ship. However, in January 1971, a fire broke out while she was being converted which spread to the whole ship and she heeled over and sank.

Two years later she was broken up. An ignominious end to the greatest ship the world has ever known.

The United States Line was another company caught with a not quite completed ship when the Second World War started. The steamship AMERICA was being built by the Newport News Ship Building & Dry Dock Corporation. It had been intended to use her on the North Atlantic but this was to be delayed. AMERICA was 26,450 tons and 723 × 93 feet, with Parsons geared turbines driving twin screws. Accommodation was for 543 Cabin, 418 Tourist and 241 Third Class passengers. On 10 August 1941 she started cruising between New York and the West Indies, but in 1941 she was taken over by the US Navy for troop transport duties and renamed the WESTPOINT. In July 1946 she was returned to her owners who had her overhauled and restored with her original name AMERICA. On 14 November 1946 she left New York for Le Havre, her first commercial transatlantic voyage. In 1964 she was sold to D. & A. Chandris of Piraeus who renamed her the AUSTRALIS. After a refit as a one-class ship for 2,300 passengers, she sailed in August 1965 from Piraeus to Sydney and two months later did a round the world voyage.

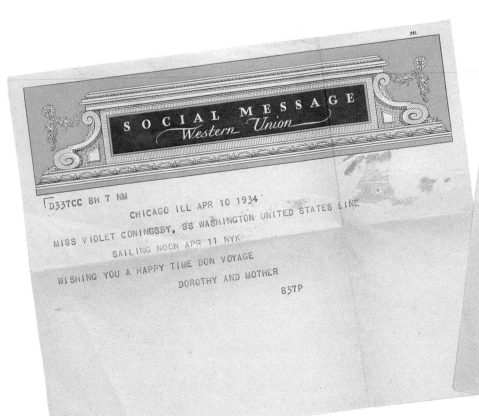

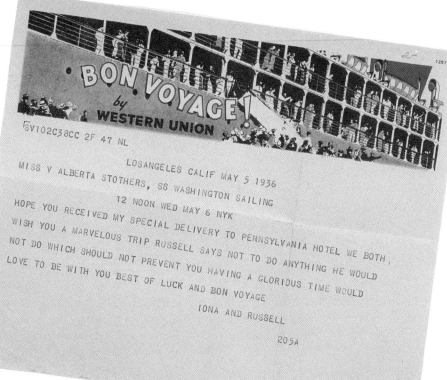

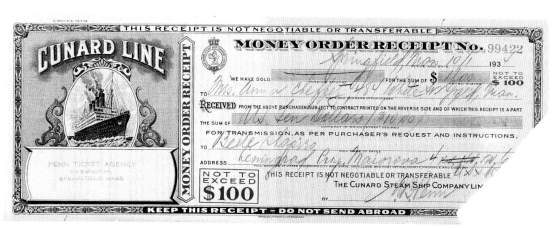

Four items of
1930s ephemera

Page 175
19 matchbox tops
produced by the various
shipping lines

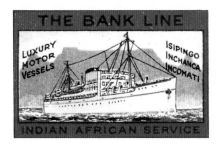

CHAPTER 11

Post-War 1947–1950

SHAW SAVILL
LINE

Official Card
of
Race Meeting
to be held on

SATURDAY, 2ND. AUGUST, 1947

FIRST RACE AT 6.30 P.M.

- - - -

JUDGE: SIR H.TWYFORD, KBE.

STARTER: MR. F.HANNAFORD

TOTE OFFICIAL: MR.R.OLIVER

STEWARDS:

MR. R. CUNNINGHAM
MR. V.HOPKIRK

R.M.S. "CORINTHIC"

Shaw Savill
race card

As might be expected during a time of world war, no major steamships were built between 1941 and 1946. The Shaw, Savill & Albion Line had one of the first steamships built after the Second World War. The CORINTHIC was built by Cammell Laird of Birkenhead and was 15,700 tons and 560 × 71 feet, with geared turbines driving twin screws. She had accommodation for 85 First Class passengers only and left Liverpool on 12 April 1947 for her maiden voyage to Sydney before beginning on the London to New Zealand service. In 1965 her passenger accommodation was removed so that she carried cargo only. She was broken up in October 1969.

The PRESIDENT OF CLEVELAND was built by the Bethlehem Alameda Shipyard for the American President Lines of San Francisco. She was 15,350 tons and 609 × 76 feet with a turbo-electric power unit driving twin screws. She had accommodation for 324 First and 454 Tourist Class passengers. On 15 December 1947 she left San Francisco on her maiden voyage to Hong Kong. In January 1973 she was laid up before being sold to a Hong Kong shipping company who registered her as owned by Oceanic Cruises Development and renamed her the ORIENTAL PRESIDENT. It would appear that this venture was not a success as in June 1974 she was broken up.

The first post-war Cunard White Star liner was the MEDIA. Built by John Brown of Clydebank she was 13,350 tons and 531 × 70 feet with geared turbines driving twin screws. She had accommodation for 250 First Class passengers. She sailed from Liverpool on 20 April 1947 on her maiden voyage to New York and continued on this service until October 1961 when she was sold to the Cogedar Line of Genoa who renamed her the FLAVIA. She was rebuilt, her outward appearance modernised and her passenger accommodation altered to 1,224 in one class for the emigrant trade.

CORINTHIC
15,700 tons
560 × 71 feet
Shaw, Savill & Albion Line
1947

In September 1962 she made her first voyage from Genoa to Sydney. In 1963 she started making round the world voyages from Rotterdam, via Panama, New Zealand, Australia, Suez, Mediterranean and back to Rotterdam. In 1968 she started cruising and the following year she was sold to Costa Armatori of Genoa and operated cruises from Miami, USA. In 1982 she was sold to Flavian Shipping of Panama and renamed the FLAVIAN. She was later laid up in Hong Kong.

The ARGENTINA STAR was built by Cammell Laird of Birkenhead for the Blue Star Line. She was 10,700 tons and 503 × 68 feet with Parsons geared turbines driving a single screw. She carried 51 First Class passengers only. On 14 June 1947 she sailed from London on her maiden voyage to Buenos Aires and sailed on this route until October 1972 when she was broken up. Her sister ship, the BRASIL STAR was also scrapped in 1972.

The steamer PATRIA was built by John Brown of Clydebank for Cia Colonial of Lisbon. She was 13,200 tons and 531 feet x 68 feet with Parsons geared turbines driving twin screws. She had accommodation for 114 First Class, 156 Tourist and 320 Third Class passengers. She sailed from Lisbon in January 1948 on her maiden voyage to Cape Town and Mozambique (Portuguese East Africa). In August 1973 she was broken up.

1948 saw the introduction of the first post-war liners for the Union Castle Line. Both were built by Harland & Wolff and were identical sister ships – the PRETORIA CASTLE and the EDINBURGH CASTLE. They were 28,700 tons and 747 × 84 feet, with geared turbines driving twin screws. Accommodation was for 214 First and 541 Tourist Class passengers. The PRETORIA CASTLE left Southampton in July 1948 on her maiden voyage to Cape Town and Durban. The EDINBURGH CASTLE made her maiden voyage in December 1948. In February 1966 the PRETORIA CASTLE was sold to the South African Maritime Corporation and renamed SA ORANJE although her sailings remained the same. In 1975 she was sold to shipbreakers. The EDINBURGH CASTLE remained with Union Castle until the end when she too was sold to ship-breakers in 1976.

EDINBURGH CASTLE
28,700 tons
747 x 84 feet
Union Castle Line
1948

The next line to register their first post-war liner was the Orient Line with the ORCADES being built by Vickers-Armstrong of Barrow-in-Furness. She was 28,150 tons and 670 × 91 feet with geared turbines driving twin screws. She had accommodation for 733 First and 772 Tourist Class passengers. She sailed from London on 14 December 1948 for her maiden voyage to Sydney and made the voyage in 26 days – ten days

PRETORIA CASTLE
28,700 tons
747 × 84 feet
Union Castle Line
1948

S A ORANJE
(formerly PRETORIA CASTLE)
South African Maritime Corporation
1966

ORCADES
28,150 tons
670 × 91 feet
Orient Line
1948

GOTHIC
15,900 tons
561 × 782 feet
Shaw, Savill & Albion

quicker than the pre-war time. In August 1955 she started sailing round the world – London, Panama, Australia, Suez, London. At the time of a refit she became a one-class ship with accommodation for 1,635 passengers. In October 1972 she was laid up at Southampton and sold for breaking up in 1973. A sister ship the ORONSAY was delivered in 1951.

Shaw, Savill & Albion had the fourth of four sister ships delivered in 1948. She was the GOTHIC, built by Wigham Richardson of Newcastle-upon-Tyne and was 15,900 tons and 561 feet × 72 feet with geared turbines driving twin screws. Accommodation was provided for 85 First Class passengers. The GOTHIC sailed from Liverpool on 23 December 1948 for her maiden voyage to Sydney, after which she entered the London to New Zealand service. In 1951 she was sent to Cammell Laird at Birkenhead to be refitted as the Royal Yacht for a royal visit to Australia and New Zealand, which did not take place because of the death of King George VI. In 1953 she was again fitted out to act as the Royal Yacht and was used by Queen Elizabeth II and the Duke of Edinburgh on their visit to Australia and New Zealand in September and October 1953. In 1968 she was damaged by fire and a temporary repair was carried out in Wellington. She made one more trip to New Zealand after her return to the United Kingdom and was then sold to ship breakers.

In 1949 and 1950 the Blue Funnel Line added eight very similar new ships of around 10,100 tons to their fleet. The HELENUS was built by Harland & Wolff of Belfast and was 10,150 tons and 522 × 69 feet with

geared turbines driving a single screw. She had accommodation for 29 First Class passengers only. The HELENUS left Liverpool on 14 November 1949 for her maiden voyage to Brisbane. After 1964 she and her three sister ships serving the Australian route carried cargo only, and these four, the HELENUS, the JASON, the HECTOR and the IXION were broken up in 1972. The other four in the group, the PELUS, the PATROCHUS, the PERSEUS and the PYPHRUS all sailed on the Far East service to Japan, and they too were broken up in 1972 and early 1973.

The Cunard White Star Line had one new ship in 1949. This was the fine-looking CARONIA which was

HELENUS
10,150 tons
522 × 69 feet
Blue Funnel Line
1949

Matchbox cover

IXION
10,150 tons
522 × 69 feet
Blue Funnel Line
1950

PERSEUS
10,109 tons
516 × 68 feet
Blue Funnel Line
1950

CARONIA
34,200 tons
715 x 91 feet
Cunard White Star
1949

built by John Brown of Clydebank. She was 34,200 tons and 715 feet x 91 feet, with geared turbines driving twin screws. She had accommodation for 581 First and 351 Cabin Class passengers. She sailed from Southampton on 4 January 1949 on her maiden voyage to New York. She was designed as a dual-purpose vessel, either for North Atlantic service or cruising. On one of her world cruises she had trouble entering Yokohama on 14 April 1958 and damaged her bow. In May 1968 she was sold to the Universal Line SA of Panama and handed to her new owners who renamed her the COLUMBIA. A few months later her name was changed again to the CARABIA and she was used for cruising until she was laid up in New York in March 1969. Nearly five years later she was broken up.

The MAGDALENA was both the first ship built for the Royal Mail Line after the Second World War and their last steamship. She came from Harland & Wolff and was 17,550 tons and 570 feet × 73 feet with geared

LIBERTAD
(formerly
17 DE OCTOBRE)
12,650 tons
530 × 71 feet
Cia Argentina de
Nav Dodero
1950

turbines driving twin screws. Her accommodation was for 133 First and 346 Third Class passengers. She left London on 9 March 1949 on her maiden voyage to Buenos Aires. On 25 April on her homeward voyage she ran into trouble off Rio de Janeiro and broke in two while being salvaged.

In 1950 Vickers-Armstrong built three ships for Cia Argentina de Nav Dodero of Buenos Aires. The third of these was 17 DE OCTOBRE. She was 12,650 tons and 530 feet x 71 feet with geared turbines driving twin screws. She had accommodation for 96 First Class passengers. She left London in October 1950 on her maiden voyage to Buenos Aires. Later she ran from Hamburg. In 1955 she was renamed LIBERTAD following the fall of President Peron. In 1962 she was refitted to carry 400 Tourist Class passengers. She was laid up in 1974 and sold to ship-breakers a year later.

The second large ship built for P & O after the Second World War was the CHUSAN from the yard of Vickers-Armstrong. She was 24,200 tons and 673 feet × 84 feet with geared turbines driving twin screws. She had accommodation for 475 First and 551 Tourist Class passengers. She was the first steamship to be fitted with Denny-Brown stabilising fins from new. The CHUSAN left Southampton on 1 July 1950 for her maiden voyage which was a cruise. Her first scheduled voyage was from London which she left on 15 September 1950 for Bombay. For all subsequent voyages she worked through from Bombay to Japan. From 1960 onwards her voyages continued to the USA and sometimes round-the-world. In 1973 she was sold to shipbreakers.

CHUSAN
24,200 tons
673 x 84 feet
P & O
1950

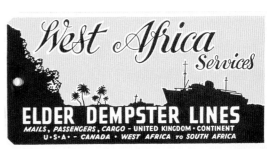

11 post-war luggage labels

10 post-war luggage labels

CHAPTER 12

Let's go on a Cruise 1951–1960

In 1951, Furness, Withy & Co. took delivery of the last steam liner built for them by Vickers-Armstrong. The OCEAN MONARCH was 13,650 tons and 516 × 72 feet with Parsons geared turbines driving twin screws. She had accommodation for 414 First Class passengers. On 18 April 1951 she left London for her maiden voyage to New York and early the next month started regular duties from New York to Bermuda. In 1966 she was laid up in the United Kingdom and sold in August the following year to Balkanturist of Varna, who renamed her the VARNA and used her for cruising. In 1971 she was laid up until sold in 1979 to Dolphin (Hellas) Shipping SA and renamed the RIVIERA. During a refit she was renamed again as the REINA DEL MAR. However, before this work was complete, she caught fire and was towed out to sea and sank.

One of the largest liners built for a USA shipping company, the INDEPENDENCE was built by the Bethlehem Steel Company of Quincy for the Export Lines of New York. She was 23,700 tons and 682 feet x 89 feet with geared turbines driving twin screws. Her accommodation was for 295 First, 375 Cabin and 330 Tourist Class passengers. Her maiden voyage was a cruise and she sailed from New York on 11 February 1951 for the Mediterranean. On her return she started sailing from New York to Genoa and later to Naples. In 1959 she had a refit which provided extra First Class accommodation. In 1968 she was chartered by an American travel agency who used the INDEPENDENCE as a cruising 'fun ship'. She was laid up in 1969 until sold to Atlantic Far East Lines of Monrovia who renamed her the OCEANIC INDEPENDENCE and used her as a one-class cruising liner. In 1976 she was laid up in Hong Kong. In 1979 she was sold to American Hawaiian Cruise Inc., repaired and refitted and in 1980 was cruising in Hawaiian waters. In 1982 she was sold to American Global Line Inc., returning to her old name of INDEPENDENCE, but still being used for cruising.

The Holland-America Line took delivery of a new liner the RYNDAM in 1951 from her builders Wilton-Fijenoord of Schiedam in the Netherlands. She was 15,000 tons and 502 × 69 feet, with geared turbines driving a single screw. Her accommodation was for 39 First and 854 Tourist Class passengers. She sailed from Rotterdam on 16 July 1951 on her maiden voyage to New York. In 1966 she started working from Bremerhaven to New York and two years later she came under the wing of a Holland-America subsidiary

OCEAN MONARCH
13,650 tons
516 x 72 feet
Furness, Withy & Co.
1951

INDEPENDENCE
23,700 tons
682 x 89 feet
Export Lines
1951

and was renamed the WATERMAN. Five months later she was back with the parent company under her old name and was put to work again on the North Atlantic. She was laid up at Schiedam in 1971 and the following year sold to a Pan-American company, World Wide Cruises. After being rebuilt in Greece she started Mediterranean cruising in May 1973. In 1981 she was sold to the Hellenic company and renamed the ATLAS.

In 1951-52 the Union Castle Line had three new steamers built by Harland & Wolff. The first one was RHODESIA CASTLE and was 17,050 tons and 576 × 74 feet, with geared turbines driving twin screws. She had accommodation for 526 Cabin Class passengers. In November 1951 she left London on her maiden voyage and thereafter operated a 'round Africa service'. In May 1967 she was laid up in England and sold to ship-breakers four months later. The other two were the KENYA CASTLE and the BRAEMER CASTLE.

The French ship owners SGTM had two new ships in 1951-52. The second one the BRETAGNE was built by Penhoët and was 16,350 tons and 581 × 73 feet, with Parsons geared turbines driving twin screws. Her accommodation was for 149 First, 167 Tourist, 606 Third Class in cabins and 368 Third Class in dormitories. She made her maiden voyage from Marseilles to Buenos Aires on 14 February 1952. In November 1960 BRETAGNE was chartered for a trial period by D. & A. Chandris and her passenger accommodation was rearranged at Genoa to take 150 First Class and 1,050 Tourist Class. In May 1961 she left Piraeus for Sydney. In September, Chandris bought the BRETAGNE, re-registered her at Piraeus in the name of the Europe-Australia Line and she straight way made a first voyage

RHODESIA CASTLE
17,050 tons
576 x 74 feet
Union Castle Line
1951

for her new owners from Southampton to Brisbane and later to Sydney. Early in 1962 her name was changed to BRITTANY. In March 1963 she went to a Greek ship yard for engine overhauls, and after she had been there eleven days a fire broke out and she was destroyed. Her sister ship, the PROVENCE, was sold to Costa Armatori and renamed the ENRICO C, was used for cruising.

The British India Line had two ships built by Barclay, Curle & Co. of Glasgow – the KENYA in 1951 and her sister the UGANDA in 1952. UGANDA was 14,450 tons and 539 × 71 feet, with geared turbines driving twin screws. She had accommodation for 167 First and 133 Tourist Class passengers. She left London on 2 August 1952 on her maiden voyage to Beira in Mozambique and operated this service until 1967 when she was rebuilt in Germany as a scholars' educational cruise liner. At the end of February 1968 she set out on her first scholars' cruise with accommodation for 1,224

RYNDAM
15,000 tons
502 x 69 feet
Holland America Line
1951

UGANDA
14,450 tons
539 x 71 feet
British India Line
1952

children. In 1973 ships of the British India Line (which was a subsidiary of P & O) were transferred to the parent company. In 1982 at the time of the Falklands crisis the UGANDA was cruising in the Mediterranean with a full complement of children, when she was requisitioned by the British Government as a troop transport for the conflict. She was rapidly prepared for these duties and in a very short time joined the task force heading for the South Atlantic. Fortunately she was undamaged and on her return was put back to her scholastic duties, before being laid up in 1985 and sold to breakers the following year. Her sister ship, the KENYA, had an uneventful life and was sold for scrap in 1969.

In 1952 CGT of Le Havre had a new liner, the FLANDRE delivered by A et CH de France of Dunkirk. She was 20,450 tons and 600 × 80 feet, with geared turbines driving twin screws. She had accommodation for 402 First, 285 Second and 97 Tourist Class passengers. She sailed from Le Havre on 23 July 1952 on her maiden voyage to New York. On her return she was withdrawn from service until April 1953 because of mechanical and electrical faults. After these were rectified she returned to the North Atlantic. From 1962 onwards she was transferred to the Caribbean service and also used for cruising. In February 1968 she was sold to Costa Armatori of Genoa, renamed CARLA C and fitted out to take 750 passengers all in one class. In 1969 she started cruising from American waters. In June 1974, the CARLA C went to Amsterdam and had diesel engines fitted thereby becoming a motor vessel.

The FLANDRE's sister ship, the ANTILLES, sank in January 1971 after catching fire off the island of Mustique. The passengers were taken off by the QE2 and other ships.

The UNITED STATES was the fastest transatlantic

liner of all time, built by the Newport News Ship Building & Dry Dock Company for the United States Lines. She was 53,350 tons and 990 × 101 feet, with Westinghouse geared turbines driving quadruple screws. She had accommodation for 871 First, 508 Cabin and 549 Tourist Class passengers. When she was designed it was envisaged she should be a dual-purpose ship, namely either a magnificent floating hotel or a fast efficient troop ship that could carry 14,000 personnel. To this end the designers made great efforts to reduce weight as much as possible. The greater part of the superstructure was aluminium and wooden finishes were kept to a minimum. These efforts seem to have paid off for on 3 July 1952 the UNITED STATES left New York on her maiden voyage to Southampton and on this first trip beat the QUEEN MARY's 1938 record (of 3 days, 20 hours and 42 minutes) with a time of 3

OLYMPIA
23,000 tons
612 × 79 feet
Greek Line
1953

days, 10 hours and 40 minutes, an average speed of 35.59 knots. On her return voyage she took 3 days, 12 hours and 12 minutes or 34.51 knots. But alas, the aircraft was taking over! The UNITED STATES worked the Atlantic until 1969 when in November she was laid up. In 1973 she was bought by the US Maritime Administration, but was not put to sea.

In 1952 the Holland-America Line of Rotterdam took delivery of the MAASDAM built by Wilton-Fijenoord of Schiedam, her sister ship RYNDAM having been completed a year earlier. The MAASDAM was 15,000 tons and 502 × 69 feet, with geared turbines driving a single screw. She had accommodation for 39 First and 842 Tourist Class passengers. She sailed from Rotterdam on 11 August 1952 on her maiden voyage to New York. In February 1963 she was damaged on entering Bremerhaven and went to the North German

Lloyd repair yard. In April 1952 she made her first voyage from Bremerhaven to New York. In 1966 she was transferred to the Rotterdam to Montreal service. In 1968 she was sold to Polish Ocean Lines of Gdynia and renamed STEFAN BATORY. 11 April 1969 saw her first voyage from Gdynia to Montreal.

In 1953 Italia San, Genoa had the ANDREA DORIA built for them by Ansaldo, Sestri Ponente. She was 29,100 tons and 700 × 90 feet, with Parsons geared turbines driving twin screws. Accommodation was for 218 First, 320 Cabin and 703 Tourist Class passengers and the ANDREA DORIA was the largest Italian-built liner since the REX and the CONTE DI SAVOIA of 1931 and 1932. She sailed from Genoa on 14 January 1953 on her maiden voyage to New York. The ANDREA DORIA and her sister ship, the CHRISTOFORO COLUMBO, plied the Atlantic until 1956 when disaster struck the ANDREA DORIA. On 25 July she was rammed by the Swedish-American Line motorship STOCKHOLM 100 miles east of New York and so badly damaged that she sank 12 hours after the accident. She was rumoured carry great wealth in her First Class safe and in 1983 a diving expedition salvaged the safe, but unfortunately the only treasure was sea-sodden bank notes.

The Greek Line's OLYMPIA was built by Alexander Stephens of Glasgow. She was 23,000 tons and 612 × 79 feet, with Parsons geared turbines driving twin screws. She had accommodation for 138 First and 1,169 Tourist Class passengers. She sailed from Glasgow on 15 October 1953 on her maiden voyage to New York. A little over a month later she sailed again for New York but this time from Bremerhaven which was to be her normal European port until 1955, when she started sailing from New York to Piraeus. In 1961 she extended her service to Haifa.

Built by John Brown, the Cunard Liner SAXONIA

MAASDAM
15,000 tons
502 × 69 feet
Holland America Line
1952

ANDREA DORIA
29,100 tons
700 × 90 feet
Italia San
1953

SAXONIA
21,650 tons
597 × 80 feet
Cunard
1954

ARCADIA
29,750 tons
721 × 90 feet
P & O
1954

and her three sisters were the last new ships acquired by the company before the QUEEN ELIZABETH 2. She was 21,650 tons and 597 × 80 feet, with geared turbines driving twin screws. She had accommodation for 110 First and 819 Tourist Class passengers. She sailed from Liverpool in April 1954 on her maiden voyage to Montreal. In 1961 she switched to the Southampton to New York run. In 1963 she had a refit at John Brown and in April made her first voyage from Rotterdam to Montreal, while in the winter she began cruising from the USA. In 1967 she was only used for cruising. In October 1971 she was laid up and offered for sale, being bought in 1973 by Nikrels Maritime Corporation of Panama on behalf of the Soviet State Shipping Company who renamed her LEONID SOBINOV. In February 1974 she sailed from Southampton to Sydney and was then used for cruising from Australia in Far Eastern waters. The SAXONIA's three sister ships were the IVERNIA (later FRANCONIA), the CARINTHIA and the SYLVANIA. By 1974, the FRANCONIA (IVERNIA) had been sold to the Russians, and the CARINTHIA and the SYLVANIA to Fairland Shipping.

The ARCADIA was built for the P & O Line by John Brown. She was 29,750 tons and 721 × 90 feet, with geared turbines driving twin screws. Accommodation was for 675 First and 735 Tourist Class passengers. The ARCADIA sailed from London on 22 February 1954 on her maiden voyage to Sydney. In October 1959 she started sailing round the world, London–Sydney–Panama–London, interspersed with cruising. She was broken up in 1979.

A tourist cabin on the ARCADIA

Ivernia
(later Franconia)
21,650 tons
597 x 80 feet
Cunard
1954

Carinthia
21,650 tons
597 x 80 feet
Cunard
1954

Sylvania
21,650 tons
597 x 80 feet
Cunard
1954

SOUTHERN CROSS
20,000 tons
604 × 78 feet
Shaw, Savill & Albion
1955

The Pacific Navigation Company's REINA DEL MAR, built by Harland & Wolff, was 20,250 tons and 601 × 78 feet, with Parsons geared turbines driving twin screws. Accommodation was for 207 First, 216 Cabin and 343 Third Class passengers. On 3 May 1956 she sailed from Liverpool on her maiden voyage to Valparaiso (Chile) and she was, without doubt, the finest ship sailing to this destination. In 1963 she was chartered to the Travel Savings Association for Mediterranean cruising and in 1964 was rebuilt by Harland & Wolff for cruising with accommodation for 1,042 passengers all in one class. She continued to sail for the Travel Savings Association under the management of the Union Castle Line and was painted in Union Castle colours. From the end of 1964 she was used exclusively for cruising from Southampton and from Cape Town in winter (their summer). In September 1973 she was sold to the Union Castle Line but two years later was again sold this time to a ship-breaker.

In 1955, the SOUTHERN CROSS, built by Harland & Wolff for Shaw, Savill & Albion, was a revolutionary vessel in outward appearance for a passenger liner. She was 20,200 tons and 604 × 78 feet, with geared turbines driving twin screws. She had accommodation for 1,160 passengers all in one class. She was also unusual in that she carried no cargo and was built for a round-the-world service. She sailed from Southampton on 29 March 1955 on her maiden round-the-world voyage. In June 1971 she cruised from Liverpool and in November was laid up. In January 1973 she was sold to Cia de Vap Cerulea Sa, Ithaka, Greece and renamed the CALYPSO. In 1980 she was sold to the Eastern Steamship Lines Inc. and renamed AZURE SEAS.

The last pair of Canadian Pacific 'Empresses' were the EMPRESS OF BRITAIN and the EMPRESS OF ENGLAND delivered in 1956 and 1957. The EMPRESS OF BRITAIN, built by Fairfield Engineering, was 25,500 tons and 640 × 85 feet, with geared turbines driving twin screws. She had accommodation for 160 First and 894 Tourist Class passengers. She sailed from Liverpool on 20 April 1956 on her maiden voyage to Montreal. Early in 1964 she was sold to the Transoceanic Navigation Corporation (Greek Line) but not handed over until the later part of the year, when she was renamed the QUEEN ANNA MARIA. She had a refit at Genoa

REINA DEL MAR
20,250 tons
601 × 78 feet
Pacific Navigation Co.
1956

EMPRESS OF BRITAIN
25,500 tons
640 × 85 feet
CPR
1956

OXFORDSHIRE
20,600 tons
613 × 78 feet
Bibby Line
1927

STATENDAM
24,300 tons
642 × 81 feet
Holland-America Line
1957

and in March 1965 started sailing between Haifa and New York as well as doing some cruising. In January 1975 she was laid up at Piraeus until December when she was sold to Carnival Cruise Lines of Panama and renamed the CARNIVAL, before being put to work cruising in the Caribbean in the following year. The EMPRESS OF ENGLAND, built by Vickers-Armstrong of Newcastle-upon-Tyne, did similar duties to her sister. In February 1970, she was sold to Shaw, Savill & Albion and renamed the OCEAN MONARCH, making one trip to Australia before being refitted for cruising. In October 1971 she started her cruising life in the Mediterranean, but four years later, in July 1975, she was sold to ship-breakers.

In 1957 the Bibby Line took delivery of a new steamer the OXFORDSHIRE, which had been built by Fairfield Engineering and partly paid for by the British Ministry of Transport. She was 20,600 tons and 613 × 78 feet with Parsons geared turbines driving twin screws. She had accommodation for 220 First, 100 Second and 180 Third Class passengers, plus 1,000 troops. Until 1962 she sailed between the United Kingdom and various Commonwealth countries under government contract. In 1963 the Bibby Line chartered OXFORDSHIRE to the Fairline Shipping Corporation for six years and in May she was sent to Wilton-Fijenoord for a refit. The following March she was purchased by Fairline, renamed the FAIRSTAR and moved to Southampton for completion of the refit, which gave her accommodation for 1,870 passengers. After a first voyage from Southampton to Brisbane in

May 1964 she continued on this service until August 1973 when she commenced cruising only from Sydney.

In the same year, the Holland-America Line took delivery of a new steamer the STATENDAM built by Wilton-Fijenoord. She was 24,300 tons and 642 × 81 feet, with Parsons geared turbines driving twin screws. She had accommodation for 84 First and 867 Tourist Class passengers. She was not named until she made her delivery voyage in 1957. She sailed from Rotterdam on 6 February 1957 on her maiden voyage to New York via Southampton and Le Havre. From 1966 onwards she was used almost entirely for cruising. In 1982 she was sold to a Panamanian company and renamed the RHAPSODY.

In 1958 the Grace Line of New York took delivery of the sister ships SANTA ROSA and SANTA PAULA. Both were built by the Newport News Ship Building & Dry Dock Company and were 15,350 tons and 584 × 84 feet, with geared turbines driving twin screws. Accommodation was for 300 First Class passengers. Both ships were used on the New York to Central America service. In 1959 the SANTA ROSA was involved in an accident and needed major repairs to the front end before resuming service. After being laid up between 1971 and 1976 she was sold to the Vintero Corporation of New York, used on their South American service and renamed the SAMOS SKY. The SANTA PAULA was sold in 1972 to the Oceanic Sun Line of Piraeus and renamed the STEELA POLARIS. In 1976 she began conversion to a hotel ship and moved to Al Kuwayt (Kuwait), opening in 1980 as the Kuwait Mariott Hotel.

SANTA ROSA
15,350 tons
584 × 84 feet
Grace Line
1958

SANTA PAULA
15,350 tons
584 × 84 feet
Grace Line
1958

A pair of ships were built by Ingalls of Pascagoula (Mississippi) for Moore-McCormack of New York – the the ARGENTINA and the BRASIL. Delivered in 1958, both were 15,000 tons and 617 × 86 feet, with geared turbines driving twin screws. They provided accommodation for 553 First Class passengers and sailed between New York and Buenos Aires. The BRASIL started her maiden voyage on 12 September 1958 and ARGENTINA on 12 December 1958. In 1972 both ships were acquired by the Holland-America Line and rebuilt at Bremerhaven. The BRASIL became VOLENDAM and the ARGENTINA became VEENDAM.

From then on their histories diverged. The VOLENDAM (BRASIL) was chartered in August 1975 to Monarch Cruises and was renamed the MONARCH SUN. In 1977 she was transferred to Volendam NV of

ARGENTINA
15,000 tons
617 × 86 feet
Moore-McCormack
1958

Panama and returned to the name VOLENDAM. In 1983 she was sold to Banstead Shipping of Panama and the following year her name was changed yet again to ISLAND SUN for continued cruising duties. In 1985 she was sold to American-Hawaiian Cruises and having been renamed yet again as the LIBERTE, she was used for cruising in the Pacific. Meanwhile, the VEENDAM (ARGENTINA) began service in 1973 between Rotterdam and New York. For most of 1974 she was laid-up until chartered by Agencia Maritima of Rio de Janeiro and renamed BRASIL (the old name of her sister ship). When the charter ended in 1985 she returned to the name VEENDAM. In 1976 she was sold to Monarch Cruises and renamed the MONARCH STAR until in 1978 she was again owned by the Holland-America Line and rechristened the VEENDAM. She continued cruising until 1983 when she was sold as a cruise liner to the Billinghurst Shipping Company of Panama and continued cruising under still yet another name, the BERMUDA STAR.

Between 1959 and 1961, the Union Castle Line took delivery of three new steamers, the PENDENNIS CASTLE, the WINDSOR CASTLE and the TRANSVAAL CASTLE. The first was the PENDENNIS CASTLE which was built by Harland & Wolff. She was 28,600 tons and 763 × 83 feet with Parsons geared turbines driving twin screws. Her accommodation was for 197 First and 473 Tourist Class passengers. She sailed from Southampton on 1 January 1959 on her maiden voyage to Durban, and ran on this route until she was sold in August 1976 to the Ocean Queen Navigation Corporation of Panama and renamed the OCEAN QUEEN. She was laid up in

PENDENNIS CASTLE
28,600 tons
763 × 83 feet
Union Castle Line
1959

ROTTERDAM
38,650 tons
748 × 94 feet
Holland America Line
1959

the Far East until being sold in 1977 to another Panamanian owner and renamed the SINBAD. Again she was not used and was broken up in 1980.

The Holland-America Line's the ROTTERDAM delivered in 1959 and built by Rotterdamsche DD MIJ was considerably larger than the vessels added to their fleet in 1957. She was 38,650 tons and 748 × 94 feet, with Parsons geared turbines driving twin screws. She had accommodation for 665 First and 801 Tourist Class passengers. She was unusual in appearance in that she had twin exhaust pipes instead of funnels, an idea later followed by other builders. She sailed from Rotterdam on 3 September 1959 on her maiden voyage to New York. After 1969 she was only used for cruising.

The LEONARDO DA VINCI was built in 1960 by

Ansaldo, Sestri Ponente for Italia San of Genoa. She was 33,350 tons and 767 × 92 feet, with Parsons geared turbines driving twin screws. She had accommodation for 413 First, 342 Cabin and 561 Tourist Class passengers. She sailed from Genoa on 30 June 1960 on her maiden voyage to New York. In 1965 she started using Naples as her home port, and later did some cruising. In 1972 she was transferred to Italia Crociere Internationali and used for further cruising. She was laid up in 1978 and two years later caught fire at her berth and sank. She was raised and scrapped in 1982.

The Union Castle Line WINDSOR CASTLE was built by Cammell Laird of Birkenhead. She was 37,450 tons and 783 × 93 feet, with Parsons geared turbines driving twin screws. She had accommodation for 191

LEONARDO DA VINCI
33,350 tons
767 × 92 feet
Italia San
1960

WINDSOR CASTLE
37,450 tons
783 × 93 feet
Union Castle Line
1960

First and 591 Tourist Class passengers. She sailed from Southampton on 18 August 1960 on her maiden voyage to Cape Town and Durban, and continued in this service until she was withdrawn in September 1977. She was sold in the same year to the Margarita Shipping and Trading Company of Panama and renamed the MARGARITA L. In 1979 she was moored at Jeddah as a floating hotel.

In 1960 the P & O-Orient Line took delivery from Vickers-Armstrong of the ORIANA, a vessel of 41,915 tons and 804 × 97 feet, which had Parsons geared turbines driving twin screws. She had accommodation for 638 First Class and 1,496 Tourist Class passengers. She sailed on 3 December 1960 on her maiden voyage from Southampton to Sydney returning via New Zealand, the West Coast of America and back home through the Panama Canal. From 1973 onwards she was employed purely as a cruise vessel until being sold in 1986 to a Japanese company who towed her to Japan for use as a static tourist attraction.

A year later P & O-Orient took delivery of the CANBERRA, from Harland & Woolf. She was 45,270 tons and 820 × 102 feet, with a turbo-electric power unit driving twin screws. She had accommodation for 548 First Class and 1,650 Tourist Class passengers. On 2 June 1961 she sailed on a similar trans-globe maiden voyage to the ORIANA. Also like the ORIANA from

CANBERRA matchbox

Deck games on the
CANBERRA

1973 onwards she was employed cruising. In 1982 the CANBERRA was requisitioned by the British Government to act as a troop ship during the Falklands conflict, where she was fortunate to escape damage, although engaged in the main troop landings. After this episode she had a refit at government expense and returned to her normal cruising.

ORIANA
41,915 tons
804 x 97 feet
P & O Orient
1960

CANBERRA
45,270 tons
820 x 102 feet
P & O–Orient

CHAPTER 13

The Decline of Steam 1961–1970

The 1960s were to see the end of the steam era and many fewer ships were built in this period. Two notable exceptions to the general decline were the mighty FRANCE and the QUEEN ELIZABETH 2.

The last 'Empress' steamer was built for Canadian Pacific by Vickers-Armstrong in 1961. The EMPRESS OF CANADA was slightly larger than the two ships built in 1956 and 1957 and was 27,300 tons and 650 × 87 feet, with Parsons geared turbines driving twin screws. She had accommodation for 192 First and 856 Tourist Class passengers. On 24 March 1961 she sailed from Liverpool on her maiden voyage to Montreal, remaining on the North Atlantic until sold in January 1972 to Carnival Cruise Line Incorporated of Panama. She was renamed MARDI GRAS and sent on her first cruise to Miami in February 1972.

In 1961 an experimental ship was completed for the States Marine Lines by the New York Ship Building Company at Camden. Her name was SAVANNAH, after the first steam vessel to conquer the North Atlantic, and she was the first civilian passenger liner to be nuclear-powered. She was 13,600 tons and 595 × 78 feet with geared turbines driving a single screw. She had accommodation for 60 passengers in one class, but so far has carried no 'fare-paying passengers'. Her maiden voyage was from Yorktown, Va to Savannah, after which she was used for experimental voyages and demonstrations. In 1964 she sailed between the USA and the Mediterranean. In 1965 she was taken over by

Atomic Ship Transport Incorporated and continued sailing to the Mediterranean without passengers. In January 1972 she was laid up at Savannah and in 1981 was opened as a museum ship in Charleston, USA.

The last of the three Union Castle Line 'Castles' built between 1959–61 was the TRANSVAAL CASTLE. Built by John Brown, she was 32,700 tons and 760 × 90 feet with Parsons geared turbines driving twin screws. She had accommodation for 728 passengers, all in one class. She sailed from Southampton on 18 January 1962 on her maiden voyage to Durban. In January 1966 she was transferred to the South African Marine Corporation and renamed SA VAAL. However, she continued on the same service and under the same management until she was withdrawn in October 1977. She was sold to the Carnival Cruise Line of Panama and under the name FESTIVALE was used for cruising.

Shaw, Savill and Albion's the NORTHERN STAR was built by Vickers-Armstrong at Southampton. She was 24,750 tons and 650 × 84 feet with Parsons geared turbines driving twin screws. She had accommodation for 1,412 Tourist Class passengers. She sailed from Southampton on 10 July 1962 for a maiden round-the-world voyage and continued in such service until sold at the end of 1974 to ship-breakers.

CGT's last big liner was the FRANCE built by Penhoët at St. Nazaire. She was 66,350 tons and was 1,035 × 110 feet with Parsons geared turbines driving quadruple screws. She had accommodation for 407

EMPRESS OF CANADA
27,300 tons
650 × 87 feet
CPR
1961

SAVANNAH
13,600 tons
595 × 78 feet
States Marine Lines
1961

VAAL
(formerly TRANSVAAL
CASTLE of the Union
Castle Line)
32,700 tons
760 × 90 feet
South American Marine
Corporation
1962

FRANCE
66,350 tons
1,035 × 110 feet
CGT
1962

First and 1,637 Tourist Class passengers. Before her maiden voyage she made a trial cruise from Le Havre to the Canary Islands. On her return she again sailed from Le Havre on her maiden voyage proper on 3 February 1962 to New York. In October 1974 after certain trade union trouble because of withdrawn government subsidies the FRANCE was laid up at Le Havre. In 1979 she was purchased by Kloster of Sweden and sent to Bremerhaven for rebuilding. She was renamed the NORWAY and, when completed in 1980 she was used for cruising from America. In 1982 her steam turbines were replaced at Bremerhaven by diesel engines. At that time she was the largest passenger ship afloat.

The Italian Line Lloyd Triestino of Genoa took delivery of two steamships, the GALILEO GALILIE and the GUGLIELMO MARCONI from CR dell Adriatico. Both ships were 27,900 tons and 702 × 94 feet, with de Laval geared turbines driving twin screws. They had accommodation for 156 First Class and 1,594 Tourist Class passengers and were used on the Genoa to Sydney service until 1976 when they started sailing to South America. Both were sold in 1983; the GUGLIELMO MARCONI to Costa Armatori of Genoa, who refitted her, renamed her the COSTA RIVIERA and used her for cruising the Caribbean from the end of 1985. The GALILEO GALILIE was bought by Chandris and was

NORTHERN STAR
24,750 tons
650 × 84 feet
Shaw, Savill & Albion
1962

GLIELMO MARCONI
GUIGLIELMO MARCONI
27,900 tons
702 × 94 feet
Italian Lloyd
1963

SANTA MARIA
14,450 tons
549 × 79 feet
Grace Lines
1963–4

became the Prudential-Grace Line. In 1980, the SANTA MARIANA was sold to the Delta Steamship Line Inc, who two years later bought both the other three ships. In 1985 the SANTA MARIANA, SANTA MAGDALENA and the SANTA MARIA were transferred to other American companies while the SANTA MERCEDES had been sold to the United States Marine Commission in 1984 as a training ship under the name PATRIOT STATE.

also refitted for Caribbean cruising under the shortened name of GALILEO.

In 1963–64 Grace Lines of New York took delivery of four container ships which had limited passenger accommodation. These were the SANTA MAGDALENA, SANTA MARIANA, SANTA MARIA and the SANTA MERCEDES. All four were 14,450 tons and 549 × 79 feet. They were built by the Bethlehem Ship Building Corporation of Sparrow's Point and had geared turbines from General Electric driving a single screw. They had accommodation for 127 First Class passengers. All four were employed on the West Coast of America to Buenos Aires route via the Panama Canal.

All four 'Santas' were taken over in the amalgamation whereby Grace Lines and the Prudential Line

In 1964 Zim Israel Navigation of Haifa book delivery of the turbine steamer SHALOM built by Penhoët. She was 25,338 tons and 629 × 81 feet, with Parsons geared turbines driving twin screws. She had accommodation for 72 First Class and 1,018 Tourist Class passengers. She sailed from Haifa on 17 April 1964 on her maiden voyage to New York. In November 1964 she was in collision with a tanker off New York. In May 1967 she was sold to the Genoa Atlantic Lines and renamed the HANSEATIC. She made her first voyage for her new owners in December 1967 from Hamburg to New York. From 1969 onwards she was only used for cruising until she was sold to Home Lines of Panama in 1973. She was renamed the DORIC and continued as a cruise liner. In 1981 she was sold to Lido Maritime Inc. and under the new name of ROYAL ODYSSEY was used for cruising.

Italia San of Genoa had two almost identical ships completed in 1965. They were the MICHELANGELO built by Ansaldo, Sestri Ponente and the RAFFAELLO built by CR dell'Adriatico at Trieste. Both ships were 45,900 tons and 906 feet x 99 feet, with geared turbines driving twin screws. Accommodation was provided for

SHALOM
25,338 tons
629 × 81 feet
Zim Israel Navigation
1964

MICHELANGELO
45,900 tons
906 × 99 feet
Italia San
1965

RAFFAELLO
45,900 tons
906 × 99 feet
Italia San
1965

OCEANIC
27,650 tons
782 × 96 feet
Home Lines
1965

EUGENIO C
30,550 tons
713 × 96 feet
Costa Armatori
1966

690 Tourist Class passengers. The MICHELANGELO left Genoa on 12 May 1965 on her maiden voyage to New York. Just short of a year later she was badly damaged in an Atlantic storm. From 1974 she was used for cruising and a year later laid up at Genoa. In December 1976 she was sold to the Government of Iran for use as an accommodation ship.

The RAFFAELLO left Genoa on 25 July 1965 on her maiden voyage to New York. After 1974 she was used for cruising and in April 1975 she left New York for the last time. In June she was laid up at La Spezia and in December 1976 she was also sold to the Government of Iran for use as an accommodation ship. She was damaged in the Iran–Iraq war.

In 1965 Home Lines of Panama had a new steamer the OCEANIC built by CR dell'Adriatico at Monfallone. She was 27,650 tons and 782 × 96 feet, with geared turbines driving twin screws. Her passenger accommodation was for 1,200 in one class. She sailed from Genoa on 3 April 1965 on her maiden voyage to New York. The OCEANIC was mainly used for cruising from New York. EUGENIO C was built by CR dell'Adriatico for Costa Armatori of Genoa. She was 30,550 tons and 713 × 96 feet, with geared turbines driving twin screws. She comprised accommodation for 178 First, 356 Second and 1,102 Tourist Class passengers. In September 1966 she started on the Genoa–Buenos Aires service as well as doing some cruising.

QUEEN ELIZABETH II
in New York harbour
65,850 tons
963 × 105 feet
Cunard
1968

HAMBURG
25,000 tons
639 × 87 feet
German Atlantic Line
1969

The now prestigious QUEEN ELIZABETH 2, familiarly referred to as the QE2, was built for the Cunard Line by John Brown. She was 65,850 tons and 963 × 105 feet with geared turbines driving twin screws. She had accommodation for 564 First and 1,441 Tourist Class passengers. There were delays in her delivery due to various builders' faults. Eventually she sailed from Southampton on 2 May 1968 on her maiden voyage to New York. In addition to working the North Atlantic she also did some cruising. On 1 April 1974 as a result of a damaged fuel pipe her boilers were put out of action and after two days her 1,654 passengers were transferred to another cruise liner. In July 1976 an engine-room fire caused serious damage while off the Scilly Isles and she had to return to Southampton. In 1982 she was requisitioned by the British Government to move troops to the Falkland Islands. However the QE2 went to South Georgia to be out of range of Argentine bombers and the troops were ferried to the Falklands in other vessels. After a refit she went back to her normal duties. This famous ship's future has been assured for many years, as the result of a major refit in Germany in 1986 when the steam turbines were removed and diesel engines filled.

The German Atlantic Line had a new one-class steamer HAMBURG built by Deutsche Werft at Hamburg. She was 25,000 tons and 639 × 87 feet with geared turbines driving twin screws and accommodation for 652 passengers. She sailed from Cruxhaven on 28 March 1969 on her maiden voyage to South America. In September 1973 she was renamed the HANSEATIC, but in December the German Atlantic Line ceased operation. She was purchased by the Soviet State Shipping Company. In January 1974 she was handed over and, renamed MAKSIM GORKIJ, has since been engaged in world cruising.

One of the main reasons why steam as the prime mover was abandoned for large passenger ships was that these were no longer 'liners' but floating Holiday Hotels cruising in quiet the waters of the Caribbean, Mediterranean or Pacific Islands. Frequent stops to go ashore meant a stop-go requirement of the machinery, more easily achieved with a diesel engine than steam turbines whose boiler pressure must be maintained even when at rest. However, steam is not dead on the high seas. The giant supertankers, which are by far the largest ships ever built, many being more than 500,000 tons, are mostly powered by steam turbines. Firstly, with the very long hulls and all the machinery at the back, the vibration of a diesel engine can cause stress cracks particularly when sailing in ballast. Secondly, at a constant speed over a long distance, steam comes into its own. In addition, when a supertanker is travelling with empty tanks, there is danger of explosion from the hydrocarbon gas given off by the sludge left in the tanks. Thus, with steam propulsion, the empty tanks can be filled, after cleaning, with the flue gasses from the oil-fired boilers, which are inert and prevent the ignition of any gasses left in the tanks.

So while the Motor Vessel holds sway in cruise ships the real giants of the oceans still use steam.

Aerial view of QE 2
and life on board

Early Steam Boats

With the advent of steam as a prime mover in the form of a steam engine in the latter half of the 18th century, several attempts were made to use this to propel ships, albeit small ones not suitable for ocean voyages. Earlier there had been Blasco Garay, who had made experiments with paddle-wheels in the harbour at Barcelona as early as the 16th century, the experiments by Prince Rupert and Savery in the Thames in the early 18th century; these were all driven by manpower. Denis Papin was the first to apply steam-power to work the paddle-wheels, followed sometime later by Jouffroy of France and by Fitch of America.

Early experiments, mostly in Scotland, were carried out with relatively small steam power units. A report in the *Scots Magazine* stated that 'on 14th October 1788 a boat was put in motion by a steam-engine. The vessel 25ft long and 7 ft broad was on the above date driven with two wheels by a small engine'. The experiment was carried out by Mr Miller of Dalswinton and came up to his expectations and afforded great pleasure to the spectators. The engine had been built by William Symington of Wanlockhead, Scotland, and after the trials was removed and placed in the Museum of Patents at Kensington.

Symington was greatly disappointed in the ending of the trials. However in 1801 he had a further chance when Lord Dundas of the Forth & Clyde Canal Company suggested using steam power for hauling boats along the canal. A boat was built for this purpose and Symington designed an engine of greatly improved character. It was direct acting, the steam powering each side of the piston, after a method invented by Watt, whose patent had by then expired. The rotary motion of the paddle-wheels was secured by means of a connecting rod and crank instead of by chains as in earlier boats. This boat was called CHARLOTTE DUNDAS. Lord Dundas was so well satisfied with the performance of the vessel that he proposed to introduce Symington

Mr Miller's Experimental
steamboat, 1788

Diagram showing
the machinery of the
CHARLOTTE DUNDASS 1801

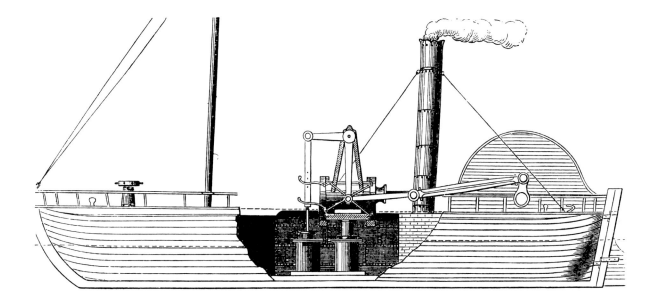

to the Duke of Bridgewater, the great canal owner. However, the proprietors of the canals became alarmed lest the banks be washed away by the waves that the steam boat raised in its wake, and prohibited further experiments.

The CHARLOTTE DUNDAS aroused the interest of other engineers and shipbuilders, particularly that of Andrew Bell, a Glasgow engineer. Later his son Henry Bell was to introduce steam navigation on the Clyde with the steamship COMET, a vessel of thirty tons built in August 1812 by John Wood & Company of Glasgow and Greenock. Before long Clyde steamers were known all over the world and the area became one of the most important shipbuilding centres.

THE COMET passing
Dumbarton 1812

Chronological List of Ships

1811	COMET	Henry Bell of Glasgow
1819	SAVANNAH	(American owner)
1827	SOPHIA JANE	Barnes & Miller
1831	ROYAL WILLIAM	Quebec & Halifax Steam Navigation Company
1837	GREAT WESTERN	Great Western Steamship Company
	GREAT LIVERPOOL	Transatlantic Steam Ship Company
1838	SIRRUS	British & American Steam Navigation Company
	ROYAL WILLIAM	City of Dublin Steam Packet Company
1839	BRITISH QUEEN	British & American Steam Navigation Company
1840	ARCHIMEDES	Ship Propeller Company
	BRITANNIA	North American Royal Mail Steam Packet Company (known as Cunard Line)
	PRESIDENT	British & American Steam Navigation Company
1845	GREAT BRITAIN	Great Western Steamship Company
	MASSACHUSETTS	R B Forbes
	MARMORA	Turkish Government
1846	CAPRI	Neapolitan Steam Navigation Company
	MOOZOFFER	East India Company
	VESUVIO	Neapolitan Steam Navigation Company
1847	WASHINGTON	Ocean Steam Navigation Company
1848	EUROPA	Cunard Line
1850	AFRICA	Cunard Line
	ARCTIC	New York & Liverpool United States Steamship Company (known as Collins Line)
	ASIA	Cunard Line
	ATLANTIC	Collins Line
	BALTIC	Collins Line
	HELENA SLOMAN	Robert M. Sloman
	PACIFIC	Collins Line
	VICEROY	New York & Galway Steam Ship Company
1851	AMAZON	Royal Mail Steam Packet Company (known as Royal Mail Line)
	BOSPHORUS	General Screw Steamship Company
	CITY OF MANCHESTER	Liverpool & Philadelphia Steam Ship Company (known as Inman Line)
1852	ADELAIDE	Australian Royal Mail Steam Navigation Co. (known as Australian Royal Mail Line)
	CHARITY	African Steamship Company
	CLEOPATRA	McKean, McCarty & Co.
	FORERUNNER	African Steamship Company
	FAITH	African Steamship Company
	HOPE	African Steamship Company
	NORTHERN LIGHT	African Steamship Company
	ORINOCO	Royal Mail Line
1852	QUEEN OF THE SOUTH	General Screw Steamship Company
	VICTORIA	Australian Royal Mail Line
1853	ARABIA	Cunard Line
	ANTELOPE	Millers & Thompson
	ATRATO	Royal Mail Line
	SYDNEY	Australian Royal Mail Line
1854	CITY OF GLASGOW	Inman Line
	CITY OF PHILADELPHIA	Inman Line
	HIMALAYA	Peninsular & Orient Company (known as P & O Line)
1855	ROYAL CHARTER	Liverpool & Australian Navigation Company
1856	GENOVA	Transatlantic Company
	PERA	P & O Line
	PERSIA	Cunard Line
	TORINO	Transatlantica Company
1857	ADRIATIC	Collins Line
	AUSTRALASIAN	European & Australian Royal Mail Co.
1858	HUDSON	North German Lloyd
	PARAMATTA	Royal Mail Line
1860	GREAT EASTERN	The Great Ship Company
	LY-EE-MOON	Alfred Dent
1861	BRITON	Union Steamship Company
	CITY OF NEW YORK	Inman Line
	MOOLTAN	P & O Line
1862	'CHINA'	Cunard Line
	'SCOTIA'	Cunard Line
1864	CUBA	Cunard Line
	NYANZA	P & O Line
1865	IMPERATRICE EUGENIE	Compagnie Generale Transatlantique (known as C.G.T.)
	JAVA	Cunard Line
	RUAHINE	Panama, New Zealand & Australian Royal Mail Company
1866	MANHATTAN	Liverpool & Great Western Steamship Company (known as Guion Line)
1867	COLOMBIAN	West India & Pacific Steamship Company
	LAMONT	Jardine, Matheson & Company

1868	NEVA	Royal Mail Line
1869	DECCAN	P & O Line
1870	ABYSSINIA	Cunard Line
	ALGERIA	Cunard Line
	JOHN ELDER	Pacific Steam Navigation Company
	PARTHIA	Cunard Line
1871	ATLANTIC	Ocean Steam Navigation Company (known as White Star Line)
	BALTIC	White Star Line
	EGYPT	National Steamship Company
	EUROPE	Ryde & Company
	NORTHUMBERLAND	Money, Wigram & Son
	OCEANIC	White Star Line
	VICEROY	Green & Company
1872	ADRIATIC	White Star Line
	BALTIMORE	North German Lloyd
	BERTHA	C. M. Norwood & Company
	CELTIC	White Star Line
	CITY OF MONTREAL	Inman Line
	COLOMBO	Thomas Wilson & Sons
	OTHELLO	Thomas Wilson & Sons
	POONHA	P & O Line
	REPUBLIC	White Star Line
1873	CITY OF CHESTER	Inman Line
	LEOPOLD II	Ryde & Company
	SANTIAGO	Ryde & Company
1874	BOTHNIA	Cunard Line
	CITY OF RICHMOND	Inman Line
1875	CITY OF BERLIN	Inman Line
	LAKE CHAMPLAIN	Canadian Shipping Company (known as Beaver Line)
	LAKE MEGANTIC	Beaver Line
	LAKE NEPIGON	Beaver Line
1876	ZEALANDIA	Pacific Mail Company
1877	GERMAN	Union Line
1879	ORIENT	Orient Steam Navigation Company (known as Orient Line)
	ROTOMAHANA	Union Steamship Company
1880	KINFAUNS CASTLE	Castle Mail Packet Company (known as Castle Line)
	TROJAN	Union Line
1881	CITY OF ROME	Inman Line
	PARISIAN	Allan Line
	QUETTA	British India Steam Navigation Company
	SERVIA	Cunard Line
1882	AUSTRAL	Orient Line
1883	OREGON	Guion Line
	PEMBROKE CASTLE	Castle Line

1884	AMERICA	National Line
	ARAWA	Shaw, Savill & Albion
1885	ETRURA	Cunard Line
1887	BRITANNIA	P & O Line
	VICTORIA	P & O Line
1888	ARCADIA	P & O Line
	CITY OF NEW YORK	Inman Line
	OCEANIA	P & O Line
1889	AUGUSTA VICTORIA	Hamburg-America Line
	CITY OF PARIS	Inman Line
	TEUTONIC	White Star Line
1890	DUNOTTER CASTLE	Castle Line
	EMPRESS OF INDIA	Canadian Pacific Railway Company (known as Canadian Pacific Line)
	MAJESTIC	White Star Line
1891	OPHIR	Orient Line
	SCOT	Union Line
1893	CAMPANIA	Cunard Line
	LUCANIA	Cunard Line
1894	CALADONIA	P & O Line
	NORMAN	Union Line
1895	ST LOUIS	American Line
	ST PAUL	American Line
1896	CANADA	Dominion Line
	DUNVEGAN CASTLE	Castle Line
1897	GASCON	Union Line
	KAISER WILHELM DER GROSSE	North German Lloyd
1898	CYMRIC	White Star Line
	KAISER FRIEDRICH	North German Lloyd
1899	AFRIC	White Star Line
	KINFAUNS CASTLE	Castle Line
	MEDIC	White Star Line
	OCEANIC	White Star Line
	PERSIC	White Star Line
1900	BRITON	Union Line
	DEUTSCHLAND	Hamburg-America Line
	INVERNIA	Cunard Line
	MINNEAPOLIS	Atlantic Transport Company
	MINNEHANA	Atlantic Transport Company
	SAXON	Union Line
	SAXONIA	Cunard Line
	VADERLAND	International Marchantile Marine Company (known as Red Star Line)
1901	CELTIC	White Star Line
	KRONPRINZ WILHELM	North German Lloyd
	RUNIC	White Star Line
	SUEVIC	White Star Line
	ZEELAND	Red Star Line

1902	ATHENIC	White Star Line
	CORINTHIC	White Star Line
	FINLAND	Red Star Line
	KROONLAND	Red Star Line
	WALMER CASTLE	Union Castle Mail Packet Company (known as Union Castle Line)
1903	ARAMDALE CASTLE	Union Castle Line
	CEDRIC	White Star Line
	IONIC	White Star Line
	KAISER WILHELM II	North German Lloyd
	KENILWORTH CASTLE	Union Castle Line
	KRONPRINZESSIN CECILIE	North German Lloyd
	MARMORA	P & O Line
1904	BALTIC	White Star Line
	MACEDONIA	P & O Line
1905	ARAGON	Royal Mail Line
	VICTORIAN	Allan Line
	VIRGINIAN	Allan Line
1906	AMAZON	Royal Mail Line
	ARAGUAYA	Royal Mail Line
	EMPRESS OF BRITAIN	Canadian Pacific Line
	EMPRESS OF IRELAND	Canadian Pacific Line
	KAISERIN AUGUSTE VICTORIA	Hamburg-America Line
	LA PROVENCE	C. G. T.
1907	ADRIATIC	White Star Line
	AVON	Royal Mail Line
	LUSITANIA	Cunard Line
	MAURETANIA	Cunard Line
	PRESIDENT GRANT	Hamburg-America Line
	PRESIDENT LINCOLN	Hamburg-America Line
1908	ASTURIAS	Royal Mail Line
	CHIYO MARU	Toyo Kisen K K
	MOREA	P & O Line
	TENYO MARU	Toyo Kisen K K
1909	MALWA	P & O Line
	MANTUA	P & O Line
	ORSOVA	Orient Line
	ORVIETO	Orient Line
	OSTERLEY	Orient Line
	OTRANTO	Orient Line
	OTWAY	Orient Line
	VASARI	Lamport & Holt
1910	BALMORAL CASTLE	Union Castle Line
	EDINBURGH CASTLE	Union Castle Line
1911	FRANCONIA	Cunard Line
	MALOJA	P & O Line
	MEDINA	P & O Line
	OLYMPIC	White Star Line
	REMEURA	New Zealand Line
	SHINYO MARU	Toyo Kisen K K
	VANDYCK	Lamport & Holt
1912	ARLANZA	Royal Mail Line
	DARRO	Royal Mail Line
	DEMERARA	Royal Mail Line
	DESEADO	Royal Mail Line
	DESNA	Royal Mail Line
	FRANCE	C.G.T.
	LACONIA	Cunard Line
	OXFORDSHIRE	Bibby Line
	TITANIC	White Star Line
	VAUBIN	Lamport & Holt
	VESTRIS	Lamport & Holt
1913	ANDANIA	Cunard Line
	ANDES	Royal Mail Line
	CERAMIC	White Star Line
	DRINA	Royal Mail Line
	EMPRESS OF ASIA	Canadian Pacific Line
	EMPRESS OF RUSSIA	Canadian Pacific Line
	IMPERATOR	Hamburg-America Line
	NELLOR	P & O Line
	ULYSSES	Blue Funnel Line
1914	ALCANTARA	Royal Mail Line
	AQUITANIA	Cunard Line
	BRITANNIC	White Star Line
	CAP POLONIO	Hamburg-South America Line
	CAP TRAFALGAR	Hamburg-South America Line
	KAISER-I-HIND	P & O Line
	KASHMIR	P & O Line
	LLANDOVERY CASTLE	Union Castle Line
	LLANSTEPHEN CASTLE	Union Castle Line
	METAGAMA	Canadian Pacific Line
	MISSANABIE	Canadian Pacific Line
	VATERLAND	Hamburg-America Line
1915	ALMANZORA	Royal Mail Lines
1917	LANCASHIRE	Bibby Line
1919	MAJESTIC	White Star Line
1920	NALDERA	P & O Line
	NARKUNDA	P & O Line
	ORMUZ	Orient Line
1921	ARUNDEL CASTLE	Union Castle Line
	AUSONIA	Cunard Line
	CAMERONIA	Anchor Line
	LARGS BAY	Commonwealth Government Line of Australia
	MORETON BAY	Commonwealth Government Line of Australia
	PARIS	C.G.T.
	SAMARIA	Cunard Line
	SCYTHIA	Cunard Line
	VANDYCK	Lamport & Holt
1922	ANDANIA	Cunard Line
	ANTONIA	Cunard Line

	DIOGENES	Aberdeen Line
	EMPRESS OF AUSTRALIA	Canadian Pacific Line
	EMPRESS OF CANADA	Canadian Pacific Line
	ESPERANCE BAY	Commonwealth Government Line of Australia
	HOBSONS BAY	Commonwealth Government Line of Australia
	HOMERIC	White Star Line
	JERVIS BAY	Commonwealth Government Line of Australia
	LACONIA	Cunard Line
	SOPHOCLES	Aberdeen Line
	TUSCANIA	Anchor Line
	TYRRHENIA	Anchor Line
1923	AUSONIA	Cunard Line
	CALIFORNIA	Anchor Line
	DORIC	White Star Line
	FRANCONIA	Cunard Line
	OHIO	Royal Mail Line
	SARPENDEN	Blue Funnel Line
	VOLTAIR	Lamport & Holt
1924	AURANIA	Cunard Line
	ORAMA	Orient Line
1925	ALAUNIA	Cunard Line
	ASCANIA	Cunard Line
	CALEDONIA	Anchor Line
	CARINTHIA	Cunard Line
	CATHAY	P & O Line
	CHITRAL	P & O Line
	COMORIN	P & O Line
	LLANDOVERY CASTLE	Union Castle Line
	ORONSAY	Royal Mail Line
	OTRANTO	Royal Mail Line
	RAJPUTANA	P & O Line
	RANCHI	P & O Line
	RANPURA	P & O Line
	RAWALPINDI	P & O Line
	TRANSYLVANIA	Anchor Line
1927	CAP ARCONA	Hamburg-South America Line
	ILE DE FRANCE	C.G.T.
	LAURENTIC	White Star Line
	LLANDAFF CASTLE	Union Castle Line
	MALOLO	Matson Navigation Co.
1928	DUCHESS OF ATHOLL	Canadian Pacific Line
	DUCHESS OF BEDFORD	Canadian Pacific Line
	DUCHESS OF RICHMOND	Canadian Pacific Line
	ORFORD	Royal Mail Line
1929	BREMEN	North German Lloyd
	DUCHESS OF YORK	Canadian Pacific Line
	ORONTES	Royal Mail Line
	PENNSYLVANIA	American Line
	STATENDAM	Holland-America Line
	VICEROY OF INDIA	P & O Line
1930	EMPRESS OF BRITAIN	Canadian Pacific Line

	EMPRESS OF JAPAN	Canadian Pacific Line
	EUROPA	North German Lloyd
1931	MONARCH OF BERMUDA	Furness Withy Co.
	HILARY	Booth Line
	L'ATLANTIQUE	Cie Sudatlantique
1932	CARTHAGE	P & O Line
	MARIPOSA	Matson Navigation Co.
	REX	Flotta Ruinite
1935	NORMANDIE	C.G.T.
	ORION	Orient Line
1936	AWATEA	Union Steam Ship Co of New Zealand
	CITY OF BENARES	Ellerman Line
	QUEEN MARY	Cunard-White Star Line
1938	CANTON	P & O Line
	NIEUW AMSTERDAM	Holland-America Line
1939	ANDES	Royal Mail Line
	MAURETANIA	Cunard-White Star
	PASTEUR	Cie Sudatlantique
1940	QUEEN ELIZABETH	Cunard-White Star Line
1941	AMERICA	United States Line
1947	ARGENTINA STAR	Blue Star Line
	BRASIL STAR	Blue Star Line
	CORINTHIC	Shaw, Savill & Albion
	MEDIA	Cunard-White Star Line
	PRESIDENT OF CLEVELAND	American President Line
1948	EDINBURGH CASTLE	Union Castle Line
	GOTHIC	Shaw, Savill & Albion
	ORCADES	Orient Line
	PRETORIA CASTLE	Union Castle Line
1949	CARONIA	Cunard-White Star Line
	HELENUS	Blue Funnel Line
	PELUS	Blue Funnel Line
	PYRRHUS	Blue Funnel Line
1950	CHUSAN	P & O Line
	JASON	Blue Funnel Line
	PATROCLUS	Blue Funnel Line
	PERSEUS	Blue Funnel Line
	17 DE OCTOBRE	Cia Argentina De Navigation Dodero
1951	INDEPENDENCE	American Export Line
	KENYA	British India Line
	OCEAN MONARCH	Furness Withy & Co
	RHODESIA CASTLE	Union Castle Line
	RYNDAM	Holland-America Line
1952	BRAEMAR CASTLE	Union Castle Line
	BRETAGNE	Société Generale de Transports Maritimes (known as S.G.T.M.)
	FLANDRE	C.G.T.
	KENYA CASTLE	Union Castle Line
	MAASDAM	Holland-America Line

	UGANDA	British India Line
	UNITED STATES	United States Line
1953	ANDREA DORIA	Italia San – Genoa
	OLYMPIA	Greek Line
1954	ARCADIA	P & O Line
	SAXONIA	Cunard Line
1955	IVERNIA	Cunard Line
	SOUTHERN CROSS	Shaw, Savill & Albion
1956	CARINTHIA	Cunard Line
	EMPRESS OF BRITAIN	Canadian Pacific Line
	REINA DEL MAR	Pacific Navigation Co.
1957	EMPRESS OF ENGLAND	Canadian Pacific Line
	OXFORDSHIRE	Bibby Line
	STATENDAM	Holland-America Line
	SYLVANIA	Cunard Line
1958	BRASIL	Moore-McCormack
	ARGENTINA	Moore-McCormack
	SANTA PAULA	Grace Lines
	SANTA ROSA	Grace Lines
1959	PENDENNIS CASTLE	Union Castle Line
	ROTTERDAM	Holland-America Line

1960	LEONARDO DA VINCI	Italia San – Genoa
	ORIANA	P & O-Orient Line
	WINDSOR CASTLE	Union Castle Line
1961	CANBERRA	P & O-Orient Line
	EMPRESS OF CANADA	Canadian Pacific Line
1962	FRANCE	C.G.T.
	NORTHERN STAR	Shaw, Savill & Albion
	SAVANNAH	States Marine Lines
	TRANSVAAL CASTLE	Union Castle Line
1963	GUGLIELMO MARCONI	Lloyd-Triest
	SANTA MAGDELENA	Grace Lines
	SANTA MARIA	Grace Lines
	SANTA MARIANA	Grace Lines
1964	SANTA MERCEDES	Grace Lines
	SHALOM	Zim Isreal Navigation
1965	MICHELANGELO	Italia San Genoa
	OCEANIC	Home Lines
	RAFFAELO	Italia San Genoa
1966	EUGENIO C	Costa Armatori
1968	QUEEN ELIZABETH II	Cunard Line
1969	HAMBURG	German Atlantic Line

General Index

Index of Named Ships